RECLAIMING THE OLD TESTAMENT FOR THE CHRISTIAN PULPIT

Reclaiming the Old Testament for the Christian Pulpit

DONALD E. GOWAN

John Knox Press
ATLANTA

Acknowledgement is made for quotations from the following:
G. Ebeling, *The Word of God and Tradition*, copyright © 1968 Wm. Collins & Co. Ltd., London and Fortress Press, Philadelphia; reprinted by permission of Fortress Press.
Klaus Koch, *The Growth of the Biblical Tradition*, copyright © 1969 Charles Scribner's Sons, New York.
J. Magonet, *Form and Meaning: Studies in Literary Techniques in the Book of Jonah*, copyright © 1976 Verlag Peter Lang, Bern.

Library of Congress Cataloging in Publication Data

Gowan, Donald E
    Reclaiming the Old Testament for the Christian pulpit.

    Includes bibliographical references.
    1. Bible. O.T.—Homiletical use. 2. Bible.
O.T.—Sermons. 3. Sermons, American.
4. Presbyterian Church—Sermons. I. Title.
BS1191.5.G68   251   79-87743
ISBN 0-8042-0166-8

To Doug and Pam

Preface

The word "reclaim" suggests that a resource has been lost or has become unusable. It has not been applied to the place of the Old Testament in contemporary Christian preaching without careful consideration of its appropriateness. For example, I am not aware of any modern preachers who have been able to put the Old Testament to use quite so easily and extensively as the medieval preacher, Bernard of Clairvaux, who produced eighty-six homilies on the Song of Songs alone. He could preach the Old Testament with such ease because he used the allegorical method of interpretation, which allowed the preachers of the past to find all the Christian doctrine they liked in it. But with the rise of the historical-critical approach to the Scriptures, allegory and typology began to go out of favor and, unfortunately, no adequate new hermeneutic, which would enable the Old Testament to retain its place in Christian preaching, appeared to take their place. The resulting general neglect of that part of the Scriptures by the average preacher in our day is too well-known to require documentation here.

It took me a long time to learn to preach from the Old Testament in a way which could take full advantage of modern, critical methods of study as an aid to Christian understanding. But eventually I did develop a method (or a combination of methods) which works for me, and this book presents it to other preachers in the hope that it may be helpful to them. My approach has been developed in the course of teaching the Old Testament at Pittsburgh Theological Seminary with a continual concern to show students how exegesis bears fruit in preaching. At the same time, I have been putting it into practice in regular supply preaching, and have found that several opportunities to serve nearby churches as an interim pulpit supply, allowing me to preach to the same congregation Sunday after Sunday, have been especially valuable in testing its usefulness.

Some of those sermons are included in this book as examples of the methods I have developed. I realize how risky this is; most books on preaching tend quite wisely to emphasize negative examples (drawn from other people's sermons) so that the readers get a very clear picture of what not to do. But few of them contain more than one or two examples of the method being advocated, and many contain none at all. This book, in contrast, presents few negative examples and a good many which are intended to be positive (in full awareness that my sermons thus become available for citation by others as how not to do it). They have been edited slightly for publication, but in essentials they are the "real thing"; not something worked over and polished for weeks, but sermons I wrote on a Saturday morning for delivery the next day, with all the imperfections that style of writing may be expected to have. Since that is about the way most pastors have to do it, they seemed to me to be the most useful type of example I could provide.

For the stimulus of critical discussion of some of the issues presented in the book I owe thanks to my colleagues at Pittsburgh Seminary, and especially to Robert Ezzell, Assistant Professor of Homiletics, who has invited me on occasion to join him in teaching courses on preaching from the Old Testament, and who has provided helpful insights from his own perspective. The students in these classes and in the exegesis courses which I teach every year have given me the opportunity to try out this approach on those who are just learning to preach. I am also grateful to the congregations who have listened to my own sermons, and especially to the people of the Middlesex United Presbyterian Church, to whom I have preached for several months at a time on two separate occasions, and who have seemed not only willing but even enthusiastic about hearing sermons from the Old Testament every other Sunday. Finally, to my family, Darlene, Doug, and Pam, my appreciation for agreeing to let me write another book.

Donald E. Gowan

Contents

Preface

Introduction: Yes, You Can Preach the Old Testament   1
      Tradition History as a Key to Preaching the Old Testament
      Form Criticism as the First Step in Approaching a Text

Chapter I: Preaching from Historical Texts   15
      What Israel's History Means to Us
      What and How to Preach from Historical Texts
            A Sermon on 2 Kings 11
            A Sermon on Exodus 13:17–14:31

Chapter II: Preaching from Saga   35
      What Are Biblical Sagas Trying to Say?
      How to Preach from Saga
            A Sermon on Genesis 6:9–9:17
            A Sermon on Genesis 12:10–20

Chapter III: Preaching from Short Stories   54
    Daniel 1–6
    Excursus: The Story of Joseph
    Esther
    Ruth
        A Sermon on Ruth
    Jonah

Chapter IV: Preaching the Law   79
    Jesus and the Law
    Paul and the Law
    The Christian and the Law
    Preaching the Laws of the Old Testament
        A Sermon on Leviticus 17:10–14

Chapter V: Preaching from Wisdom Literature   100
    Who Were the Wise Men and What Did They Do?
    The Techniques of Wisdom
    What to Preach from Wisdom Literature
    Orthodox Wisdom: Psalm 1
        A Sermon on Proverbs 4:1–9
    Questioning Wisdom: Job and Ecclesiastes
        A Sermon on Ecclesiastes 9:1–12; 5:18–20

Chapter VI: Preaching from the Prophets   119
    Who Were the Prophets?
    New Light on the Prophets from Form Criticism
    What Can We Preach from the Prophetic Books?
    Preaching Judgment and Promise from the Prophets
    Amos 2:6–16
        A Sermon on Isaiah 1:2–9
    Jeremiah 31:31–34
        A Sermon on Isaiah 7:1–17

Epilogue   145

Abbreviations   149

Notes   150

Scriptural Index   161

INTRODUCTION

Yes, You Can Preach the Old Testament

When I visit a church as a pulpit supply—as I often do—and preach from an Old Testament text—as I do about half the time—I frequently hear this kind of comment afterward: "I really enjoyed hearing you preach that *Old Testament* sermon." That often repeated remark is not so innocuous as it seems at first, for it is really saying these two things: 1. that it is unusual for them to hear a sermon on an Old Testament text, and 2. that there are riches in the Old Testament which are quickly appropriated and deeply appreciated by the people in the pew when they are offered access to them. Both of those statements are true, but it seems to me that most books on the Christian use of the Old Testament have tended to dwell on the former truth, the neglect of that part of the canon in large portions of the church's life; they diagnose the problems which the Old Testament has presented to Christians and struggle with various solutions. I intend to emphasize instead the latter truth, the abundance of preaching material in the Old Testament and the ways in which modern scholarship as applied to these texts may reinvigorate the preacher's work. The "problem of the Old Testament" will not be dealt with in this book; instead it will be approached as a treasure-house to which we have gained some new means of access.

Instead of beginning like the typical book on preaching from the Old Testament, then, with a description of the neglect of that part of the canon in Christian preaching and a discussion of the historic problems which the church has wrestled with in trying to use it as a Christian book, I intend to short-circuit that familiar approach. It will be assumed that the people who read this book do so because they are already interested in the Old Testament and are concerned about effective preaching from it, so that they do not need to be lectured about the church's failings in this respect. Furthermore, since it is written to propose and illustrate *a method*, it does not seem necessary to provide a treatise on other methods. Both kinds of material can be found effectively presented in other recent works.[1] This is more a tract than a treatise, more a how-to manual than a full introduction to the subject of Old Testament preaching. It has grown out of the experience of finding that "Biblical Criticism" as practiced in the last third of the twentieth century is neither a hinderance to nor irrelevant for the preacher, but that it offers resources which if neglected can only impoverish preacher and congregation alike.

For most preachers in service today I assume that the "Biblical Criticism" they learned in seminary was essentially the Documentary Hypothesis of the composition of the Pentateuch (JEDP) plus the similar results of the historical-critical approach to the other Old Testament books. And I dare say that material has been either rejected as untrue or put to one side as irrelevant to the work of a pastor. Seldom can one imagine the Documentary Hypothesis adding fire to one's preaching. Those who have attended seminary recently have been exposed to form criticism as an exegetical tool and have struggled to understand what is meant by traditio-historical criticism, rhetorical criticism and most recently structuralism. Sometimes they are offered help in applying those newer exegetical approaches to their work in preparing sermons, but so far I have seen no systematic effort to show how such new techniques can solve some of the old problems everyone has faced in trying to preach the Old Testament, and so I fear that form criticism, *et al.*, may take their place along with the Documentary Hypothesis as pedantry best left out of the way when a sermon is to be preached. I have learned otherwise from my own preaching experience, however. I have found that two of these critical methods, especially, form criticism and traditio-historical studies (or history of tradition) can be extremely valuable techniques for learning what to preach from the Old Testament and for discerning how to preach it most effectively. The two methods will be introduced briefly for this purpose in the remainder of this chapter, and the rest of the book will try to show by means of numerous examples how learning to use these approaches can make it possible to preach valid and relevant Christian sermons on any part of the Old Testament.

This is a sweeping claim to make, and immediately it must be qualified somewhat. I do not mean to suggest that any and every verse can necessarily become a valid text for a Christian sermon. Some verses probably ought never to be preached. Neither is the method a monolithic one, to be applied in the same way to every passage; indeed, one of the lessons of form criticism is that the type of literature in the text should determine the approach one takes to it. It tries to be a way of finding what the text itself has to say and to appreciate its distinctive way of saying it, so as to avoid the common tendency of approaching Old Testament texts with a conviction about what they *ought* to say, then of finding a method of discovering just that, or, if the method fails, putting that part of the Old Testament to one side as unpreachable.

Let me remind you briefly of some of the problems facing those who would preach from the Old Testament, then make some promises which the remainder of the book will try to fulfill:

1. The Old Testament has presented Christians with a whole series of moral problems. We tend to assume that the heroes of that book should be good guys, then find out that Abraham lied about his wife (Gen. 12:10–20), that the Israelites slaughtered the Canaanites without mercy, and that David committed adultery. As I was telling a college class about Elijah slaughtering the prophets of Baal at Mt. Carmel, a student raised her hand and said, "Was this before or after the Ten Commandments were given?" (She needed to do some reviewing.) She had a real problem with an Old Testament hero, who knew about "Thou shalt not kill," doing away with all those prophets. A similar attitude has produced the attacks on the Bible's moral standards by Mark Twain and by the representatives of a certain type of religious liberalism.

Part of that problem is simply based on a misapprehension of what the Bible is all about, but unfortunately that point of view has been perpetuated by much of our preaching and teaching. We have wanted to use the Bible as a set of moral examples, then when we run across *real people*, such as Jacob or David, whose behavior was sometimes far from exemplary, we don't know what to do. We shall see that there are some people in the Old Testament who actually are held up as examples to follow, such as Daniel, but that most of the book presents, not models of perfect behavior, but the story of how God deals with ordinary, imperfect human beings. But there is another aspect of the problem which is more difficult. What do we do when God himself is quoted as commanding the Israelites to slaughter all the Canaanites, or when the law of God permits slavery? The two most common responses in our day are: (a) not to read those parts, or (b) to take a "progressive revelation" approach; i.e. ascribe the Old Testament material to a primitive level which is eventually corrected by the New Testament. The sections on History, on Saga and on Law in this book will offer some other ways of dealing with such problems; approaches which use the insights form criticism provides concerning the intention and use of certain types of literature (so that we understand whether a given text is intended to provide a model for behavior, for example), and which, by their emphasis on history, show that some of the quandries alluded to have been produced by our unhistorical treatments of the Bible.

2. The cultural differences between the Old Testament and our society have made much of it apparently irrelevant to us. We don't need instructions on how to sacrifice animals, we don't need to be warned against alliances with the Assyrians and we don't have any regular use for a list of the descendents of Aaron. In the old days, when people read the whole Bible and thought it all should be

important to them, the favorite method of dealing with this problem was *allegorizing*; anything which on the surface of it appeared to be irrelevant or improper was assumed to be in reality a symbol of a spiritual truth.[2] So, the list of creatures which may not be eaten, in Leviticus 11, was explained by saying that each creature really was a symbol of a vice which Christians should avoid. And the scarlet cord, hanging from Rahab's window, which saved her house from destruction (Josh. 2:18) was taken to be a message that we are saved by the blood of Christ. The great pitfall of allegorizing is, of course, that it *imports* these messages from the general teachings of the church or the interpreter's own head, the words of the text do not contain them and thus can exercise no control over them (How do we know that a swan is really a symbol for hypocrisy, and that anything red is really a symbol for the blood of Christ?), and thus the Bible can be made to say anything we like. In the present, when we hear less of allegorizing, the usual treatment of culturally strange material seems to be just to ignore it, or to try to modernize it, as if Abraham really was just like the modern businessman.[3]

The approaches suggested in this book will attempt to show how we can preserve the integrity of those Israelites as people with their own life and outlook without thereby making this literature which they produced an archaic document with no relevance for the twentieth century. Form criticism helps us to understand their culture better, to appreciate why it is different in some respects and to recognize where we are alike in our basic humanity. The history of tradition emphasizes the real continuity which does exist between us and the Old Testament, despite the cultural gaps which should not be denied. A first effort to explain that continuity will be found in the next section of this chapter.

I have found that the tradition history approach provides such a natural way of discerning the real connections between the Old Testament and New Testament, between "Bible times" and our own, that I no longer find it necessary to struggle quite so painfully with the familiar questions concerning the "Christian use" of the Old Testament, concerning when it is legitimate to preach Christ on the basis of an Old Testament text, etc. Most texts lead in a very natural way through the Old Testament tradition and that of intertestamental Judaism to the New Testament's tradition concerning Christ. I do not have to search for a New Testament text to link up with one in the Old (largely because I have not ignored all that lies between them), nor do I need some technique for "finding" Christ in the Old Testament (historically he is not there, but viewed historically it is clear that those texts are on their way toward him). But if the tradition does not lead directly to some New Testament text or I see no historical relationship with something Christological, I do not worry about that or consider that part of the Old Testament to be unpreachable. It is still a part of the broader, canonical tradition preserved for us by the believing community and so a valuable witness to what it means to believe in the God and Father of our Lord Jesus Christ.[4]

3. Another problem preachers face is that much of the Old Testament seems to be "untheological." The New Testament is conveniently filled with "doctrine" and perhaps Gen. 1–3 and parts of the prophets can easily be read as theology, but what can be preached from Joshua, Judges or Proverbs (not to mention Song of Songs or Esther)? I hope to provide enough concrete examples of how to discover what such materials meant in Israel's theology that it will become easier to recognize why it was essential for Israel and the church to preserve them as part of the canon of Scripture, and thus to offer some clues to how they may be effectively preached to a modern congregation.

Such claims, that there is a way by which every major portion of the Old Testament may be approached with the expectation that in it may be found a message which is actually contained in the text and is also preachable, should be made with some diffidence. It is for that reason that an unusual number of examples of full sermons are included here and that rather often the texts which are chosen are not easy ones. The sermons are not presented as great examples of pulpit artistry nor have the texts been chosen to demonstrate my cleverness in getting something out of nothing. They are simply intended as demonstrations that the method works.

That this is intended to be a comprehensive approach to preaching from the Old Testament may be seen by a glance at the Table of Contents, which shows that the book is organized according to the major types of literature in the Old Testament. The preacher's Old Testament, in this book, includes more than Genesis, Psalms and Isaiah. It is also possible to preach from Leviticus, 2 Kings and Proverbs—and to preach what is really there. I do take the whole canon as the subject for Christian preaching rather than trying to devise some principle for judging what is preachable—which then sets up a standard outside Scripture, even though it claims to be drawn from Scripture. To cite two examples briefly, Luther judged the books of the Bible by the standard of what leads one to Christ. James didn't fit that standard very well because of its differences from Pauline theology, so was declared an epistle of straw. Despite that, some of us find material of real value in James. The search by modern scholars for the *kerygma* has led some to restrict full revelation in the Old Testament to the recital of the acts of God in history, thus suggesting that material such as the wisdom literature is of questionable value for preaching. But the community which has given us the canon has found these books to be necessary, too, and I hope none of our theories will keep us from hearing what they have to say.

So this is in part an essay in getting more truth and more vitality in our preaching from the familiar and easy parts of the Old Testament, but it is also a reclamation project, intending to show that there are presently untapped riches to be found in every part of it by the preacher who will take the time to learn to wrestle with the text in new ways. These two most useful approaches to biblical interpretation will now be described briefly so as to provide a general introduction to the detailed explanations of how they can help the preacher at work which will be developed in the ensuing chapters.

Tradition History as a Key to Preaching the Old Testament

The central problem which has faced modern preachers who attempt to use the Old Testament faithfully is *discontinuity*. It is a foreign land which they enter when they open the pages of one of those archaic books—no Christ, no Church, worship by sacrificing animals, strange peoples with strange customs—and to find a way to bridge the gap has been a concern of Christians since early times. I have already mentioned the cultural and moral discrepancies we feel between ourselves and the Old Testament, and have noted how the allegorical method of interpretation provided a way of dealing with that problem which the church accepted for many centuries. There was also an obvious discontinuity between the *religions* of the Old and New Testaments which the church recognized from the very beginning. The religion of ancient Israel is by no means identical with Christianity and that has produced a gap which has sometimes been widened into a gulf. Modern scholarship has probably aggravated these old problems, if possible, by expanding greatly our knowledge of the nature of Israelite society and Hebrew thought, making it harder to read our own presuppositions back into the Old Testament and making the differences between us and Israel more evident than ever before.[5]

All these problems have been dealt with over and over again, in works on Old Testament theology, on hermeneutics, on the inspiration and authority of the Old Testament and on homiletics, yet the average preacher I encounter is still not quite sure how (or whether) the Old Testament can be used as a text for a Christian sermon. My proposal, then, is to try a different track; not to go on wrestling with these familiar problems, real as they are, but to get hold of a real element of *continuity*, and to use it for all it's worth.

The element of continuity is *history*; we really are the descendents of people whose beliefs and actions have determined (to a great extent) who we are, what we believe, and what we can and cannot do. Our "effective" history extends back a long way; to Jesus Christ and his disciples, for Christians, and far beyond that, for they could not have done what they did without Judaism, without Israel. Now, a part of that history has its effect on us whether we know about it or not (e.g., the genes we inherited and many cultural mores which we never think about), but much of it needs to be *understood*, since it only influences us to the extent that it is affirmed. Consider, for example, the increasing awareness of the effects which a knowledge of black history can have on the consciousness of American blacks. So it is with nearly all of the Christian heritage; it must be understood and affirmed in order to be effective—it must be preached. An important part of preaching, from the whole Bible but especially from the Old Testament, ought to be to show how we really are connected with our fellow believers of the past—and the connection need not be created by our ingenuity; it is there, physically and spiritually, in the generations who have transmitted their faith to those who have come after. That is to say, none of us comes to the Bible *de novo*. We cannot jump over all the centuries that separate us from Israel and encounter the God of Israel face to face in the Old Testament, as if nothing had happened since the Exodus. Exegesis has often attempted to do that, of course, and it is that effort of ours which has created, unnecessarily, a part of that historical, cultural, and theological discontinuity which we struggle with. But in fact *we* cannot *go back* to meet with Jacob at Bethel; *he comes* to us, transmitted to us by generation after generation of believers to whom Bethel meant something, who have transmitted not just what happened at Bethel, but what it meant and continues to mean.

This is an approach to preaching which takes with the utmost seriousness the *history of tradition*. It is not *bound* by tradition, in the sense that we say only what our fathers taught us; it is "Protestant" in that it seeks to evaluate one's own heritage and to compare different strands of tradition (acknowledging that Catholic tradition also grows, hence changes), so as ultimately to make the decision where the contemporary believer should stand with reference to the past. But it acknowledges that no one's faith comes directly from the Bible without human mediators (for that to happen, translations would even be ruled out, for example), but that we have received it from the Bible as interpreted and re-interpreted by the believing community. What the community of faith has delivered to us we receive gratefully, but also critically, for they have been human beings, subject to error and in need of correction, under the guidance of the Holy Spirit, by subsequent generations.

The believing community to which I refer has its beginning with the earliest parts of the Old Testament, and it is the transmission, with its accompanying interpretation of tradition, *within the Bible* that is of the greatest importance to the Christian preacher. However, the 1,900-year process of transmission which links us with the latest parts of the Bible should not be ignored, for the generations which succeeded the New Testament church have also contributed much to our identity as Christians in the twentieth century.[6]

Readers who look elsewhere for material on the history of tradition approach to the study of the Old Testament, or "traditio-historical" criticism, as it is sometimes called, will encounter a certain potential confusion in the use of the term.[7] As Gerhard von Rad, to take an example of German scholarship, or Ivan Engnell, as a representative of the Scandanavian school, use the term it normally refers to the *pre-history* of our Old Testament texts, to the process of the transmission of traditions before they eventually were fixed in their present, written form. But, it must be acknowledged that written texts may continue to create a tradition of their own (in addition to their mere physical transmission as part of a book), in that they influence subsequent thinking and writing. The

Germans call this the *Nachgeschichte*, the "post-history" or better the "continuing history" of a text,[8] and it is this aspect of the history of tradition which is important as a hermeneutical key for the preacher, for this is what links us, in an almost physical sense, with the text. Hence it is this less common use of the term which will concern us exclusively in this book.

My tradition-history approach to the preaching of the Old Testament involves several theological presuppositions, which must now be made explicit. If the presuppositions cannot be accepted, the value of the rest of the method will be limited. However, I think it need not be completely vitiated by such a disagreement, except for some whose theologies are quite radically different from mine. I propose to list and explain, at this point, a series of premises for preaching from the Old Testament:

1. The God who is revealed in the Old Testament is the God and Father of our Lord Jesus Christ. Since he has revealed himself as having established a special relationship with Israel, then I, as a Gentile, may believe that I have access to the Old Testament and the God of Israel only through Jesus Christ. But since I believe the promises made through Jesus, I believe that as an adopted son I am permitted to use the Old Testament as my book of Scripture.

2. We have no meaningful, direct, personal access to God, or to Christ, except through the word of Scripture. Although it may be possible to encounter God directly through the Spirit, *who it is* that we have thus encountered is made known to us only through Scripture.

3. From the beginning the Scriptures have been produced and preserved by a community of believers. They are thus not only a revelation of God but also a reflection of the faith of the believing community. God has revealed himself always *through* something human: human words (Greek and Hebrew), human societies (Israel and the Church), human beings (prophets and ultimately Jesus the incarnate Son of God). Hence the words of the Bible present to us not only the voice of God but also the voices of our fellow believers.[9]

4. When we join the believing community we affirm for ourselves that their faith is true and accept for ourselves their standards of truth, which include the Scriptures. Thus we do not come to the Scriptures *de novo*; because we have accepted the faith of the believing community we must take seriously what the Scriptures have meant to those believers who have come before us.

5. Therefore we ask of each text not merely, "What does this mean to *me*? First we ask, "What *has* this meant to the believing community throughout the centuries since it was first produced?" and then finally, after hearing and weighing all these testimonies, "What does this *continue* to mean to us, and does it say anything new to us?"

6. Scripture interprets Scripture. Our guide to what is of lasting value in a text is to be found in the use which subsequent texts make of its themes and concerns. Some elements in every text are incidental and ephemeral: details of

geography, history, chronology, biography, natural science, customs and even religious practices. We judge these things to be ephemeral not by our own standards or opinions (ephemeral in themselves) but because we discover that the believing community which is testifying to us within the Scriptures did not find it important or necessary to reaffirm these things generation after generation as essentials of the faith. So we look for the elements of our text which they *did* reaffirm, see how they added to or subtracted from it and how they reapplied it to new situations. From this "history of tradition" we then find a guide to help us to reaffirm and reapply the text for our own day.[10]

7. Scripture is not static. It is the Living Word and it is on the move. So one thing we look for in the history of tradition is *direction*, for if we discern that correctly within the scriptural witness and our interpretation moves in that same direction we should not go too far wrong in understanding what God intends to say to us through that text.

To borrow and modify a diagram used by a colleague of mine in discussing the question of authority in the church,[11] we may see that preachers have three elements available to them as they seek a message to deliver to their congregations: a text from the Bible, tradition—which for our purposes now includes the rest of the Old and New Testaments plus subsequent Christian history, and experience. Now, the preacher may take a text and tell what that *meant*, but never

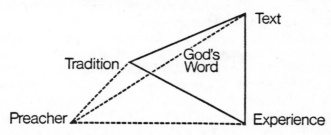

find a way to relate that to our own contemporary experience—we have heard such "sermons." Or the sermon may draw largely from present experience and only tag it with a text—we have heard even more of that kind. But let us not be hypercritical, for how to connect the two is not obvious and is often very difficult. The older methods of allegory and typology were devised to solve the problem, but modern scholarship has destroyed their effectiveness for most. The older ways remained generally faithful to tradition but often did great violence to the texts they were supposedly interpreting. Modern preaching, on the other hand, has tended to make experience its canon and to take text and tradition rather lightly. The method being proposed here intends to root every sermon in a text and to find its central message there and nowhere else. It aims to find a message for *us*, to speak to the experience of the congregation gathered in a particular place on a particular day. And it seeks to find the most faithful way of bridging the gap between the text and our present experience by tracing that text's own history and the history of its themes. So tradition does not govern what is proclaimed; it is the servant of the text and ultimately of experience as well, for if we find that the church has always taught something which we simply cannot accept, then the triangle is broken. But if we find that we can affirm the way tradition has interpreted the text as being true for us, then we have a message to preach which is not just the product of our own ingenuity or the echo of what we have always been told, but a message which is the result of the testimony of both Bible and Church.

This understanding of the way God reveals himself to us is not the same as Catholic teaching, which places the tradition of the Church on a level equal with Scripture.[12] On the contrary, Scripture remains primary, since it records how it all began, it provides everything that later generations interpret. Neither is this a form of progressive revelation, in which God keeps adding to the knowledge and insight which he has offered humanity. The role of tradition in my understanding of revelation may be illustrated by means of this allegory:

The Bible plus the entire history of what the Bible has meant to the believing community, from the beginning until today, might be compared to an immense symphony. It is very long—unfinished as yet—and all of us are players in the orchestra. The symphony is unbelievably complex, for it is made up of an uncountable number of variations on a theme. The theme is God's—he composed it. But his theme is played in human history in many variations, on every kind of instrument, in assorted keys, harmonies, counterpoints, rhythms and volumes. Some distort the theme so badly it can no longer be recognized. But in every variation which can be called a faithful rendition, God's theme can be heard by new players and taken up to be repeated in their own version. It is heard in several variations already in the Pentateuch, is taken up in distinctive ways in the prophets and the psalms, and it breaks forth with unparalleled vigor in the New Testament. The church has composed its own versions, over and over again. And our work, in tracing the Bible's tradition, is to discern God's theme within all that variety. We never hear the pure theme as is—that belongs to God—but we try to hear and follow the variations produced by our fellow instrumentalists so that the variation we produce will not be too much distorted, so that others will be able to hear and join in producing celestial music on earth.[13]

As G. Ebeling has concluded, in an article referred to earlier:

It is not the Word of God which, in the history of the Church, is subject to change and movement—Jesus Christ is the same yesterday, today, and for ever—but the interpretation of this same Word of God in all the heights and depths of the world and human existence. . . . From the theological point of view the remarkable thing about this course of events is that the Church, although she remains one and the same, undergoes a manifold change of form; thus the witness to Jesus Christ in the history of the Church does not consist in the mere repetition of Holy Scripture and in imitation of the way in which disciples followed him; but in interpretation, that is, in ever new usages and forms, thoughts and decisions, sufferings and victories, and hence in an unfolding of the richness and power of the Word of God, and in ever new victories for the hidden kingdom of God.[14]

Form Criticism as the First Step in Approaching a Text

Before we begin to trace what a text has continued to mean to believers throughout the history of belief, however, we must approach that text on our own, in order to find out where it belongs in that great symphony of which I spoke. The methods devised by *form criticism* have provided for us ways of picking up overtones we had missed before and of avoiding distortions due to our lack of understanding of what it means that the Bible is not all written in one literary form. For New Testament studies form criticism has been a somewhat problematic subject, the value of which has been questioned by many, largely because of the way it was used in the work of Rudolph Bultmann. But Old Testament form criticism has never been put to the service of a program such as Bultmann's, hence its usefulness can be made clear without the kind of debate which has gone on in New Testament scholarship. Other introductory works must be consulted by those readers who may be unacquainted with the form critical method;[15] in this brief section it must suffice to describe it in outline and to move quickly to its application to sermon preparation.

The basic principle of form criticism is that the *use* or *function* of language and the *form* it takes tend to correspond with one another very closely. That is, legal documents use forms of speech which are appropriate for that use (e.g., contracts, wills, subpoenas) but which would seem inappropriate in any other place in life. A service of Christian worship uses forms which are appropriate for what is happening there (hymns, prayers, sermons) but which would seem totally out of place in a sales conference or at a basketball game. Certainly freedom does exist in our use of language and the forms which are typical of a certain life setting are not always rigidly confined to it, but it is a general truth that the *form of speech* which is chosen corresponds both to the *setting* in which it is used and to the *content* which is being conveyed.[16] If we may be pardoned for taking a trivial example, let us consider the riddle. There are several typical forms in which riddles may be posed, so that when the setting is appropriate and we are asked a question in that form, we know what kind of answer is expected. "What's the difference between a ghost and a crippled sailor?" should not be answered by reference to logic or the dictionary. (One is a hobgoblin; the other a gob hobblin'.) Neither should "Why is a lame dog like a schoolboy adding six and seven?" (Because he puts down three and carries one.) But the freedom which does exist in our use of language means that we can play with the form. In my high school days we took the riddle and effectively emptied it of content. "Why is a stove?" "Because the more you polish it, it gets." Or, one can play with the fact that the same form can be used for a serious question as well as a riddle, so that the setting or intention is the sole determiner of meaning. "What's the difference between an egg and an elephant?" (Since it sounds like a riddle you give the expected answer:) "I don't know." "If you don't know, I'd hate to send you to the store for eggs."

These are examples of typical forms of modern speech which are obvious to us, because we have grown up using them in their natural setting and we instinctively know what is happening when their use is modified, as in the last example. But in the Old Testament we enounter speech forms which are unusual to us, and that should not surprise us, since they reflect a culture very different from ours. The funeral song and the war song as found in the Old Testament are not used by us; our customs at funerals and wars are different from Israel's and our literature differs correspondingly. Hence we may not immediately recognize what kind of literature we are reading in a portion of the Old Testament and the place in life from which it came may remain hidden from us. If that is true, then it will be even less likely that we will understand cases like my twisting of the riddle form, as, for example, when a prophet takes the form of the funeral song and puts it to an entirely new use.

The value of the analysis of the literary forms used in the Old Testament for the interpretation of the Scriptures can be tremendous. At the most elementary level its attention to opening and closing formulas and to internal structure helps one to determine the exact limits of the pericope which is being studied, and there are cases where what one thinks of the meaning of a passage does depend on where it begins and ends. Next, once a passage is classified as to its literary genre, we can immediately add to it all the passages of that same genre which occur elsewhere in the Old Testament, thus providing comparative material which often sheds light on the function of the genre and which may offer parallels which will elucidate difficult parts of the chosen text. Clarification of the function and setting of the genre helps one to understand what *kind* of message is intended. To offer a simple example, if a text has been identified form critically as a short story then one would not expect it necessarily to connect up with the history of Israel as it is recounted in the historical books nor to offer important historical information, and if such material does appear it will be understood to be incidental to the story's purpose and not the "ore" for which it should be mined. To take one explicit case, once we have identified the Book of Jonah as a short story, we will not then be led to consider the reference to a prophet named Jonah in 2 Kings 14:25 as the historical key to the meaning of the book, for even if there is a historical connection, the purpose for the writing of a short story is not the same as the purpose for writing history.

Form critical study has made it clear that the Bible is not all of the same kind of literature and that different literary types are used for different purposes, hence they should be treated in accordance with their intention and not forced to fit one single pattern. Law is not functioning in the same areas of life as Saga, and its message is not the same. If we look to both of them for predictions of the Messiah, or for moral examples or spiritual insights, if we approach each of them just hoping to distill two, three, or four preachable points of doctrine, then we do violence to their quite specific kind of message for a definite type of human situation.

This book takes up six of the major genres of literature in the Old Testament: History, Saga, Short Story, Law, Wisdom, and Prophecy. These are very broad categories; prophecy, especially, puts a wide variety of smaller genres to its service, but the point concerning the homiletical use of form criticism can be made without having to treat every literary type the Old Testament contains.[17]

So far I have been stressing the value of form criticism for interpretation, for discovering what the message of the text really is, and many examples of that will be given in the body of the book. But there is another side of it which is useful specifically to the homiletician. The ancient writer used the genre which was best suited to convey the particular message which burdened him, and the question is, can that help the preacher who wants to speak to contemporaries as effectively and persuasively as possible? Preachers are limited, ordinarily, to a single, rather rigid genre—the sermon. Take a text, or maybe two, stand alone before a quiet and one hopes attentive audience and expound it for twenty minutes. Some variations have been tried, of course, but the dialogue sermon and dramatizations remain in a small minority. Most preachers use the traditional sermon most of the time, but within that genre considerably more variety is possible than is often used. Here is where attention to the varieties of speech within the Bible can be helpful. Should a sermon based on a lament be didactic in form? Hasn't something of the biblical message itself been lost if the power of the biblical language cannot be echoed in the sermon?

That is not to say that one must always try to reproduce the same genre which appears in the text; one must not necessarily compose a lament as a sermon on a biblical lament and it is probably impossible to create a modern saga which could function the way the sagas of the Old Testament did. But sometimes the text's own form of speech can be followed; for example, something which is essentially a story may, if one is good at story-telling, be presented most effectively by a sermon in narrative form. When so simple a correspondence as that is not possible, one may still become sensitive enough to the speech patterns which appear in our culture as well as to those in the Bible that one will be able to choose a modern genre which functions in our life the way the text functioned for ancient Israel. An effort to do something like that will be found in my sermon on the Flood, in which references to certain types of novels and films are made in the conviction that they express the same instincts which were given their classical expression in the saga of Genesis 6–8.

These brief and all too general remarks about tradition history and form criticism as aids to the preacher are intended only to raise some questions and perhaps suggest some possibilities, but I assume that for many readers the application of the method will be far from clear as yet. That can only be done with reference to specific literary types and by a series of examples. Because history has already been emphasized as a key to our homiletic application of the Old Testament, and because modern Old Testament theologians have tended to make history central to their work, we shall begin with it. Sagas and short stories, which have usually been taken for history in the past, will follow. Law and Wisdom make up substantial parts of the Old Testament and deserve separate treatment because of their theological importance and difficulty for the preacher. Prophecy brings the circle round, as its connection with history will be emphasized. This will make it possible to focus on the central messages of the prophetic books in spite of the great variety of types of literature which they contain.

CHAPTER I

---

*Preaching
from Historical Texts*

The historical books of the Old Testament contain some of the most difficult materials for the average preacher to deal with homiletically. They are for the most part so political and contain so little that is obviously theological that the question surely must have been raised by many whether there is any theology to be found in them, thus whether there is anything to preach from them. Modern Old Testament theologies do indeed speak of the kerygma of these writings and can help us to appreciate what they meant to ancient Israel,[1] but we still have some steps to take before we are ready to say what they mean to us in our day.

First, however, it is necessary to define "history-writing" form critically. A negative is called for at the beginning. By "history" the form critic need not be separating what really happened from what is fictional.[2] The definition of history-writing as I offer it here has to do with form not with truth; indeed it might well be that an author could write a completely fictional piece in the *form* of history. The judgment about facticity must be made equally about materials written in the form of history and those in the form of saga or legend or short story, and should not be prejudged in accordance with the form-critical label which is attached to them.

The form which history-writing takes will be defined with special reference to three parts of the Old Testament: the so-called Succession Narrative (2 Sam. 9–20, 1 Kings 1–2), 1 and 2 Kings, and 1 and 2 Chronicles, with the characteristics of more modern histories also kept in mind.

1. History-writing takes *public affairs* as its subject. It deals with organized groups of people, usually with nations. The subject-matter is normally the rise, internal and external affairs, and fall of governments. Individuals appear in their roles as public servants. Incidents in their private lives may be recounted at

times but normally that is only when their personal affairs have some effect on the destiny of the people whose history is being recorded. For example, due to the differences between the monarchy and a democracy it is much more likely that the family affairs of a king will become part of the history of a nation than the private life of a president.

2.   The events which are recorded in a history are dateable; i.e. they can be associated with other public events in chronological order and also in synchronisms. This is a deliberate part of the historian's work; he wishes to show the reader how events are related temporally. An early example of this concern appears in the regular mention of the lengths of reigns and of synchronisms between the kings of Israel and Judah in 1 and 2 Kings.

3.   History-writing involves more than the record of one event; it intends to connect events and to show continuity over a period of time. The historian not only connects events chronologically, as already mentioned, but in cause-effect relationships. So the writer of the Succession History recounts a long series of events in the lives of David and his sons in order to explain how it came about that Solomon eventually became the next king of Israel.[3]

These characteristics have been isolated partly by comparing Old Testament materials with modern works which everyone calls history-writing and partly by contrasting a work such as 2 Kings with a book such as Genesis. The distinction between history and other narrative literary genres may become more clear when the definition of saga is read in the next chapter. The three lengthy works mentioned earlier are historical writings; there is a question, however, about how other parts of the Old Testament should be classified. There are sections which contain a mixture of elements characteristic of history and of saga, and we must look at them at this point, presupposing some of what will be said about saga in the next chapter.

The account of the Exodus deals with a public event involving a nation and part of its slave population and it is recorded in a reasonably well-connected account of some length. Most of the events which are told of Moses' private life are directly related to his role as leader of the runaway slaves, although there are some exceptions to this (e.g. Exod. 4:24–26). The present form of the work is much like history-writing, but many of the materials which it contains still bear characteristics of saga and legend. The Wilderness narrative is less well-connected, more episodic and difficult to follow, either geographically or chronologically. It is probably fair to say that the motives which led to the collection and arrangement of these materials were partly those of the historian, but it is not a good example of the craft.

The story of the Conquest of Canaan records public events, clashes between peoples, in a connected fashion, and is nearer to the genre of history-writing than the materials which precede or follow it, although it also contains other genres within it. The Book of Judges is again more episodic, centering on individual heroes, with the events difficult to date or to relate to one another. The careers of Samuel and Saul plus the early parts of David's life make use of saga-like units which have been connected, rather than rewritten, by an editor whose interests are the history of Israel, not merely to make a collection of hero stories.[4] Hence we must move with considerable care through these books of the Old Testament, since the pericope we are interested in may prove to be a good example of saga or legend, but on the other hand its main value in the work as a whole may be in what it contributes to an attempt to write a comprehensive historical work. We shall look at examples both from this transitional material and from unquestioned historical writing.

What Israel's History Means to Us

Some parts of the historical books are relatively easy for the preacher to interpret and bring to life in a sermon. For example the Exodus event, the institution of the Passover or the covenant with David (2 Sam. 7) are passages which carry a heavy theological freight, which are interpreted more than once within the Old Testament and which have obvious carry-overs into the New. But what shall one do with Jehu's rebellion or with the exploits of Samson? If the allegorical method is ruled out, then the biographical approach which normally looks for examples of good or bad behavior is almost the only expedient which has been left to us. And there are chapters where even that fails us. Worse yet, even when we can use a character as an example the question remains whether that has anything to do with what the text really wants to say. Most of the Bible quite clearly does not present other human beings to us as models of behavior, although there are some exceptions to that. The problem, with the historical books, is that there are long sections where the author's purpose is not explicit to the casual reader. If he is writing theologically, he does so without even mentioning God in episode after episode, let alone spelling out clearly what God is doing in and through that history. Yet, this is not secular history. Modern studies have elucidated the theology of what is now often called the Deuteronomistic Historical Work (Joshua, Judges, Samuel, and Kings) and have shown it to be a large-scale, carefully thought through effort to create a theology of history.[5] It was produced during the exilic period and has as its message first an explanation of why Israel lost its promised land, including a justification of God's part in that, and second the recurrent theme of "turn-return" from which even those who had lost everything might find a basis for hope.

That was directly relevant for Jews in exile and the theological context provided a framework into which each of the events in the history could be set, but we are not Babylonian Jews and even when Old Testament theologians have brought to light the kerygma of works such as this (or of the Chronicler, to mention another case) it remains ancient history, Israelite theology. And the anti-historical bias which infects so many Americans creates a tremendous gap which the preacher needs to bridge somehow—and first of all in the preacher's own mind.

One mental bridge that I have found helpful depends on the question of identity which concerns so many people. The question "Who am I?" is such an important one to us because it is largely a question concerning self-respect. It asks, "Am I someone of value?" There are many ways of trying to answer the question. The existential posture need not concern us long, for it is meaningful to few; viz. the negation of the past and of one's surroundings as of no value and the conviction that what one is is determined from moment to moment by one's decisions as to what to do and be. More common by far is the definition of identity according to one's gifts. Those whose talents are overwhelming seldom question who they are; they are musicians, or chess players, or athletes. For those of us whose gifts are less impressive that may not suffice and it may fail the talented when talents themselves begin to fail. A similar answer is provided by vocation, a sense of calling to a particular work so strong that it determines the course of one's whole life. People with strong vocations seldom worry about who they are. But there is another kind of answer to the identity question which is more complex and more subject to the intellect and will. Who we are is determined in part by our relationships. I am a child of my parents, a husband of my wife, and a father of my children. I am a neighbor, a citizen, a Presbyterian, etc., and all of these aspects of my identity are determined by varying kinds of relationships with individuals or with groups. And these relationships are not just present tense affairs. My parents are dead, but I am still no less their son, and I cannot deny the influence that relationship has on my present and future, as well as on my past. That is to say, my *history* is one of the relational factors which determines who I am.

Now, there are two kinds of personal history which contribute to our identities: that of which we may be unconscious and that of which we must be conscious and about which we may make decisions. Certain facts about our past affect us whether or not we are aware of them. Our ancestors have passed on their genes to us whether or not we know who the ancestors were or what their genetic characteristics were like. We are affected by the laws and customs of our society whether or not we know how and why they originated, and psychologists tell us that the way we were brought up has an unconscious effect on our deeds and our feelings.

The other kind of personal history which we all have is the past which we are aware of, and to which we refer in our efforts to understand who we are. This kind of history is to some extent under our control and under the control of others. There is no determinism in it, for in order to be effective in our lives it has to be thought about and affirmed or denied. This means that there are options for us in the past as well as the future, and they are important options, because what we think about the past will determine our futures. For example, my biological history would go back for about three generations in America and then would transfer to Great Britain, from which my ancestors came. But the history of 19th and 18th century Britain is of little relevance for my present existence; *my* history as an American, the history which affects the way I live from day to day, includes the Civil War, the adoption of the Constitution, the Revolution and the Pilgrim Fathers, things which happened long before any member of my family came to these shores. In terms of the physical past all that has nothing to do with me, but it is not artificial or fictional to say that *my* personal history includes the Civil War. My ancestors had nothing to do with the American institution of slavery (they didn't even live here at the time), but for my present existence they might as well have been Southern slaveholders, for the way black-white relationships affect my life is determined by the fact that I am a citizen of a country which once enslaved blacks, and not by anything my own ancestors really did. Conversely, when we lived in England for a year my son became very interested in history and quite naturally it was English history that he read, for while we lived there it was the history of that country which determined the conditions of our existence and so, to a limited extent it became our history.

Now, if our history—and especially that part of the past which is consciously accepted as our history—enables us to determine our identity and establishes the conditions of our existence at a given time and place, then we have a way of explaining what a twentieth century American Christian has to do with Joshua or Rehoboam. We aren't descended from them genealogically. I am descended from some wild Gaelic tribes, some of you are descended from wild Slavic tribes or wild African tribes, or maybe from civilized Greeks or Romans, but all of us, except for the occasional Jewish Christian, have ancestors not very far back who worshipped idols. But at some time they came in contact with Jesus Christ, and when they began to worship him they became worshippers of the God of Abraham, Isaac, and Jacob. The church, in the name of Jesus Christ, assured them that the God of the Hebrew patriarchs was not merely a family deity, but was Creator of heaven and earth and ruler of all nations. Through Jesus the God of Israel became accessible to them, and this was a God with a history, the history of Israel. Our pagan ancestors learned that through Jesus they could be engrafted into that history, that they could dare to believe that God's promises to Israel were offered to them as well. Paul's analogy of the olive tree in Romans 11 forms the obvious scriptural basis for this way of describing our history, as Gentile Christians. Paul assumes, as the gospel had taught him, that our fate is not predetermined by the past in such a way that we have no control over it. He actually says that we can be given a new history, that Israel can become our ancestors, in the way that our ancestors function effectively in our consciousness to make us who we are. The change is described in spatial imagery in Eph. 2:11–19:

Therefore remember that at one time you Gentiles (were) . . . separated from Christ, alienated from the commonwealth of Israel, and strangers to the covenants of promise. . . . So then you are no longer strangers and sojourners, but you are fellow citizens with the saints and members of the household of God.   (vss. 11a, 12, 19)

Two other analogies are introduced here which show that this is something that really happens, not just imagination. Citizenship is alluded to, and immigrants really do take on a new identity with a new history when they accept the laws, customs, and outlook of their new country. We are also said to become members of the household of God, and this reminds us of the adopted child, who is given a name, a family, a history by which to identify himself. My own children are adopted, and this has given me some insights concerning this. Once I told my son that we were going to see a certain village in England and, when he asked why, I told him it was because that was where his great-great-grandfather had lived. But there was a momentary mental reservation; was that man really my adopted son's great-great-grandfather? The answer I quickly gave myself was yes; for among the things I gave my son was a family, and that family includes ancestors. When he, like any other child, became a member of our family he gained the right to participate in its history, including the making of its future history. He may one day decide to reject his heritage, of course, just as some natural born children do, and that only reminds us that each of us must decide whether to accept our personal history. It is not forced upon us; we choose it.

That is not to say we are free to make up any kind of fiction we like and say, This is who I am. What really happened does matter; history is not all in our heads. What is in our heads is the *functioning* of history, the effect upon us of our acceptance as valid or our rejection as harmful of what really happened. Here is where the preaching of our history as the people of God becomes essential. When the faith is just "me and Jesus" we remain subject to every wind that blows. We need the believing community to save us from the multitude of errors the unguided individual can fall into and to provide support when unbelief becomes strong. But the present community is not support enough unless it has roots which it understands, appreciates, and reaffirms. The roots which nourish, admonish, warn, correct, encourage, and challenge are to be found in the history of the people of God during that classical period (recorded in the Old and New Testaments) when God was forming his people. We best know who we are as Christians and what our relationship is with God when we understand ourselves to be in the company of all those other believers.

Thus I approach every historical text with the thought: This is a part of *my* history. Because this happened I am to a certain extent who I am. Then I begin asking: How did this event affect the course of the history of God's people? From that study I may expect to find something that ought to be preached.

This is not the way people normally look at their past and it may take some careful explaining in a sermon to help them appreciate that Ahab and Jezebel are part of their own personal histories. But in a time when America has passed its Bicentennial Year with all its emphasis on history, when Alex Haley's *Roots* has brought to light the vital importance which having a history has come to mean to the black community in America, in a time when other ethnic heritages are being affirmed in the search for identity, it may be easier than it once was to help people to understand how discovering and affirming their "spiritual histories" as Christians can make them better Christians and sounder persons.

What and How to Preach from Historical Texts

Let me offer some brief examples before taking two passages for extended treatment. It seems most natural to preach from a historical text when we actually see the results of that past event in effect in the current life of the people, and that happens more often than one might expect. I preached from 1 Kings 12:1-24, concerning the division of the monarchy after Solomon's death, in a church which was soon to consider a merger with another congregation. That old schism, unhealed since 922 B .C., can be seen as the beginning of a long history of schisms within God's people, and I described briefly some of them along with the continuing evidence that despite the good reasons for many of them, there remains always the desire for healing. As one example I spoke of the prominence of the number 12 throughout the Bible as a symbol of God's whole people, despite the fact that the twelve tribes of Israel did not exist as a political unity after 922 B.C. But I did not use this as a basis for lecturing the people on the necessity of merger. I concluded with reference to the vow to work for "the peace, unity and purity of the Church" as a way of formulating the tensions which have existed throughout history between schism for the sake of purity and the deep-felt conviction that God desires unity. And I left it for them to ponder the troubled history of God's divided people as they look forward to negotiations with another congregation.

A sermon on Ezra 3, the account of the beginning of the rebuilding of the temple in 520 B.C., emphasized the abrupt ending of the narrative, with its reference to the weeping of those who had once seen Solomon's temple, as a clue that the writer wished us to give that event more than a passing thought. They were the people who had experienced it all: the fall of Jerusalem, the exile and the restoration, and on that triumphant day they wept. The Bible so strongly connects repentance for national sins with the fall of Jerusalem that I thought it justified to connect that weeping with what those returned exiles had learned from their own history. I then looked to other Old Testament passages which make explicit those lessons learned from the experience of exile and restoration and drew from them two things to emphasize: the acceptance of responsibility and the belief in God's gracious power. I tried to show how it was precisely the returnees' acceptance of responsibility and faith in God's power that has made possible our existence as believers in that same God, by noting briefly their subsequent history, then moved to the necessity for each generation to learn the same lessons. Since this congregation was soon to call a new pastor, I concluded by suggesting their new beginning may also include the mingling of weeping and laughter, but it is just then that we need to recommit ourselves to our responsibilities with faith in God's gracious power.

A sermon on the sad history of David and Absalom can scarcely avoid commenting on David as an example of how a father should not raise his son, but if only that was said, would we have touched on what the Bible wants to say? I think not. So the framework of such a sermon should point out that this is not just biography; it is an essential part of Israel's history, and its implications are not just political (who will succeed David?), for the succession has strong theological overtones because of Nathan's prophecy (2 Sam. 7). We do hear something about God in this text, even though it is implicit. The Bible records this family scandal because it was needed to cope with another great scandal—the eventual failure of God's promise that David would never lack an heir to sit on the throne of Jerusalem. We are being told that there was an unhealthiness in that family which began with David's own failures as a father. The family endured longer than it could have been expected to, thanks to God's patience, but it did not have the inner strength to endure forever. And this tension between the just results of human failings and God's patience which corrects many of our errors is a consistent part of the experiences of believers from David's time to our own day.

A Sermon on 2 Kings 11

I decided to try to preach on this chapter precisely because it is so political and so untheological. It does conclude with the making of a three-way covenant involving God, the king and the people, but the main event is a palace revolt, and there is nothing very spiritually uplifting about that. For the exegete the passage is very simple. There are no difficult problems with the text, with the composition (there is no evidence of multiple authorship), or with the reconstruction of the event described. The revolt against Athaliah is told in a straightforward and circumstantial way. The problems here are strictly homiletical and so the chapter provides a simple example of how I apply the method of preaching from historical texts which has just been described.

The sermon which follows was preached at the Trinity Presbyterian Church, a small, inner-city congregation in Pittsburgh, Pa., on June 26, 1977. I already had it planned when I was reminded that it was to be a communion service and at first blush I thought I would have to start over with another text, but on thinking about the direction the development of the sermon was taking I realized that it was leading me to say something about the Communion of the Saints, a theme which I like to emphasize as part of the Lord's Supper. This led me to use Hebrews 11:32–40 as the New Testament lesson, a decision which might not have been made under other circumstances.

This is an example of a sermon developed exactly along the lines described earlier. The author provides no explicit theological interpretation of the events he records and so we face the difficult question of what can be "read out" of the text, knowing that anything theological we say about it is in real danger of being "read into" it. What can be read out of this text is supplied for us by the broader context in which it appears, the work of the Deuteronomistic Historian, and the interpretation of the theology of that work provided by Gerhard von Rad in his *Old Testament Theology* was of great help to me. He points out how so much of 2 Samuel, 1 and 2 Kings reads like "secular" history in that God is seldom mentioned by the author; with the exception of the prophetic legends about Elijah and Elisha there are no miracles to speak of and people live by their wits in a world ruled by human decisions and behavior. But the grand plan of the work does not ignore God by any means; it intends to show how Israel failed its responsibility to the covenant and why it eventually had to suffer the consequences of disobedience to the God of the covenant. This chapter is an incident in the conflict between those who were overtly opposed to the acknowledgment of Yahweh as the sole God of Israel and those who attempted, for one reason or another, to maintain the old covenant relationship. In attempting to learn what they may have to do with us I tried to think of this event as a part of my personal history as a Christian and to lead the congregation in similar reflections. This kind of text has a certain shock effect which may or may not be helpful homiletically, for here we must consider what violent political activity may have contributed to our faith and to us as individuals of faith.

The incident recorded here raises some difficult theological problems which are not discussed by the author. He speaks in a matter of fact way about violence, the overthrow of a government, and murder. The issues that he raises cannot be ignored in a sermon, but I tried to use them helpfully without being judgmental. It is not for us either to apologize for the actions of people in the past nor to condemn them, but to learn from them, the more so since we are their heirs. I briefly took up the question of violence largely to remind comfortable American Christians that similar ethical issues face some modern Christians, with whom we ought to be in empathy, and to show them how difficult the ethical decisions may be in life or death situations.

The second main emphasis of the sermon was drawn from von Rad's insights concerning the hiddenness of God's action in much of this historical work, using that as a basis for affirming God's work behind the scenes in the apparently thoroughly secular world in which we now live.

The Thin Line

2 Kings 11:1–21   Hebrews 11:32–40

We might be pagans today if it were not for the event recorded in this text, for the worship of our God had been narrowed down to a thin line of faithful people in 837 B.C. If Joash had been killed, would there have been a Jewish faith one day? If there had been no Jewish faith would there have been a Jesus, the Christ? If there had been no Jesus would we still be worshipping the idols of our ancestors?

Actually we cannot answer such questions, for in fact there was a Jesus, there was a Jewish people, there was a Joash, but to ask the questions helps us to realize how much we owe to things that people in the past have done. In a peculiar sense that palace revolt in the far off city of Jerusalem, 2,814 years ago, was carried out for *our* sakes. It is part of *our* history.

This is the kind of history, however, which we might prefer to forget: plotting to overthrow the government, violent revolution, and murder. We'd rather not have anything to do with that, and yet it seems we owe something to those plotters. That is why we ought to spend some time thinking about what they did and why, and to try to learn if we can what God was doing in the midst of all this.

The overthrow of Queen Athaliah of Judah was a kind of reaction to the backlash to a revolution. It had all begun a generation earlier when Queen Jezebel of the Northern Kingdom of Israel had tried to make the worship of her god, Baal of Sidon, the dominant religion in Israel. The resistence to her missionary efforts eventually took a political form and one Jehu led a revolution which wiped out the members of the royal house and massacred every Baal worshipper he could find in the country. Jezebel's son was on the throne of the Northern Kingdom at that time and another relative was king in Judah. Both of them were assassinated and Jehu became king in the North, but in Judah the mother of the dead king, Athaliah, a strong character, grasped the throne for herself and ruled for six years as queen. She led the backlash to the revolution which I mentioned. In revenge for the death of her son and her other relatives she attempted to kill every member of the house of David, the traditional dynasty which had ruled from Jerusalem for 200 years. She almost succeeded. Only the little boy Joash, one year old, was saved from her wrath, hidden away in one of the rooms of the temple. For six years Athaliah reigned while the supporters of the house of David bided their time. Finally they decided the moment had come for the coup, and you have heard the results.

We thank God that we do not live in such a time and place, that we live under a government which offers us freedom of religion and that we, with all the problems that we do face, are not up against the kind of life and death situation which we read about this morning. But it is not so for all believers in our day. We think especially of the Christians in Uganda who are being actively persecuted for their faith. Even now they have no choice but to discuss whether it could be permissible for a Christian to plot against a head of state. Could it be right to attempt to assassinate Idi Amin so as to save the many lives that will otherwise be taken if he continues to rule? That is the terrible issue which faces some of our brothers and sisters in Christ today. And only a generation ago the same issue confronted the German Christians, with some of them concluding they could not in good conscience take violent action against Adolph Hilter, no matter how much suffering he was causing, but with others deciding that as Christians they had the terrible duty to try to take his life.

From the Christian point of view, killing, even of a tyrant, can never be done with an easy conscience. Yet some Christians have decided that there are times when for the sake of humanity one must take blood guilt upon himself. We don't know whether Jehoiada had a struggle with his conscience over the killing of Athaliah or not, but we do know that we have benefited because of it.

God was at work in this terrible event and he had the power to bring benefit to humanity even out of plotting and murder. This is something we need to be reminded of, for we tend to identify the work of God only in those human actions which we believe God approves of, but Old Testament history teaches us something different.

God is usually at work in secret among us and we do not understand what he has done until much later. In Jerusalem on the day of that palace revolt there must have been people who saw Athaliah as the rightful queen and who agreed with her cries of treason. Only afterward could it become clear that what happened that day contributed something to God's purpose for humanity and did not work against it.

God works that same way today. We tend to think of conversions and healings as the work of God and the rest of what we do as our business. But God is involved with what the congress is doing and with the decisions of the President and his cabinet. God is involved with the Russian Politburo and the Indian parliament. God is involved with our local union meetings and with meetings of boards of directors.

That does not mean he condones or justifies everything those groups do, but it does mean he is at work in them and behind them. And we live by faith that he is indeed at work when he works in secret.

Human power often seems so strong that the government and big business can do anything they like and we are at their mercy. The Athaliah's of this world come on so strong it is hard to believe that God is really there and really doing something. But the conclusion of the eleventh chapter of Hebrews reminds us what a strange and mixed company that thin line of the faithful makes, and reminds us of the varied ways God works in our history. Rebels, who put foreign armies to flight, and martyrs, who suffered mocking and scourging, are both used to advance God's purpose.

Today, at the Communion table, we sit in their presence. With the presence of the Risen Christ we experience the Communion of the Saints, as the old service in the Book of Common Worship clearly reminds us. It is a motley group with whom we share this faith, Jehoiada and Joash included among them. But if it were not for them we would not be here.

The author of Hebrews found a way to read history backwards as well as forwards. He says that not only are our ancestors in the faith essential to us, but we are also essential to them, for if we do not keep the faith all they did was in vain. In the belief that we are keeping faith with them we come to this table.

A Sermon on Exodus 13:17–14:31

This passage is very different from the previous example. It is fraught with problems, literary, historical, and philosophical, and it carries a heavy theological freight. It is probably composed from more than one source, it makes use of several separate traditions, and it has a long and rich history of interpretation. So the preacher is here working with a passage full of homiletical possibilities, but one about which a whole series of decisions must be made before a coherent sermon, soundly based in the text, can emerge.

I have taken this passage to be essentially historical in its intent, for it deals with events on a public scale, involving one of the great nations and its slave population, and it even shows some interest in dating, since 13:18 tells us this happened to the fifth generation of Israelites sojourning in Egypt. The complexity of the text plus the occurrence in it of supernatual elements lead me to suggest some principles for the homiletical appropriation of any passage of this type:

1. Since it purports to describe a historical event, one cannot escape asking the question, What really happened? If it claims by its form and intent to be history, then it does matter whether the event recorded really happened or not. If it didn't, then we have nothing to preach about it. Certainly truth may be conveyed in other ways—through parable, allegory, etc., things which never happened in history, and this is often done in the Bible—but if it claims to be conveyed through the record of an event, a non-event won't do. So we must do some historical work on this text.

2. The preacher should work through all the literary and historical difficulties, but they shouldn't all be paraded before the congregation in one's sermon. In the classroom, where there is time for discussion and careful re-reading of the passage, that could be done with members who are interested in Bible study, but the pulpit is an inappropriate place for it. The sermon must have something to proclaim, not to debate, so one needs to work to find out what the text says

which one is sure about and which the people will be able to recognize as true for themselves. This is not a counsel to hide the mysteries of biblical scholarship from the congregation, but to choose the appropriate setting for it. On the other hand, the preacher ought to be open, honest, and humble enough to be able to admit to the congregation that some things remain uncertain and that there are parts of the Bible which we still cannot explain.

3. We haven't been given a full, circumstantial account of what actually happened at the Sea. We cannot reconstruct it in detail as we could the enthronement of Joash, without adding a great deal which is not in the text. Here again, a textbook or a Bible study class will find it necessary to try out some such reconstruction, and sermons sometimes have to make some use of them. The example which I am offering does some of that. But I think one should be very cautious about offering a re-telling of the event according to one modern idea of what really happened as if that were just what the Bible says. Two unfortunate results are likely: They may take what you said as if it were Scripture and never realize the difference, or they may be very conscious of the difference and thus be led to discount everything else you say. I recall a sermon on the feeding of the 5,000 in which the preacher said that when the people saw the boy's generosity they brought out and shared the food which they had with them but had been hiding up until then—and said it as if he knew that's what really happened, rather than indicating that this was one possible rationalizing explanation. That is not playing fair with the intelligence of the congregation. It is the same with the crossing of the Sea. We cannot avoid speculating about the natural processes involved; whether it could have been caused by the eruption of Santorini (Thera) and a resulting tidal wave,[6] or by a local earthquake or something else, and in addition to discussing these ideas in the classroom they may sometimes be mentioned in a sermon when appropriate, but they are such modern concerns that they tend to distract from what the Bible is talking about. For the fact is that the Bible shows no interest in providing that kind of explanation, and if we are satisfied with one such hypothesis as telling us "what really happened" we are very likely to miss what the Bible itself wanted to say about that event.

4. This is not to deny that sometimes a sermon may need to deal explicitly with peculiarly modern questions about the ancient texts, such as whether we can still believe in miracles or in supernatural beings. When that kind of message seems to be needed, it also should be textually grounded as far as possible, but it should be clear that it is not proclaiming the text's own message. My example does take up the question of the loss of the sense of the miraculous in our age, but does not deal with it philosophically or scientifically; rather, it tries to stay close to the text to see whether something of that sense can be recaptured.

How then shall we approach such a text in order to preach it? I have suggested that first we must work as historians, to find out as best we can what happened. The pericope begins just after the exodus proper, the escape from Egypt, and records the near abortion of the escape, so that it could be taken as a triumphant appendix to the exodus-story, or as the first and worst of the many dangers from which God saved Israel in the wilderness. However, in Israelite tradition the crossing of the Sea is connected with the exodus rather than with the wilderness materials. And the Old Testament regularly testifies that it was with the exodus that Israel's existence as a people began. There can be little reasonable doubt of the historicity of the exodus-event; i.e. of an escape from Egypt of a group of slaves who became the nucleus of later Israel. Any other explanation of the existence of Israel is much harder to believe. No one need have any uncertainty about proclaiming the occurrence of the exodus and what it meant for the life of Israel. But the incident at the Sea is not always included in Old Testament references to the deliverance from Egypt (e.g. Deut. 6:21–23, 26:5ff.; Ps. 105; Ezek. 20), and so the question has been raised whether the exodus-event originally included such a feature.[7] It has been suggested that the original "crossing of the water" occurred at the River Jordan (Josh. 3–4) and that this theme was later transferred to the exodus setting. However, the tradition connecting the Sea with the defeat of an army is a very old one, as indicated by the Song of Miriam (Exod. 15:21), and this could not have its home in the Jordan materials. Also, the theme is so often connected with the Pharaoh and Egypt that one is on reasonably safe ground in affirming that a victory at the Sea was an original part of the exodus-event. As to the details of this pericope, that is another matter, as the ensuing work will show, and one may feel very uncertain about any step-by-step recreation of the incident.

An event in itself cannot be preached; what is to be preached is what the event means, and here we have an abundance of material from the Old Testament and later interpreters to help us. But we begin with, and concentrate on, the immediate text itself, of course. The complexity and confused nature of the account suggests that it may have been compiled from two or three original sources (e.g. are the Israelites to stand firm or to strike camp? vss. 13, 15), so one looks to traditional source analysis for help. But the process is very difficult in this part of Exodus and the results are less secure than they are in other parts of the Pentateuch. Childs suggest the following:[8]

> J: 13:21–22; 14:5b, 6, 9aα, 10bα 11–14, 19b, 21aβ, 24, 25b, 27aβb, 30, 31
> P: 13:20; 14:1–4, 8, 9aβb, 15–18, 21aαb, 22–23, 26, 27a, 28–29
> E: 13:17–19; 14:5a, 7, 19a, 25a

The result of this division is to produce one source (J) in which the Israelites hold their ground while Yahweh causes movements of the water which catch the Egyptians and drown them. The other main source (P) speaks of the waters dividing and the Israelites marching through, pursued by the Egyptians who are drowned by the returning waters once the Israelites have safely passed through. Hence we have two conflicting accounts of exactly what happened, although there is agreement on essentials, that the Egyptian army was wiped out by divine intervention at the Sea. Should one then choose one source or the other and say this is the authentic one, and on what principle? One might prefer J because it is presumably older, or P because its version is more consistent with other parts of the Old Testament. But here we have taken a wrong track. J, by itself, is not Scripture, nor is P. The canonical account of the victory at the Sea is this composite form, as it appears in the Book of Exodus; that is the testimony which all those generations of believers to which I have referred earlier wished to pass on. So we look to the analysis of sources not seeking some prior authority, but to help us better to understand the present, canonical form of the text.[9] The character of the redaction will be appealed to again when we come to the listing of messages which can grow out of the study of this passage.

Some major and minor themes might be noted at this point. We have already observed that the centrality of God's action is to be found in each source. A minor theme is the reference to the bones of Joseph (13:19) connecting the departure from Egypt with the promise to the patriarchs. This section is also connected with the account of the plagues in Egypt by the references to the hardening of Pharaoh's heart (14:4, 8), and with the subsequent wilderness traditions by the theme of the Israelite murmuring against God and Moses (14:10-14). These are important subjects but one would probably choose different texts if one intended to make them the basis of a sermon. Another wilderness theme, the guidance which God provides for his people through an unknown and trackless region by means of the pillar of cloud and fire, is introduced here, but it serves a different purpose at the heart of this story, to hide the Israelites from the rapidly approaching Egyptians. The motif of protection is dominant in this passage rather than that of guidance, as in the wilderness traditions. Finally, there is an unusual note at the end when we are told that the Israelites believed in Yahweh *and in his servant Moses*.[10] This is the only place where faith in Moses is mentioned in the Old Testament. Although it became basic to Samaritan theology in later years, it was not reaffirmed in Judaism, so we will not make too much of it.

Next we ought to trace the use of the major theme of this passage, deliverance from the Egyptian army at the Sea, elsewhere in the Old Testament to help us to understand what it continued to mean to Israel and to begin tracing the history which connects us with that event. Probably the oldest reference to the event is the song of Miriam:

> Sing to the LORD, for he has triumphed gloriously;
> the horse and his rider he has thrown into the sea. (15:21)

Many scholars consider this short song to be contemporary with the event itself.[11] A somewhat later development of the theme appears in the longer song in Exodus 15:1–18, in which the concept of Yahweh as a warrior developed and which adds to the victory at the Sea materials dealing with the wilderness sojourn, the conquest, and the election of Zion. This appears to be one of the early poetic expressions of the conviction that the exodus was the foundational event for the entire subsequent existence of Israel. Elsewhere, in clearly later materials such as Josh. 24:6–7, the victory at the Sea appears as part of the recital of the mighty acts of God, beginning with the promise to the patriarchs and concluding with the occupation of Canaan. As noted earlier, however, references to the exodus do not require any mention of the crossing of the Sea. In the Psalms the theme is used to praise the power of God and in contexts confessing Israel's failure to respond to him with obedience (Ps. 78:52f., 106:9–12, 114, 136:13–15). That the crossings of the Sea and of the Jordan were thought of together is shown in Psalm 114. A new use of the theme appears in Deutero-Isaiah. References to the past-saving act of God are made the basis for the promise of a new act of redemption of that same kind (Isa. 43:16f.). Furthermore, this prophet's strong emphasis on Yahweh as the Creator God leads him to combine the bringing of dry land out of the watery chaos in the act of creation with the provision of dry land by which the Israelites could cross the Sea. He also does not hesitate to introduce mythological elements from the creation materials common to the Near East, as in Isa. 51:9–10:

> Was it not thou that didst cut Rahab in pieces,
>   that didst pierce the dragon?
> Was it not thou that didst dry up the sea,
>   the waters of the great deep;
> that didst make the depths of the sea a way
>   for the redeemed to pass over?

So the exodus and the crossing of the Sea have become "types" of God's redemptive work in the past and the future and proofs, along with creation, of his power to free his people from exile, bring them back to the promised land and make the desert become a fertile garden. The exodus taught Israel how God "typically" behaves.

The kind of work which has been done thus far on the passage can proceed with the help of the usual commentaries and with a concordance. What comes next, tracing the use of the tradition in post-bibilical Judaism and through the New Testament into the church, requires a bit more in the way of resources and may have to be done in a very sketchy way for the average sermon. Fortunately there is a commentary on Exodus which seems designed to aid the homiletical process I am suggesting: B. S. Childs' *The Book of Exodus: A Critical, Theological Commentary*, and from it we can glean materials from the history of tradition which will help us to see what the victory at the Sea has continued to mean to believers in our effort to preach what is faithful to the text and its ongoing meaning. Childs has found three primary uses of the theme in the rabbinic literature: to emphasise God's protection of his chosen people, to celebrate the result of the event—which is freedom, and to exalt the promise which God made to the patriarchs as the reason for his intervention to save Israel from the Egyptians.[12] The New Testament partly uses the theme as it appears in the Old Testament (Acts 7:36, 13:16ff.; Heb. 11:29) but also follows the lead of Second Isaiah in making it the type of a new redemptive event, greater than the first, viz. the coming of Christ (Matt. 2:15). Paul also allegorizes the crossing of the Sea and makes it a symbol of baptism in 1 Cor. 10:1–13, but his main point in the passage is similar to the one found in those psalms which confessed Israel's sin: As Israel passed through the waters of the Sea the church has passed through the waters of baptism, but just as Israel afterwards disobeyed and put God to the test so the church is in danger of doing. The Church Fathers picked up the baptism allegory and used it as virtually the only meaning which the crossing of the Sea had, thus losing much of the richness of the tradition. Theirs is an example we will not want to follow although we may not deny completely that there is a certain aptness to the parallel; both baptism and the Sea mark the beginning of a new people.

More could be added to that part of the work, but it is long enough and more than can be done with a reasonable amount of effort for many parts of the Old Testament. We now have an abundance of material to aid us in the interpretation of the passage for homiletical purposes and the next question is to choose the theme which seems best to meet a need recognized in the congregation to be addressed and which the preacher feels some enthusiasm about developing. At this point I shall simply list some of the possibilities and then go on to justify the route taken in the example which follows.

The exodus is the archetypal salvation-event in the Bible. Here typology is certainly an appropriate interpretive method, for both Old and New Testaments use the event in this way, and the imagery most often chosen when speaking of the exodus comes from this chapter, from the crossing of the Sea. The typical elements of God's saving work which have been stressed by interpreters all through history are: the unbelief of God's people, God's undeserved and unaided intervention in order to save, the character of the act, viz. setting captives free, and the appearance of belief *after* God has saved.

The exodus as a beginning might be emphasized, in line with much of the Old Testament's witness and taking a clue from Paul's use of it in 1 Corinthians. That event, unnoticed at the time on the world scene, not only changed the destiny of a little band of slaves but changed the course of world history. It was the constitutive event for the existence of the people of God, Israel (hence for us, as well), and because there was another equally world-shaking event of the same initiatory character, the coming of Christ, it is appropriate to compare them.

My example developed from combining the traditional use of the chapter as the classical type of God's deliverance of his people with a question about human reactions to such things. Rather than the reactions stressed in Scripture and tradition: belief (Exod. 14:31) or forgetfulness and disobedience (Ps. 78, 106; 1 Cor. 10), I turned to the modern problem of disbelief or uneasiness with the miraculous. The idea and the approach came from pondering the historical problems posed by the text and trying to determine, from looking at source analysis and from careful reading of the final redaction just what *they* thought had really happened. I finally concluded they didn't really know, then found a similar comment in M. Buber's book, *Moses: The Revelation and the Covenant*: "The situation itself cannot be reconstructed from the narrative."[13] I found Buber's entire chapter on this passage to be of great help in my effort to reconstruct the feeling of the text, and his statement, "The concept of miracle which is permissible from the historical approach can be defined at its starting point as an abiding astonishment" became the motif of the sermon.[14] The sermon was preached at the Hanover United Presbyterian Church, an open country church in western Pennsylvania, on October 13, 1974.

Wonder

Exodus 14:5–31

My subject this morning is the miracle in our lives. It's not a biblical word—miracle—and so the title of this sermon comes from the way the Bible talks about things we call miracles; it calls them "signs and wonders." But there doesn't seem to be much that's wonderful left for us. We've seen it all: men walking on the moon, Evel Knievel jumping two dozen buses on his motorcycle, unbreakable athletic records broken with ease—there's not much left that could surprise us. After the moon, what do we do for an encore? We are not unlike the bad, old joke I remember reading in *Boy's Life* magazine many years ago. A teacher is trying to explain to a pupil what a miracle is. "If a man climbed to the top of a ten story building, jumped off and landed on the sidewalk, got up and walked away without a scratch, what would you call that?" "A fluke." "Well, suppose he immediately climbed to the top of the building again, jumped off, landed on the sidewalk, got up and walked away without a scratch, what would you call that?" "A fluke." "But suppose the same man, three times in succession, jumped off the top of a ten story building, got up and walked away without a scratch, would you still call that a fluke?" "No, I'd call it a habit."

The sense of wonder is almost gone from us, and we are poorer for it. We still see it in tiny children and rejoice for that, but even children now lose it very early. We parents have been disappointed more than once to find that when we give our children the opportunity to have an experience that once thrilled us, it means nothing to them. And over against that stands the Bible with its "miracles." We don't quite know what to make of them because we don't quite know what they are. I believe that Martin Buber was correct when he said that what the Bible calls signs and wonders were those events which produced an abiding sense of astonishment. And if that's true, it's not that miracles don't occur anymore, it's just that we don't experience them.

This morning I would like for us to see if we can experience for ourselves one of the wonders recorded in the Old Testament, and by doing so to open ourselves to the new possibility of being enriched by the sense of wonder at what God is doing for us now; for the other thing Buber defined as the essence of miracle, which makes the astonishment *abiding* is the recognition that the remarkable thing which has happened was done *by God*.

The Book of Exodus, in its account of how the Israelites crossed the Reed Sea and were delivered from the Egyptian army, recounts one of the great things God has done *for us*. It is ancient history, true, but it is a part of our own history, for from the exodus came Israel and from Israel came the Christ who is our savior. They were our spiritual ancestors who were delivered from the Egyptians that day and so as we try to recapture what it was like for them we shall do so not as a secular historian, not as a scientist, not as Cecil B. De Mille making a movie, but as people *for whose sake* all this happened.

To understand just what happened at the Sea is very difficult. This part of Exodus is not completely clear and straightforward. At one point Israel is told to stand firm and watch the Lord destroy the Egyptians and at another they are told to strike camp and march. There is a cloud, there is wind, there is the clogging of chariot wheels—and as we ponder the confusing details we begin to realize that confusing is the way it was.

It was a mob scene, to begin with. Moses didn't bring a close-knit, well-disciplined group out into the wilderness; he led what the Bible calls a "mixed multitude," a motley group of slaves, some Hebrew, some not. Most of them had never been in the desert before, they had grown up in the lush vegetation of the Nile delta, but now they were feeling the awesome desolation of the wilderness. They had followed obediently enough until they came to a marshy area of lakes and swamps where Moses had them camp. And then the Egyptians arrived! They saw the clouds of dust raised by the chariot wheels from afar, and panic set in. People running wildly about, giving contradictory orders, clutching children and possessions, Moses yelling at the top of his voice trying to make himself heard, arguing with some who were accusing him of leading them into a death trap, wild rumors about what was happening, because in the milling crowd few could see anything.

Eventually things calm down a little, because the Egyptian army does not come charging into the camp. It is dusk and something has made them stop and wait; darkness falls quickly. Through the night there was more confusion, Moses shouting orders again, a violent wind blowing, noise, fear, mud and water, stumbling and pushing movement somewhere—and finally daybreak. They were on the other side! They were safe! And along the shore were the corpses of what was left of the Egyptian army!

Celebration!

That is how God works, in the midst of the turmoil and confusion and uncertainty of life as we also experience it. Mysteriously he brings deliverance. We, like the Israelites, often can't describe in step-by-step detail just what has happened, but we know we're on the other side! And it's quiet. And all we can do is wonder, and rejoice.

I stood in line behind a severely handicapped woman the other day, one who was mentally as well as physically deficient. For once, in addition to feeling sorry for her, which is as far as we usually go, it occurred to me to marvel that I have a brain which works reasonably well and I rejoiced in something which I almost always take for granted—being able to think. God's special blessing at the moment was that sense of *wonder* which made life sweet just then.

Do you remember trembling for a time after a close call in which you might have been hurt or killed? What caused it—fear? The danger was past. No, what caused it was that awful awareness of how horribly wrong things could have gone just then and that wondering sense of relief that they didn't.

Have you ever been tempted to do something really wrong, to steal something big or to hurt someone badly? Have you, somehow or other, found yourself safe on the other side, even though you didn't know where you could find the strength to resist? And felt that wondering relief at being delivered?

There is cause for wonder all around us. God, our maker and our deliverer is at work in and for us. But our senses are so dulled that it takes a shock of some kind for us to feel the power around us, so we don't rejoice very much. But the age of miracles isn't past. Whenever something wonderous happens to you, and you've been delivered, and you know that God has done it, that's a miracle.

And then we ought to sing.

CHAPTER II

Preaching from Saga

"Saga" is not one of the everyday words in our language and I would expect that to introduce the word in a sermon would produce more confusion than enlightment. Fairy tales we understand and a man may be a "legend in his own time" but what is saga? As a matter of fact its origins are far removed from us; it is an Icelandic word, but it has been taken up into the vocabulary of Old Testament form criticism and I believe that preachers who understand the kind of literature which this term denotes will find that they can make these parts of the Old Testament speak with a peculiar directness to their congregations, whether or not the individual listener can define the term. Saga was, after all, a type of folk literature; it originated in and spoke to the deepest and most common needs and concerns of the people, and it maintains that ability despite the cultural barriers which separate us and the people of Israel.

The sagas of the Bible were first given an accurate form-critical description by Hermann Gunkel in the introduction to his commentary on Genesis.[1] As a type of folk literature, essentially oral in its origin and character, it is related to other genres of folk literature such as legend, myth, and fairy tale, but unfortunately students of folklore have never succeeded in making sharp distinctions among these terms.[2] Attempts to apply these somewhat vague labels to the materials of the Old Testament (which has a long history of *written* transmission) have sometimes been more confusing than helpful. But nevertheless the term saga can be used in a helpful way to denote a type of literature which is different in form, content, and intention from history-writing, so different that it ought to be preached in a distinctive way.

For our purposes most of the Book of Genesis can be classified as saga. The primordial history in chapters 1–11, which some have been tempted to call myth, is so different in many ways from the ancient Near Eastern materials universally recognized as myth that it seems better to call them types of saga. The largest section of Genesis which does not fit this category is the Joseph cycle in chapters 37–50, which is a continuous, well-plotted story of some length, called by some scholars a *novella*.[3] It belongs more appropriately in our chapter called *short story* than in this chapter. As noted in the first chapter, there are elements of saga appearing elsewhere in the Old Testament, but we shall confine our attentions to Genesis.

What are Biblical Sagas Trying to Say?

The form critical characteristics of saga will be described with reference to the three main aspects of history-writing given in the previous chapter so as to clarify the difference between them, then the oral and family-centered nature of saga will be developed further in order to show how these formal results can lead to a type of interpretation which is appropriate to the genre.

1. Saga deals primarily with the affairs of private life. The basic unit is the family and the events which typically occur are births, marriages, family quarrels, and deaths. Seldom does a group of any size appear and normally there are only two or three characters with speaking parts. Political history is largely ignored; e.g. there is no clue given to the personal identity of the Pharaoh who appears in Gen. 12:10–20. Occasionally a king is named, such as Abimelech of the Philistines and Melchizedek of Salem, but we are told nothing of them except for their personal relationship with the patriarch who is the center of the saga. The campaign of the four kings described in Gen. 14:1–17 has aroused an inordinate amount of interest in scholars because it is the closest to a "historical" event which can be found in Genesis, but so far even it has baffled attempts to link it with other historical sources. Saga, then, is concerned with things which are of intense interest to those close to its heroes, but which don't make the history books. It is "family history."

2. To expand on what has just been said, the events recorded in sagas cannot be associated with "public" events and thus cannot be dated. Even the named kings are not identified in such a way as to make it possible to connect them with political history, for that is not the interest of saga. There are few chronological notes except for indications of the ages of the characters, again a matter of personal interest, and the time intervals which may be thought to have elapsed between sagas are usually very uncertain.

3. Sagas are typically short units, often concentrating on only one episode and usually poorly connected with one another. So, although we have a cycle of sagas about Abraham leading from some unspecified time in his adulthood until his death, this in no way represents a continuous biography, but is a collection of episodes loosely related both thematically and chronologically. There are some long units, such as Genesis 24, but this still concerns a single incident,

how Isaac's wife was obtained.[4] There is no effort to connect a series of units so as to show cause and effect continuity, such as we find in the Succession History of David.

None of these remarks should be taken as somehow critical of saga as if it were poor history-writing. It is another kind of thing and doesn't intend to write history; the contrasts made above are a first attempt to delineate its own character. We can proceed now to some more positive statements by asking, What is saga really about? The two most important clues for obtaining an answer to that question are its family-centered character and its transmission via oral tradition.

a) The largest number of biblical sagas deal with the patriarchs, i.e., the "fathers" of Israel. When the Israelite spoke of Abraham he was talking about his grandfather, but more than that, he was talking about his own self. Even for us, in our individualistic age, statements about one's family are, more than any other kind of reference we may make to the past, statements about oneself. Why do people trace their genealogies? Why do they take pride in discovering noble blood or outstanding achievements in their family history? Is it not because they think this tells them something about their own worth? And do we not regularly refer to characteristics or behavior of our parents or grandparents as a way of accounting for the way we behave? Statements about one's ancestors are not so much statements about the past as they are about the present; they are self-affirmations.

If this can be true of us, with our strongly developed individualism, how much more powerful it must have been for the Hebrew mentality, which normally thought first in terms of one's family group as the basic unit of one's identity and then only secondarily of oneself as an individual. This form of self-understanding, which we try to explain by calling it "corporate personality," extended not only to the presently living family group but also into the past and the future.[5] The Israelite thought of himself as really having been present in the loins of Abraham and of his own character and personality as really living on in his posterity. So when he spoke of Abraham, Isaac, and Jacob he was not speaking only of individuals who lived in the past but was speaking of Israel in the present, of which he was a part. Perhaps the converse is also true; he might find that the most appropriate way to express his own experiences as an Israelite was to speak in terms of Abraham rather than of anything in the present.

b) This is where the probability that the sagas of Genesis originated as an oral genre becomes important. We should probably not think of them as stories composed by someone, then memorized and retold word-for-word as accurately as possible for generation after generation. It is more likely that they were re-composed over and over, using a traditional theme and a great deal of traditional language, including standard story-telling formulas. This sort of thing is done by experts in societies which value the oral transmission of their heritage; they know all the valuable traditions of their people thoroughly and have mastered all the stock phrases and formulas, but in addition they have the gift of being able to produce orally an artfully told story.[6] The stories were often entertaining, but we understand from what has just been said about family history as self-affirmation that they were also deeply meaningful. And the saga-teller, in re-composing them as he told them, had the opportunity (which we assume he used) to make them directly relevant to the present each time they were told. This helps to explain the characteristic of the Genesis sagas which has been so frustrating to historians who try to date the patriarchs—the sagas contain authentic features from widely separated historical periods. Abraham has been dated in the 18th century, the 15th century, and even later, depending on which elements are emphasized. The reason for this is that the sagas were living things, they changed as they were retold, with new material being added from time to time so that they reflect various periods, and this is not to be taken as a distortion or corruption of some pristine original, since they were never intended to be relics of the past. Their function was to serve as living, present affirmations of what it meant to be a son of Abraham.

> . . . This means firstly that the saga has a different effectiveness from that of historical writing, bridging the gap between the present and the past, and showing that what appears as past events contains a hidden relevance to the present. The narrator and his hearers identify themselves with the deeds and sufferings of their forebears. God's intervention in favour of their forebears is intervention in favour of themselves. Those who learn about the danger which threatened the ancestress of Israel are made conscious of the inherent danger to themselves from the established peoples in Canaan by whom they are surrounded. They hope for divine protection also. The warriors who tell of David's courage identify him with their present leader, who will be granted Jahweh's favour as David and the other earlier leaders were. Thus it is natural that in the course of the transmission history the later narrator's experiences of God and the world affect the stories of earlier periods. The saga is a repository for the economic, intellectual and religious experiences of countless generations. It draws all periods together, and compresses the events into a language with highly symbolical overtones.[7]

As Koch says, saga is a "repository" for various kinds of information from many ages, so, if we insist, we *can* mine it for historical data, and the tendency in recent scholarship has been to do just that and only that. We attempt to discover whether Abraham and the rest were real persons and to date them if possible; i.e. to do just what I said must be done with history-writing. And for the person who is attempting to reconstruct the earliest periods of Old Testament history that must be done with sagas, also.[8] That is not the preacher's work, however, and we must ask whether, having found the historical nucleus of a saga we have learned anything about what the saga *means*? Have we been faithful to what that type of literature intends to say? That is the question which form criticism forces us to ask.

Therefore it is wrong to take out the supernatural, and perhaps also the unlikely elements of a saga, thus reducing it to its historical core and making it part of a historical investigation as if it were nothing but an extravagant elaboration of historical events. The literary type of the saga evolved for quite other reasons. It is more concerned with the present than the past. It aims to give the hearer an unconscious awareness of his own place in the world, for he is inspired, moved, and warned by the events, and emboldened by the praises which are sung for the hero. He is swept off his feet, and taken up into the events as they are described. Every saga is the work of a definite social group, unconsciously expressing its desires and ideals. It is the voice of the people. Thus as soon as it is written down it dies.[9]

This is what has created many of the problems we have in understanding Genesis, because we do not experience the book the way living sagas are experienced by the people who use them. We experience it instead as a story about the past written down in a book, and then we have to try to imagine what it was really all about. This is why a preacher is needed.

If the written sagas in Genesis are the record of generations of self-affirmation of Israel's personal experiences with the God of Abraham, then our hermeneutical tack is first, to learn to appreciate what their testimony was, and then to see whether there is anything in our own experience which reflects the same kind of experience of God, so that the saga can become self-affirmation for us, too. Some of the sagas may do that for us directly and without the help of an interpreter, because of the power of the imagery they employ, but often, because of the cultural and chronological gap which separates us from ancient Israel, some study and imagination are required.

Consider, before we turn to some specific examples, what this approach to the interpretation of saga says to some of the apparent peculiarities of the materials in Genesis. Saga tends to speak of God as appearing to human beings under quite ordinary circumstances, as speaking to them (in Hebrew), as strolling in the garden of Eden, even as sitting down and eating with them. Does this mean that God was different in that age, or that those people were different from us? Perhaps not. Perhaps it is saga's unique way of speaking about the God who was the God of all Israelites, in all ages, and thus about the same God we know now. The Israelite who expressed his faith in the form of living sagas was a person who believed in the nearness of God, personally, who had experienced the presence of God in daily life, who believed that God revealed his will to human beings, who talked to God in prayer and knew that God answers prayers. How were such convictions and experiences expressed by an Israelite? Not in philosophical or mystical terms. They spoke in concrete terms about their ancestors who represented all Israel and in whose lives they discovered and expressed the meaning of their lives. In a concrete, pictorial way they described how the God of Israel is present to those who believe in him. To say that Abraham walked and talked with God and to put it in visual terms is saga's way of saying that the

Israelite walks and talks with God, though he does not see with the eyes or hear with the ears. Perhaps, then, Abraham's experience with God was no different from that of David, Nehemiah, or Timothy, but it was only transmitted via a different form of speech, and the patriarch is thus not a strange bird with privileges denied the rest of us, but very much one of us in the community of believers. If so, then, a sermon on Genesis will by no means emphasize the peculiar or supernatural elements of the sagas but will strive to help people to discover what the story expresses which they can recognize and respond to as their own self-affirmation. It is something about our own existence which the saga expresses, if it speaks to us at all.

How to Preach from Saga

I once took as a test case of this approach the story of Hagar and Ishmael in Gen. 21:1–20. These figures are *not* ancestors of Israel, but outsiders; today a Muslim would claim to be their heir. Can this saga then be interpreted legitimately as a representation of part of Israel's spiritual experience which is recapitulated again and again? Careful study of the language of the text, enlightened by other parts of the Bible which also deal with "outsiders" suggests an answer. Isaac, not Ishmael, was the child of the promise, and we believe ourselves to be Isaac's spiritual descendents—the chosen. Yet of Ishmael God says to Abraham, "He too is your son," and to Hagar, "I will make him a great nation." At the end we are told that *God was with him*, and these are blessings of the kind that elsewhere God gives his chosen people. Are not the chosen ones then being taught something by such words? I quoted Amos 9:7 to show that elsewhere in the Old Testament the God who is not known by the foreign nations is nonetheless the moving factor in all their history, and he blesses as well as judges. Here, Paul's words in Rom. 1:20f. and Acts 17:26–28 offer appropriate ways of developing this theme of God's universality. And I concluded that we *need* to be reminded of Ishmael and Esau and the other "outsiders" so that we insiders may not become too proud of what we have—by God's grace—and to assure us that, "There's a wideness in God's mercy, like the wideness of the sea. . . . For the love of God is broader than the measure of man's mind" (from the hymn by F. W. Faber).

The development of what I took to be the major theme of the Hagar/Ishmael story could proceed with scarcely a reference to the miraculous elements in it. The supernatural is far more important in Gen. 32:3–31, the account of Jacob's night of wrestling at the Jabbok. But the description of what was happening in the dark leaves many things unclear, so let us permit them to remain in mystery. Whether he was wrestling with a man, an angel, or Christ doesn't matter. The keys to the saga's meaning are the setting (feverish preparations for the meeting with his brother whom he had wronged) and his acknowledgement the next day that he had encountered God. Does this not immediately bring to the surface the struggles we also have had with our guilty consciences and is not the story's account of a sleepless night before the day of decision the most vivid way possible of bringing our own guilt and selfishness together with the anxiety of the archetypal "look out for number one" man, Jacob? And of course the gospel in the story is that God didn't wait until a really good man came along; he chose a notably flawed human being and made him *Israel*, the father of the chosen people.

The two extended examples which follow involve different kinds of self-affirmation, as will be explained in more detail shortly; the first, of something which is a part of universal human experience, and the second, of something unique to the covenant people.

A Sermon on Genesis 6:9–9:17

The first eleven chapters of Genesis differ from the rest of the Bible in that they do not deal with the covenant people, but with all humanity. Perhaps only apocalyptic literature has a comparable, universal outlook, but despite its world-wide vision apocalyptic still focuses on the covenant people, while in the primordial history of Genesis all humanity is on an equal footing. It is thus fitting that the material the Old Testament uses in this section is not peculiar to Israel but also appears in a variety of forms in the folklore of many cultures. At least 68 different flood stories were known already to Frazer when he produced his *Folklore of the Old Testament* and a great many creation stories have also been discovered.[10] So when Westermann reaches the question of the place in life of the flood story in his commentary on Genesis, he concludes that it belongs to the fundamental cultural heritage of mankind.[11]

When we consider what is preachable in these chapters, then, it is appropriate for us to ask, What universal human experiences are reflected here? It is the intention of this kind of saga to talk about just that: humanity in general. This is not always a safe procedure to follow in reading the rest of the Bible, for most of it deals quite explicitly with a certain people who lived in a specific time and place—and we are in many ways not identical with them. We are the spiritual heirs of Israel, as I emphasized in the first chapter, but that does not mean that all of their experiences are recapitulated in us. Certainly there are other places in the Bible where we may expect to find general truths about the human condition; the wisdom literature is a good example of this, but we must be careful to respect the uniqueness of the biblical message in most of its parts. But in Genesis 1–11 the concern is to deal with types of problems which are characteristic of the human condition generally and it is appropriate to ask, What do I find of myself and my culture here?

That is the first question but it must be followed by one which acknowledges that *Israel* took such material and made it a part of the covenant people's testimony to their and our God; i.e. we must go on to ask what special use Israel

made of the story. Before looking with care at the text we can provide a prelimi-
nary answer to that question based on the structure of the Pentateuch. The Flood
is not a part of salvation history, which begins with Abraham, but is used along
with other materials which could fit a similar purpose to produce a history of the
fallen state of humanity. Consider the Garden of Eden and the Tower of Babel
as two other ways of commenting on what has gone wrong with the world which
God needs to set right. As these materials have been used by the biblical authors
they have taken on a distinctively Israelite form and theology so that it is not as
if we were dealing with material that is somehow "neutral."

The text of the Flood story has been worked over exegetically hundreds of
times, but we need not rehearse all the problems and approaches and hypotheses
in order to discover what is preachable in it. We are not concerned with its historicity, because form criticism tells us that is the wrong question to ask, and so
most of the questions asked about the story turn out to be irrelevant for preaching. It does not matter, for what the story wants to tell us, whether the flood
covered the whole earth or how long it lasted or how many animals were in the
ark or how big the ark was or whether it is still resting on Mt. Ararat. If it intended to be history-writing we should want to know those things, but the meaning of saga is to be found at another level. The source analysis of the passage,
which locates a J version and a P version, is of a bit more interest for it enables
us to see how each source used the story in its presentation of the general human
predicament, but it does not turn up the kind of puzzling differences which we
encountered in dealing with Exodus 14. In looking for a clue to the kind of universal experience which might be reflected in the saga I found that P's version
was most explicit about it, and it was in reflecting on 6:13; 7:11, 21–23 that I
recognized the real pathos of the story. The language reminds us of Genesis 1,
the creation story according to P, and when we compare the two passages we
make the terrifying discovery that P is talking about the undoing of all God's
creative work. Chaos is breaking in upon the ordered world again. Note especially that 7:11 speaks of the "fountains of the great deep" bursting forth, so
that the flood is not just the result of a big rain storm, but involves the surging
up of *Tehom*, that chaotic watery mass which God brought under control with
creation.

Now, if we ask what universal human experience is reflected here, the next
move is not difficult, for we all seem to be fascinated with catastrophes. The
newspapers depend on it regularly and a lot of money was earned by film makers
when they discovered the popularity of the disaster movie. But there is a special
kind of disaster, the world-wide cataclysm, which forms the exact parallel to the
biblical flood, and if we begin to ask why that kind of literature flourishes it
leads us to recognize that there is a lurking awareness within us that potential
disaster of a staggering scope may be out there just beyond the edges of our safe
and ordered lives. If that is not merely pathological but a part (though a usually

unacknowledged part) of a normal human existence, then it is something for which we desperately need a word from God. I have preached this sermon several times and afterward people have come to me to offer additional examples, so it seems clear that they knew exactly what I was talking about.

To help us hear the word from God we look both at the text and at the history of its interpretation. The themes which are present are easily recognized: Noah's righteousness, world-wide rebellion against God which calls forth world-wide judgment, the remnant which is saved, and divine providence which continues to keep the world under its control despite the threat of chaos. We find these themes reaffirmed a few times only in the Old Testament, which seldom alludes to any part of the primordial history. In Isa. 54:9 the covenant with Noah is appealed to as the basis for the prophet's assurance that God will be merciful rather than judgmental toward the exiles:

> For this is like the days of Noah to me:
> as I swore that the waters of Noah
> should no more go over the earth,
> so I have sworn that I will not be angry with you
> and will not rebuke you.

Ezekiel makes a quite different use of the material; speaking before the fall of Jerusalem, he refers to three men of the past who were famed for their righteousness and says of God's impending judgment of the land, " . . . even if these three men, Noah, Daniel, and Job, were in it, they would deliver but their own lives by their righteousness" (Ezek. 14:14; cf. vs. 20). So the prophets can find in the Flood evidence for both God's judgment of the world and for his providence.

Noah and the Flood became subjects of much greater interest to the authors of the intertestamental literature and the New Testament. For our purposes we need not trace the entire history of the tradition but can turn to the New Testament references immediately. In Heb. 11:7 Noah appears as an example of faithful behavior, one who obeyed God without knowing the future. In the discourse of Jesus concerning the close of the age, the coming of the Flood upon a generation which did not expect it is used as a parallel to the suddenness of the coming of the Son of Man (Matt. 24:37–39; Luke 17:26–27). God's care for his own people in the hour of judgment is emphasized in 2 Pet. 2:4–9 by means of reference to Noah and the Flood. Finally there is an allegorical use in 1 Pet. 3:20–21, where the ark is compared with baptism as the means of salvation, with the water playing a somewhat awkward role in the allegory, since it is saving in the latter case and threatening in the former. We could trace these uses further into the history of the church but once again they are so well-known that no extensive documentation is needed. The Flood and the Ark continued to be allegorized, and to this day the Ark is a common symbol for the Church. Other aspects of the allegorical approach, such as Philo's attempt to take the parts of the Ark as symbols for the parts of the body, are better forgotten. Noah has remained one of the examples of righteousness and obedience, at least up until the time when such examples ceased to be much appealed to. But the way both Old and New Testaments use the message concerning God's judgment of the world and his rescue of the faithful remnant which was drawn from the primordial era as a word for the future seems to be the most promising aspect of the Flood story for preaching. We are assured that cataclysm is not separated from God's providence, that it is the exact opposite of the mindless chaos we fear. The catastrophe of the Flood is used for judgment, so it remains under God's control. (Here the preacher must be careful not to reinforce the common notion that every disaster is to be explained as a punishment for somebody's sin.) And God is at work to save, even in the midst of judgment. Those who escape do so not by some lucky accident, as in the fictional pictures of world disaster, but as part of God's intention to deliver the righteous. So the Flood story, as understood in Scripture and tradition, assures that such a judgment is indeed coming—by fire next time—but that nothing in heaven or on earth can harm God's faithful remnant.

The sermon was first preached at the Faith United Presbyterian Church in Trafford, Pa., on October 20, 1974, and subsequently at several other churches.

Before the Deluge

Genesis 6: 11–22; 7: 11–12, 17–24   *Matthew 24 : 37–44*

Not long ago my daughter came home from Sunday school announcing that she had to look for pictures of animals to take with her next week. When I asked her what she needed them for, she said, "We're studying Noah and we are making a picture of the ark." My response was that in this changing world some things do remain the same, for that's just what we used to do when I was in Sunday school, long, long ago. We know why the story of Noah and the Flood remains a favorite of children; it's because of the ark and the animals. But is it a story which has any place in the church outside of the primary department? What can it possibly mean to adults? Why did the Israelites remember the Flood as something which was important to them? Does it say anything to you and me that we need to know about our lives here and now?

I believe that it does. I believe it resonates to some deep feelings within us which often are hidden, but which sometimes well to the surface with great power. The parts of the story which I read to you this morning were chosen to help bring that out:

> And God said to Noah, I have determined to make an end of all flesh; for the earth is filled with violence through them; behold, I will destroy them with the earth.   (6:13)

In the six hundredth year of Noah's life, in the second month, on the seventeen day of the month, on that day all the fountains of the great deep burst forth, and the windows of the heavens were opened.   (7:11)

And all flesh died that moved upon the earth, birds, cattle, beasts, all swarming creatures that swarm upon the earth, and every man; everything on the dry land in whose nostrils was the breath of life died. He blotted out every living thing that was upon the face of the ground, man and animals and creeping things and birds of the air; they were blotted out from the earth. Only Noah was left, and those that were with him in the Ark. (7:21–23)

These are terrifying words, for they remind us of the story of creation in Genesis 1. There we are told of a watery chaos and of how God divided the waters to make a place for dry land on which animals and birds and people could live. Now that act of creation is being annulled; chaos is breaking into the ordered world again. This is far worse than Hurricane Agnes; this is the undoing of all ordered life.

This story of a world-destroying cataclysm speaks to something deep within us because we have a fascination with catastrophe. Recently I saw a TV movie called *Where Have All the People Gone?* about a family on a camping trip in the California mountains who, by coincidence, happened to be exploring an old mine when an outbreak of solar flares killed almost everyone else in the hemisphere. The bulk of the movie dealt with what one does when you are one of the last people left alive on earth. It is a familiar theme. I remember another movie in which Harry Belafonte plays a coal miner trapped underground. He finally digs himself out—and discovers his town is completely deserted! He gets a new car out of a showroom and drives the empty roads to New York—also deserted, until eventually Inger Stevens turns up. That's not too bad until a third party comes sailing into the harbor and the plot becomes the familiar love triangle. Not long ago I read a science-fiction novel called *Earth Abides*, in which, once again, something kills off almost everyone on earth, and in this case we are taken through the whole first generation of those who survived and had to build a new life.

These are examples of a whole group of pieces of modern fiction which, like the flood story, speak of a great world-wide cataclysm which wipes out almost every human being. They remind us of other familiar disaster stories such as *The Poseidon Adventure*, but they have a special quality about them in that they speak of a *universal* catastrophe. Why do such stories appeal to us?

I believe it is because they speak to an uneasiness within us, to a worrisome feeling that out around the edges of the world we experience there lurks a danger, a danger that order and reason may break down, that chaos may break in on us.

This is not a sickness in us. It is not an imaginary danger. It represents something very real. In the past there have been famines and locust plagues and the Black Death which have nearly wiped out whole populations. Today we have a wider choice of disasters to choose from: nuclear holocaust, biological warfare, strangulation from pollution, and once again the old reliable—famine.

But it does not end there. As individuals we live in awareness that the flood may come. If health is precarious we try not to think how bad it could be if sickness becomes chronic and we are left at its mercy. It is like a flood held back by a shaky dam. Every month we manage to get most of the bills paid but there are bills left over sometimes and we wonder what we'll do if that begins to happen every month and the prices keep rising and income doesn't. We can imagine being engulfed. Others are losing their jobs and although we feel thankful and somewhat secure in having a job we can't deny that one day when we don't expect it we'll be in the drink.

We'd rather not think about those things, and I'd rather not remind you (and myself) of them, but we know they are there. And the Flood is the most appropriate, the most natural, the most effective way of talking about those lurking dangers. Marc Connelly used a very apt phrase in his play *Green Pastures* when he has the Lord say as he tells Noah about the coming flood: "Everything that's fastened down is comin' loose."

What the Bible has done for us so far this morning is to bring out into the light, and express in the words of the Flood story the deep lying fears and anxieties which we have about whether our personal lives can endure, whether or our society can endure, whether our world can endure. Perhaps we'd rather not be reminded of any of those things. But what does God want to say to us about those anxieties?

He says first that the Flood was for judgment. And that means two things to us. a) It means the Flood was no accident. Catastrophes occur, but that does not mean God is not in control. He intended the Flood to come. He used it for a purpose. So the biblical flood is very different from modern science fiction in which the disasters are accidents. The Bible says God is in charge. b) But when the Bible says the Flood was for judgment it is not merely talking about some event in the mists of antiquity, for judgment is also in the future, and that means it includes us.

> As were the days of Noah, so will be the coming of the Son of man. For as in those days before the flood they were eating and drinking, marrying and giving in marriage, until the day when Noah entered the ark, and they did not know until the flood came and swept them all away, so will be the coming of the Son of man. (Matt. 24:37–39)

The Flood reminds us as it did Jesus that God holds us responsible for what we have done, that he judges our deeds and our misdeeds, and that he cannot abide evil. Judgment is coming—by fire next time—the judgment of each of us for our individual responsibilities, and the judgment of the world.

But that is not the end of God's word to us:

> If [God] did not spare the ancient world, but preserved Noah, a herald of

righteousness, with seven other persons, when he brought a flood upon the world of the ungodly, . . . then the Lord knows how to rescue the godly from trial. . . .   (2 Pet. 2:5, 9)

The ultimate message of the Flood is that God saves his people. Noah found favor in the eyes of the Lord, and so was saved. Can we claim the same privilege? The gospel is that we can. On that night when Jesus was born the angels announced ". . . on earth peace among men with whom he is well pleased." And we have been promised that in the name and for the sake of Jesus Christ we do find favor in God's eyes.

God's gracious word then assures us as it did Noah that we are not at the mercy of mysterious evil forces beyond reason or control. Even when chaos seems about to break in upon us, God provides an ark. Often when serious illness strikes and one must go into that frightening world of the hospital it seems like the flood waters are rising, like the end of the world. But time after time God has thrown us a lifeline, in the form of a loving Christian who has said and done the right things, or through some inner word of assurance. There are jobless men today in this country who have worked all their lives and who thought they were secure, until the dam burst. And for them it seems as though the world is coming to an end. Yet in places such as Seattle, where the problem is especially acute because of the cutbacks in the aircraft industry, the churches are trying to hold out a hand. Food and basic necessities are provided to people who once were well-to-do but who now go hungry. More important, in a way, the churches have gone into the employment business, to try to help those desperate men, not only by assuring them that someone cares for them but by doing something to help them find work again.

When these things happen, we know God is at work. He saves his people, but if his people believe that, then they must set to work to build the ark. For centuries the ark has been one of the symbols for the church, and it is a symbol we ought to take seriously and do something about, for the flood waters are rising in more than one life we know.

The disasters may be more widespread than those personal catastrophes I have mentioned. Economic disaster for this country, or even all the industrial nations of the world, is not an impossibility. Ecological doom may not be averted, despite our efforts to change the ways we have been destroying our environment.

If they come, they will not be accidents. They will be to a great extent our fault, and God will be using them to judge us. But if they come, the church will be there, in the midst of the flood. It will be there, perhaps in the person of *you*, a Christian who helps another to keep his head above water because you give him help and hope. And you are there with something to give because you have heard God speak to you with words of assurance, even as he spoke to the prophet, whose words inspired the hymn "How Firm a Foundation":

When through the deep waters I call thee to go,
The rivers of sorrow shall not overflow;
For I will be near thee, thy troubles to bless,
And sanctify to thee thy deepest distress.

("K" in Rippon's *A Selection of Hymns*, 1787; based on Isa. 43:2)

A Sermon on Genesis 12:10–20

Our second example comes from early in the salvation history and so our approach will differ somewhat from that used for the Flood story. This portion of the Bible begins with the call of God to Abram to leave his family and country to set out for a new land, coupled with the promise to make of him a great nation and to make him a blessing (12:1–3). Most of what follows from here until the time of David is concerned with the fulfillment of that promise. It is the thread which reappears frequently throughout Genesis and then less often but in important settings in the rest of the Old Testament. This context in which the little saga which now concerns us is placed is of great importance for ascertaining the meaning of the story, for it is the first of a long series of stories dealing with the often faulty human responses which are made to the covenant of promise and with the various ways in which its fulfillment is put into jeopardy. The context also reminds us that this is not a saga, like the Flood story, which might be meaningful to anyone; its subject is the father of the covenant people and it is to them alone that it speaks. It is our experiences as believers in the God of Abraham which we may expect to find reflected here.

The text is a very simple one compared with the previous two. It shows no sign of composite authorship and is a good example of the masterfully concise art of storytelling to be found in classical Hebrew prose. The one literary problem is caused by the context, rather than the story itself. According to the P framework in which the story now rests Sarai would have been at least 66 years old when her beauty caught the eyes of the Egyptians (cf. 17:1, 7 with 12:4), but this is probably just an accident of the editorial process and if we like we can assume that as J told the story she was thought of as a young woman.

This same, rather strange plot appears twice elsewhere in Genesis, a fact usually taken as a clear indication of the existence of various sources behind the present unity of the book. In chapter 20 Abraham and Sarah attempt to pull the same trick on Abimelech, king of the Philistines, and in chapter 26 the same king encounters the same attempted deception on the part of Isaac and Rebekah. This is of great interest for one studying the history of the composition of Genesis but of little importance for one who is preaching on one of the texts. A comparison of the version in chapter 12 with the other two does bring to light certain features of the first which might not otherwise be noticed, however. Unlike the other stories, the first one indicates no concern about the telling of a lie by Abram and Sarai nor about Sarai's chastity. Neither is there an explanation of how the Pharaoh knew what caused the misfortune which afflicted his house, since we are not told how he learned that Sarai was a married woman. These things do not interest the story-teller and he does not clutter up the swift movement from fear to deception to denoument with answers to unnecessary questions. The questions do get asked anyway, of course, by those who think about what is happening, and we see that answers begin to be provided in the other two versions. But for the preacher the issue is whether one can simply deal with it as J told it and bring home the meaning of what J had to say without getting bogged down in the problems which the passage can raise for us.

This text has no subsequent history within the Bible; i.e. it is never alluded to explicitly in the Old or New Testament except for the two parallels in Genesis already mentioned. In post-biblical literature it did become a matter of interest as a part of the tendency to exalt the patriarchs as heroes of the faith. In the Genesis Apocryphon, a re-telling of Genesis found in fragmentary form at Qumran, we find extravagant and lengthy praise of Sarah's beauty,[12] and in the later Midrash on Genesis we are assured that the Pharoah never laid a hand on her, for every time he came into the bedroom God sent an angel to beat him off with a whip.[13] These are exegetical moves which I trust we will not be inclined to follow.

But the context in which the story appears and to which it contributes has an important subsequent history. We have already noted that it functions as one of a series of descriptions of the jeopardizing of the fulfillment of God's promise to Abraham. Now, this promissory covenant, which requires nothing of the human recipient but just assures him that God has obligated himself on his behalf, plays a significant role throughout the Bible.[14] We find Israel appealing to it as a last resort when everyone understood they deserved nothing from God of their own right (Lev. 26:42; Deut. 4:31; Isa. 41:8, 51:2). Unlike the Sinai covenant, which required something of Israel, the covenant with Abraham was eternal and unbreakable. Paul makes capital of this difference between the covenants in Romans 4 and Galatians 3. But the variation on that theme which we find here, and often in Genesis, is concerned with the question whether it really could be believed that God will keep his promises, no matter what.

The tradition history of the covenant of promise thus enriches our understanding of the context in which the story rests, and that theme of the unconditional promise is one strand out of which a sermon on this text should be woven. The other is the plot of the story itself, which involves human activity which would seem to cancel out any possibility for the promise to be fulfilled. Since it is saga, we look to ourselves for the kind of anxiety about whether God really can be trusted, which appears to be the motivating factor in the transmission of such stories, And, if I am not mistaken, we find that such anxiety does exist, so maybe the text needs to be preached. Having been taught by form criticism that saga should be internalized to be understood, we then find a way to get beyond the troublesome events of this story—Abram as a liar, Sarai as an adulteress (potentially, maybe actually)—because we see that there is a level of feeling in the story which we recognize and can identify with, and it is that toward which the sermon will push.

The sermon was preached in the Brookline Boulevard United Presbyterian Church in Pittsburgh, Pa., on August 14, 1977. This is a case where the liturgy had an effect on the sermon. The order of service supplied to me called for a responsive or unison reading of Scripture and I chose from the hymnbook a New Testament passage filled with promises to which I could allude in the sermon. Had it not been that the hymnbook included a unison reading from Ephesians 1, I might have chosen some other promissory text from the New Testament to use in that part of the sermon.

In Spite of It All

Genesis 12:10–20   *Ephesians 1:3–14*

What a strange story! To think that we would find wife-swapping in the Bible! One wife for troops of sheep, oxen, donkeys, slaves, and camels. And Abraham, of all people, the father of the faith, as the central character!

If this story weren't in the Bible we would be inclined to read it as a kind of joke: how Abraham turned a liability into an asset, with the Pharaoh as a Woody Allen type for whom nothing ever works out right. The premise of the story is that to have a beautiful wife while living in a foreign country is a distinct liability, because as an alien you may easily be mistreated and even killed by someone who desires her. But a beautiful sister is another matter. If some rich man wants her for a wife there is the opportunity of negotiating a big dowry.

That's the way Abraham operates. If the Pharaoh sounds like Woody Allen, Abraham comes off at first reading as a real wheeler-dealer. Pharaoh, who seems to have acted in all innocence, ends up with a severe illness afflicting his family, short a good many sheep, oxen, donkeys, slaves, and camels, and without the new wife who was the cause of it all. But Abraham, who seems to be the guilty party, comes out better than he started!

What a story to find in the Bible! But there it is; it is a part of our heritage as Christians. Generation after generation of believers, in Christendom, in Judaism and in ancient Israel, have read or have been taught this story, and it meant something to them. It said something which was important to them—as believers—or they wouldn't have remembered it, wouldn't have preserved it and passed it on as part of the story of God's dealing with his people. This raises some problems for us as believers, but here is a place where modern biblical scholarship can help us to recognize what it meant to believers of the past, and so to enable us to hear what may be the word of God in it for us in the present.

We now know that these stories in Genesis were passed on by word of mouth from generation to generation for many years before they were finally written down. They were far more than just entertainment, although many of them are enjoyable stories to hear. In speaking of Abraham, Isaac, and Jacob, their ancestors, the Israelites found ways to express their own religious experiences. Their hopes, their fears, their faith, their doubts, all could be put into words in terms of what had happened to their forefathers. So when we read Genesis we ought not just to ask, "What happened to Abraham and Sarah?" but also, "What was Israel testifying about its continuing experience with God as it told the stories of Abraham?" and then, "Is there anything in my experience which resonates with that of Abraham and of Israel?"

That is what we shall try to do in the remainder of this sermon, and thus to look below those surface aspects of the story which I have talked about so far to see whether there are in it reflections and echoes of our own lives as believers.

On first reading, looking from the outside and judgmentally, Abraham may seem to us to have been a real rat, or now maybe he is more likely to be called the epitome of male chauvinism. From the inside, however, we see something else: terror. The man is afraid; he is in desperate trouble. There was a famine in the land. People are going hungry. Starvation is imminent. Abraham decides he must do something, not just sit and wait to die. So he folds his tents and with Sarah and his slaves and his flocks and herds heads south to Egypt. He has heard that Egypt's fields are watered by the Nile and do not depend on rainfall for their fertility, so there he hopes to find food. But he also knows that the Egyptians were notorious for their suspicion of foreigners and for their superior attitude to all others, so he worries, all the way, about what may happen when they arrive. Eventually his worry escalates into blind fear that he may be murdered.

Now, does that reflect anything that has ever happened to you? That gripping uncertainty about the future—do you know what that's like? That worry about a new place, new situation, about one's reception by new people—have you ever felt it? Fear, which blinds our better judgment—can you appreciate that?

This is a story for people who know those feelings.

The second element in this story shows us that it is for people who realize that such feelings are somehow contrary to what our faith should be teaching us. At the beginning of this chapter God said to Abraham:

> Go from your country and your kindred and your father's house to a land that I will show you. And I will make of you a great nation, and I will bless you, and make your name great, so that you will be a blessing. I will bless those who bless you, and him who curses you I will curse, and by you all the families of the earth shall bless themselves.

So Abraham came into the promised land, but in the promised land there is a famine; one cannot live there. He leaves—what good was the promise? He heads for Egypt, and it is Egypt that is the great nation, not Abraham and his little clan—what good was the promise? He knows he will be at their mercy, as an alien in a strange land—what good is the promise to bless those who bless him and curse those who curse him? He faces the loss of his wife, and has no children—what of the promise to make *of him* a great nation? He faces the loss of his own life.

This story turns everything upside down. Abraham doubts God's promise and tries to work out things his own way. "Say you are my sister, that it may go well with me because of you." Abraham never mentions God in this story; the man who later became famous for his faith appears here as one who cannot trust God to keep his promises.

Now, does that echo anything in your experience? We have been given tremendous promises; we read a beautiful summary of some of them in the New Testament lesson:

> (He) has blessed us in Christ with every spiritual blessing, . . . chose(n) us in him before the foundation of the world that we should be holy and blameless before him.
> He destined us in love to be his sons through Jesus Christ. In him we have redemption through his blood, the forgiveness of our trespasses.
> He has made known to us . . . the mystery of his will. We have been destined to live for the praise of his glory.

But that's all too glorious for the lives we live, sometimes. Sometimes we don't really feel forgiven and our sins are still very much with us. Sometimes we feel much nearer to death than to the abundant life he promises us. Have you ever heard God's promises in the Scriptures and thought to yourself, How can I believe that could be true for me? Have you ever despaired of trusting God and thought, I've got to do it my own way, whether or not the Bible and the church say it's right?

If so, then this story is for you.

The third element is the curious fix Abraham gets himself, his wife and the Pharaoh into because of his plotting. Abraham is alive and wealthier, but his future, which was to come through Sarah, is cut off. He has made sure, by what he did, that God's promises, which were to be fulfilled by a son born to Sarah, would never come true. Sarah is now in another man's harem, about to become an adulteress. Pharaoh has a new wife, and everybody in the house is sick. Abraham took his destiny into his own hands, and fouled up the lives of everyone around him.

To those of us who are parents the most obvious contemporary parallel to that kind of behavior is found in the way our children act. They can't help but think they know more and better than their parents; they can't quite believe that their parents' rules and advice are really intended for their own good. They do it their own way when they get the chance—and they get hurt. But that kind of behavior is not restricted to children; when we look carefully at ourselves we see it's just how we tend to handle our relationship with God. Have you ever thought, I'll do it my own way, and suffered the consequences?

If so, then this story is for you.

Finally, although this is a story which turns everything upside down, God is really there after all and he really does keep his promises. What Abraham has upset through his fear and doubt, God puts right again. That is the gospel in this story. Although God is only mentioned once, as usual he is the main character. It shows us that in the most bizarre of human situations, God is there and God is faithful despite our unfaithfulness.

Is any predicament beyond saving? For us, yes; for God, no. Is there any way we can foul up God's plans for us? Yes, through our fear and doubt. But is there any way we can change or thwart his plans for us? Answer: No way. Of that we are assured when we understand this strange story is our story.

I hope we never experience famine or wife-swapping or any of the other details of this story. But I know that what's really happening in the story does happen to us. We need the assurance it gives, that although fear and doubt lead us into trouble, God is still there, in spite of it all.

CHAPTER III

Preaching from Short Stories

The materials to be discussed in this chapter are clearly different from either history or saga. Unlike history-writing, they are relatively short, self-contained units with a beginning, middle, and end, and are only loosely connected with the ongoing history of Israel, if at all. They differ from saga in that they are longer, more complex in plot and structure, and seem to have been produced for different purposes. The works we shall consider, Ruth, Jonah, Daniel 1–6, and Esther (with an excursus on the Joseph chapters in Genesis), are not all classified the same way by form critics but they have enough in common (especially with reference to their homiletical use) that it seems justifiable to group them together here under the broad heading "short stories." Once again the reader should be reminded that such a term is not intended to prejudge whether these pieces are entirely fictitious—like parables, for example—or are based on actual historical events. The description is a purely formal one. It has been observed, for example, that if one uses the designation "historical novel" for such works, one still has the option of emphasizing either the noun or the adjective.[1]

We are dealing here with "literature" in a way that is not true for saga; while saga is relatively unselfconscious folk art, these pieces show clear signs of careful construction by a master story-teller.[2] They might be read and enjoyed simply for their literary value. Yet they are a part of the canon of Scripture, and we may be sure that they did not acquire that status just because they were entertaining. In preaching from this kind of material we need to get across the purpose of the story without losing the value they have as entertainment, for, after all, the authors had a reason for choosing a story as the best way to make their point. The preacher will do well to read with care some of the recent studies of the literary art of these story-tellers, for there are two kinds of lessons to be learned from them.³ First will come an increased appreciation of the range of meanings which can be conveyed by a narrative and an awareness that if one grasps at a single point and claims that it is *the* message of the story, then one is probably missing a good deal more which the story also contains. As one such study says about the Book of Jonah:

> No one single explanation satisfies all the possibilities the text raises, nor can it do so. That is to say that by choosing a narrative form to convey his ideas, the author has found a medium which forces the reader to live with some degree of uncertainty, particularly with regards the motivation of one of the central characters. . . . Thus form and content contribute simultaneously to the lesson being conveyed.⁴

Put in practical terms, if the preacher asks whether there is more than one sermon which can legitimately be preached from Ruth or Jonah, the answer is definitely yes.

Second, these modern studies of the use of language ought to make the preacher more alert to the potential power of the language used in the sermon and to suggest ways of enriching the proclamation of every kind of text. The values of the story-form for the presentation of truth are two. First, a good story captures the interest and sticks in the memory. We remember the parables of Jesus better than the didactic language of Paul's letters. If we have read Plato we remember some of his "myths" better than the dialogues proper. We all know that people hear and remember the stories we tell in our sermons better than any other part. So the story is an effective way to teach, to appeal to the emotions and to sway the will. Every course in homiletics reminds its students of this. The other value of the artfully constructed story is not so obvious or wellknown. The story is an imitation of life and if it is a *good* imitation it will convey the ambiguities and mysteries of life in a way that is impossible for discursive language. For example, the origin of evil still defies rational explanation by philosophers and theologians and sin still remains the "impossible possibility" in our theologies, yet the author of Genesis 3 was able to convey a great deal of truth about the human experience of sin and guilt by means of a story—precisely because the story could portray life as it is without having to answer the unanswerable questions: What is the ultimate source of temptation? If we are created good how can we sin?, etc. Neither does Jonah or Job or *Hamlet* or any other great work of literature answer all our questions; their heroes are real people in that we do not fully understand them any more than we understand everything about our friends or ourselves. And the literature fascinates us because it prods us to think, to try to explain what the story leaves untold.

Now, the sermon, on the other hand, is normally expected to have a clearly identifiable point, to be didactic if not hortatory, and so it may not seem appropriate to leave quite so many questions unanswered as the Book of Jonah, e.g., does. We try to *explain* the book, when we take it as a text. But there is still a place, as part of a sermon or as most of it, for a narrative which reflects an aspect of the life of faith including the ambiguities of real life, so that the people may be stimulated to ponder the options which life presents and to participate with you in working through them, rather than simply being presented with some answers. Preaching from these biblical stories presents us with the challenge of saying something *about* them, not just retelling the story without helping people to recognize what it has to say to them, but to present that interpretation without becoming completely discursive and losing the effectiveness of the story form.

There are various ways to do it. One of my students retold Jonah as a story of a modern revivalist (''Mr. Dove,'' translating the Hebrew word, *Jonah)* and made of it a funny story with a point which did not need to be belabored. My illustrative sermon on Ruth, in this chapter, devotes three-fourths of the time to retelling part of the story, without trying to modernize it, then comments on it as an example in life of what Paul is teaching in 1 Cor. 13:7. I have combined the Scripture reading with the sermon, in preaching from Jonah, so as to be able to read the entire story and to make the text itself the backbone of the sermon. I commented on the text along the way, briefly, picking out only the things which contributed to the point I wanted to emphasize, then drew some conclusions at the end. Noting that it was the communities of the Diaspora as a whole that benefitted from what Esther and Mordecai did, I told the story of Esther as it might have been heard by an imaginary family of Jews living in Babylon. One might also try a midrashic style, using a series of contemporary stories to make the same point that one wishes to emphasize in the text. But the key to a faithful use of a biblical story in a sermon ought to be preserving the interest to the listener and the nearness to reality which the original provides while also helping the listener to go beyond the level of entertainment and to recognize what it may have to say that is helpful to them.

We shall summarize briefly the conclusions of recent research on each of these stories, with suggestions concerning the benefits which they may offer to the preacher, and will present a sermon on Ruth as an example of narrative preaching.

Daniel 1–6

The first six chapters of Daniel contain six self-contained stories about the trials and successes of Daniel and his friends in the courts of pagan kings early in the exilic period. They are placed in chronological order, but aside from that there is no continuity or development as one moves from one story to the next; they could just as well appear in any other order and each one can stand separately without losing anything. Hence we are dealing not with history or biography, but with six simple and effective examples of the short story. As we examine them we discover that among the six stories there are actually only two basic plots, each of them worked out in three different ways. They may be summarized as follows:

A. A Jew is persecuted by a Gentile king for being faithful to the peculiar precepts of his religion, but he perseveres, and his God saves him, whereupon the king recognizes the superiority of the God of the Jews.

B. All the wise men in a Gentile court are unable to explain a dream or omen which has appeared to the king, but a Jew, to whom has been given superior wisdom by his God, is able to do so and is promoted to a high position because of it, while the superiority of his God is recognized by the pagan king.

Plot A, which might be called "The Faithful Exile," appears in chapters 3 and 6 and in a modified form in chapter 1. Plot B, the Court Wise Man story, appears in chapters 2, 4, and 5. All of these stories are set in the Diaspora, and that is of great importance for our homiletical use of them. Although they take place during the exilic period, near the end of the Neo-Babylonian and the beginning of the Persian era, they actually present issues which have been very much alive for most Jews from that time to the present and which have periodically been critical matters for Christian existence as well. As a matter of fact, the Book of Daniel itself, in its present form, is not likely to have been written as early as the beginning of the Persian period, but took its final shape in the Hellenistic period, near the middle of the second century B.C. The book itself, then, is already the result of the reapplication of lessons learned during the Babylonian exile to later, similar situations. This book represents one of the few cases where the date of composition is of great importance for preaching. That is because the middle of the second century is the time of the first attempt in history to stamp out the Jewish religion; the persecution of the Jews by Antiochus IV Epiphanes. As I comment on how each of these main plot types is related to our own situation as Christians in America, the value of knowing something about that setting as we preach from the book will become clear. The dating of Daniel in 165 B.C. is one of the results of biblical criticism which has been attacked by conservatives as destructive to a biblically grounded faith because such a date means Daniel did not really predict 500 years or more of history from a sixth century vantage point. However, I believe it can be shown that to make of Daniel merely a sixth century predictor of the future is to lose much of the relevance of the book for our efforts at faithful living. Actually, if the second century date can be accepted, Daniel can become an excellent example of how historical-critical scholarship is *helpful*, adds new insight and makes the Bible more alive than ever, even through such apparently pedantic questions as date and authorship.

But let us take each of the two plot types in turn and consider what these "exile stories" have to say to the modern Christian. We can pick out the following significant features from the stories of the Faithful Exile:

1. They tell something about what it is like for a Jew to live in a Gentile

environment. They have grown out of the experience of leaving a supportive culture, the Israelite monarchy in Palestine, where all were the same nationality, spoke the same language, shared a traditional, common culture, and worshipped the same God, and of being moved into a foreign country to live as a minority group amid people whose language, world-view, and religion were very different.

2. The Jews in these stories are not in prison camps or enslaved; quite the contrary. They all enjoy high positions in the Gentile government. Daniel is second only to the king and the young Jews in chapter 1 have been chosen to be trained for government service. The stories thus have a positive outlook on life among the Gentiles; they do not counsel retreat from the company of pagans or withdrawal into a closed community of believers in order to keep the faith pure. Instead they have a conception of Judaism which allows, even encourages participation in the affairs of the majority culture. The Jew has something of value to contribute to the society in which he lives, and he can also benefit from it. The outlook is world-affirming and optimistic.

3. However, the exile experience had taught the Jews that life amid an alien culture could also present serious problems to those who intended to remain faithful to Yahweh, and that is not ignored by these stories. Indeed, it is the point where Judaism may not compromise with paganism which is the central plot feature of each story. In chapter 1 it is the kosher food laws, in chapter 3 it is image-worship, in chapter 6 it is monotheism, or the refusal to acknowledge any power greater than Yahweh. And in each case the success story is threatened; each story reminds the Jew who lives in a Gentile society that times do come when to remain faithful to the Jewish way means jeopardizing position and even life.

4. The stories intend to be exemplary and take the optimistic position that despite the pressures which the alien culture puts upon Judaism it is possible to maintain one's faithfulness. They delineate, also, certain kinds of issues on which compromise is not possible. Their optimism leads them to include a scene of divine deliverance from the jeopardy into which the faithful Jew is put and to conclude with the king's own acknowledgement of the superiority of Yahweh, and the promotion of the hero(es).

Now, what shall we say about our own situation, as the faithful exile stories help us to see it, perhaps in a new light?

1. Do Christians today have anything in common with Jews living in a Gentile world? I think that we do, despite the lingering aura of the "Christian nation" idea which still entrances us, and despite the wishful thinking that our culture, including law itself, ought to be supportive of Christian values. But in fact it is not.[5] Christian ethical standards, which may have been given lip service by society at large in the past, are simply not the standards accepted by our society as a whole, despite the efforts of Christians to maintain some of them at

a level of community acceptance. And matters of theology are not even of any interest to the populace as a whole, let alone candidates for widespread understanding and acceptance. America and many other modern states, furthermore, are constitutionally pluralistic nations, so that one has no right to assume that their culture should be "Christian," and nations which are still constitutionally Christian are in fact also pluralistic to a greater or lesser extent. The Constantinian era is over, the veneer of Christian culture is peeling, and we are where the Jews of the Babylonian exile were.

2. If we are willing to face up to that (and not all of us are) it means we have to learn how to cope with being a minority group. What options do we have when we live in a society which does not reinforce our beliefs and lifestyles, and which sometimes makes life very hard because of them?[6]

a) We might try to bring back the Constantinian era; i.e. try to force everyone to accept our views by law, even though we are a minority. The efforts to get a "Christian Amendment" to the Constitution of the United States, which would declare that the country is a Christian nation, may be an example of this. That is not Daniel's way.

b) We might withdraw from participation in a world which does not accept what we believe and associate only with other Christians (to the extent that we have the freedom to do that). This is the way of sectarianism, and it is not the way of the Book of Daniel.

c) Or, we might cooperate with all that is good in non-Christian culture, might contribute to every enterprise which is valid, according to our Christian standards, and even expect that because we are Christians we may have something extra to contribute. We may expect to share in the good things the culture has to offer us (although not many of us will end up in the State Department, as Daniel did), but we will also anticipate that sometimes our faith will put us into very difficult situations. This is the way of life which the Book of Daniel advocates.

3. If what I have just described is the real situation for Christians in many countries of the world today—living in a non-supportive, but usually tolerant culture, and accepting a participatory role in that society—then the issues which confront Daniel and his friends are of direct personal relevance to us. How far can and must we go in accommodating ourselves to the beliefs and lifestyles of the non-Christian world in which we live and work? Each story warns us that there must be limits, that participation must not lead to surrender. Each of them warns us that we may be severely hurt if we do hold to our principles, but the heroes of the stories are presented as models of precisely that kind of courage.

Chapter 6 shows us how awkward our position may become when we stand on conscience, how subtly powerful the temptation to compromise may be. The king in this story is no tyrant; Darius is Daniel's friend, who obviously thinks highly of him and is extremely upset when he is tricked into signing a decree which puts Daniel into jeopardy. The decree prohibited making any petition to anyone but the king for 30 days, and that interfered with Daniel's custom of daily prayer to Yahweh. Now, couldn't he have found a way out of that? It was only 30 days; couldn't he have abstained from prayer for that short period? Or couldn't he have found a way to pray in secret? But no, he prays three times a day with all the windows open so everyone can see him. Why so stubborn about it? The king, his friend, doesn't want him killed; he sits up all night in distress when Daniel is thrown into the lion's den. Why not find some way to cooperate? The answer is that Daniel recognized the issue to be what we would call freedom of the conscience. As a Jew he could not let it even *appear* that there is any lord who can command an allegiance higher than his allegiance to Yahweh. So he must resist, and this resistance to a friend reminds us that sometimes the strongest temptations of all come not from those who are out to get us, but from those who like us and whom we like, who put us under pressure not intending to harm us but just because their ways are different from ours, and we are asked whether we can be strong enough to resist for the sake of conscience on occasions when that resistance is awkward, embarrassing, and painful for all concerned.

4. But everything works out okay for Daniel and his friends; they are rescued from the lions' den and the burning fiery furnace, and the optimism of these stories requires some special consideration, for we think of ourselves as realists, we live in a day of the anti-hero and the downbeat ending, and are very suspicious of happy endings. God intervenes at the last minute, the hero is saved, and he gets a promotion—Sunday school stories! How can an adult, who knows it doesn't work out that way, take such stories seriously? Two comments are to be made in answer to that legitimate question:

a) I mentioned earlier the date of the final form of this book, c. 165 B.C. The stories in chapters 1–6, which no doubt were created some time before this, during a period when life under pagan rule was relatively easy, were combined with the visions of chapters 7–12 in the midst of a period of religious persecution. Antiochus IV Epiphanes, of the Macedonian house of Seleucus, ruled Palestine, Syria, and much of Mesopotamia from his capital at Antioch. For reasons we don't need to go into here, he attempted to stamp out the Jewish faith, beginning in 167 B.C. with the conversion of the Jerusalem temple to the worship of Zeus, the prohibition of circumcision, the observance of the Sabbath and other holy days, and the destruction of the Scriptures.[7] Those who refused to conform and to show their allegiance to the gods of the Greeks were killed, often by torture. Eventually the Jews rose up in revolt and regained their freedom but that obviously had not yet happened when this book took its final shape. The visions show that they are still a persecuted people. Now let us consider an astonishing fact. The visionary who produced those messages for a suffering people added them to a group of traditional stories with happy endings! He presented that work to a people who knew nothing of happy endings, who were dying in torment because they "dared to be a Daniel." We may think we are realists—but how many of us have witnessed anything in life as raw as what those second century Jews were experiencing? God was *not* stepping in to rescue them at the last minute; they were dying. And they did not laugh at these optimistic stories and dismiss them as Pollyanna stuff, too good to be true. Those stories became Scripture. And if the suffering Jews of the second century heard a word from God in this, perhaps we had better listen carefully before we dismiss them saying, but we know better!

b) The other fact appears in chapter 3, in one of the few hints of what is going on in the minds of our heroes. As the king gives Shadrach, Meshach, and Abednego their last chance to bow down to the great image before throwing them into the burning fiery furnace, they respond, "O Nebuchadnezzar, we have no need to answer you in this matter. If it be so, our God whom we serve is able to deliver us from the burning fiery furnace; and he will deliver us out of your hand, O king. *But if not,* be it known to you, O king, that we will not serve your gods or worship the golden image which you have set up" (3:16b–18). They believed God would help them, *but if not . . .* They would do exactly the same thing whether or not God intervened to save them.[8] They knew God is free and cannot be coerced, even by our faithfulness, and their faithfulness did not depend on the happy ending. Rewards do come, and let us not forget that fact, in the midst of our "realism," but blessed are they whose faithfulness does not require a reward.

Although the Court Wise Man stories of Daniel 2, 4, and 5 have much in common with the stories of the Faithful Exile, they have distinguishing features which call for a different type of sermon. Whereas the stories we have just been considering grew out ot the peculiar experiences of the Jews in the Diaspora, the court wise man was a well-known figure throughout the ancient Near East and stories about him were a part of popular literature. The exploits of one of them, Ahikar, are known in Aramaic, Syriac, Greek, Old Turkish, Ethiopic, Armenian, Slavonic, and Arabic versions,[9] so we know that his story was retold and circulated from country to country for over a thousand years, until finally it appeared in the Arabian Nights. The stories were popular favorites because they dealt with contests of wits. An example is to be found in the Apocrypha, in 1 Esdras 3–4. For his entertainment the king proposes a riddling question, "What is the strongest?" and offers a reward to the courtier who can give the cleverest and most convincing answer. The first one answered, wine is the strongest, and gave an effective speech supporting his claim; the second answered, the king is strongest; and the third gave a double answer: Woman is stronger than wine or the king, but truth is strongest of all. Since the story appears in a Jewish document it does not surprise us that the third and winning speaker is a Jew and that credit for his wisdom is given to the God of the Jews.

The stories in Daniel 2, 4 and 5 depict Daniel as one of the wise men in the Babylonian court, in competition with and victorious over the local "magicians, enchanters, sorcerers and Chaldeans," to whom the king normally turned for advice. Each story calls for the interpretation of some puzzling phenomenon which requires more than rational powers, and each one declares that the God of the Jews gives to his faithful ones a gift of wisdom which surpasses all others. Hence there is much less of the imperative or exemplary in them than we detected in chapters 1, 3, and 6; instead the subject is exaltation and praise of God, the affirmation of his superiority even in the midst of a great pagan nation, told in an entertaining way.

More briefly than before, let me make some comments on characteristics of the stories which suggest their relevance for today's preaching:

1. God can be praised in many ways and some of them are entertaining. These chapters possess a bit of the extravagance that goes with story-telling for the fun of it and I think they ought to be handled with a light touch. The familiar theme of dream interpretation, which appears in chapters 2 and 4, in the Joseph story and often outside the Bible, is made unbelievably difficult in chapter 2 when the king forgets what he has dreamt. What a commission! Tell me what I dreamt and what it means or off with your head! Daniel not only outperforms his opponents but saves their lives as well, thanks to his God. In chapter 4 the great king becomes a laughingstock as he is turned into a lunatic, roaming the fields like an animal for seven years. This chapter conveniently enabled Verdi to write a "mad scene" for his opera *Nabucco* (an abbreviation of the Italian form of Nebuchadnezzar), which was loosely based on Old Testament materials concerning the exile. And chapter five's handwriting on the wall remains a riddle which intrigues scholars to this day. The king asked a double question; how to read it and how to interpret it, and this suggests that the handwriting was in the Aramaic script, consonants only, so that different readings were possible, depending on the vowels one supplied. The interpretation we know, for Daniel gave it, but the vocalization of the consonants MN' MN' TKL WPRSN is something we can still play with.

2. God works indirectly in human affairs, as these stories represent them. He does not intervene with miracles (the handwriting is an exception to this) but remains behind the scenes. All the characters are purely human and the incidents could be explained in non-religious language. Despite some bizarre elements, which I have suggested are present for their entertainment value, the "world of the Bible" is not so different from our own world. Those elements of the religion of the Old Testament which are peculiarly Israelite, such as sacrifice, references to the covenant, etc., are absent; only prayer is available to the faithful Jew. Even the people Israel, with their own special outlook and way of life, are missing. Here we encounter only individual Jews, very much on their own, living by their wits, with one thing to sustain them: prayer to the God of heaven.[10]

3. These features bring the wise man stories close to our own experiences, despite the elements in them which are strange to us. God works behind the scenes in our world, as well; he is accessible to us by prayer, and we can interpret the events in our lives from a standpoint of faith, but non-reli-gious explanations can also be offered. Most days we live by our wits, depending on the talents we were born with and have developed. Nothing comes in from outside to bail us out. And that can be seen as a part of the secularization of our time. But didn't that kind of lifestyle already exist in Daniel's time, among the wise men?[11] Apparently it did, and the wise men of the Jews gave it a religious, not a secular, interpretation. Who gave you your wits? Who is responsible for the talents you put to work every day? Their answer was that God is behind it all and that God can be served and glorified by putting our gifts to the best possible use. And prayer is available to anyone, at any time; we have the same means of access to God that the great saints have had. In certain respects the stories of Daniel 1–6 thus show us that the wisdom movement of post-exilic Judaism had already entered the "modern situation." It saw the world as pluralistic and itself as part of a minority group subject to all the pressures minorities always experience. It did not see God at work in obvious ways (despite the two big miracles in Daniel, the furnace and the lion's den, the words in 3:16–18 show us they knew you can't count on miracles), but was convinced that God is still at work behind the scenes, that he may be reached and his power tapped through prayer, and that he calls for unswerving commitment from those who bear his name. But don't the stories put it much better than the abstractions you have just been reading?

Excursus: The Story of Joseph

The story of Joseph in Gen. 37, 39–47 is an interesting example of the varying ways in which a short story may be approached, both from traditional, homiletical points of view and with the form critical method. The typological use of the Old Testament has taken Joseph to be a type of Christ, in that he was betrayed by his own people but as a result of that betrayal became their savior.[12] The whole story might be preached, then, not so much for what it says of Joseph but as a type of event which foreshadows the really meaningful event of the death of Christ. My own reaction to such an approach is to think that it loses too much that is of value in the story, and that there are better ways to preach Christ.

Parts of Joseph's career have been preached as examples of moral behavior, i.e. they have been taken to be similar in intent to Daniel 1, 3, and 6, and indeed there are similarities between the two parts of Scripture. The incident of Potiphar's wife has certainly been used for that purpose since before the Christian era (cf. Wisd. of Sol. 10:13f., 1 Macc. 2:53) and it may still have some value in that way even though sermons of that kind are less effective than they used to be. Joseph has even been seen as a paragon of virtue, almost sinless, but caution ought to be used before treating him in that way. His brothers certainly found him to be insufferably vain and the way he subjects them to his power in order to play with their emotions during their visits to Egypt suggests that he was a man who needed his revenge before he could move to reconciliation. It is unlikely, then, that the purpose of the story was to hold up Joseph as a model of moral behavior.[13]

The closest parallels between Joseph and Daniel are to be found in the court wise man elements in Gen. 40–41 and some of the same features which we emphasized earlier appear here as well. The lone Hebrew in a foreign land is helped by his God to rise to a position of power through the gift of wisdom. Unlike the rest of Genesis, here there are no theophanies; God does not appear to anyone but instead makes his will known through dreams and via prayer. So parts of the Joseph story may be preached as parts of Daniel were treated.

The presence of this short story in Genesis not only connects it with saga by means of the characters involved (mainly Jacob) but also shows an element of continuity in that one of its dominant themes is a typical theme for saga. This is the family quarrel and its resolution. Instead of a brief treatment, such as we find in the sagas of Cain and Abel, Sarah and Hagar, or Jacob and Esau, the dispute between Joseph and his brothers has been told with great literary skill, bringing out many nuances of interpersonal relationships which the saga-form could only suggest.[14] Once again, God is not an actor in the drama, as he could be in the saga of Cain and Abel, for the story is told on a purely human level and God remains in the background. But does that make it less preachable than the more overtly theological stuff in the Bible? There is a lot of this kind of material to be found in the Old Testament; in the historical and wisdom books as well as in these stories, and do we have to correct the Bible's "oversight" by providing lots of theological content via typology or allegory? The answer I gave for Daniel applies here: The world of Daniel and Joseph is the kind of world we live in, and since we need to know how God operates in our world these ought to be eminently preachable texts. In our world, getting right with God requires getting right with our families and neighbors—that's the form it takes (cf. 1 John 3:11ff.)—and it is not less-than-Christian preaching to ponder, on occasion, the subtle difficulties of maintaining intimate human relationships which are portrayed so skillfully in the story of Joseph.

The Joseph tradition is a slender one in the Bible. He is mentioned in Ps. 105:16–23, Acts 7:9–16, and Heb. 11:21f., and in the Apocrypha in Sir. 49:15, 1 Macc. 2:53, and Wisd. of Sol. 10:13f. Each of these is a catalogue of faithful ones of old, so Joseph only appears when a fairly comprehensive list of Old Testament characters is being presented. In this respect Joseph's is like the other short stories, which do not produce strong traditions within the biblical record.[15]

Esther

Probably the average Christian would pick Esther and the Song of Songs as the books of the Bible from which he is least likely to choose a text for a sermon. I confess that until recently I had not preached from either of them, although I had discussed the subject of how to preach them more than once. Esther has been a problematic book for both Jews and Christians since the first century, when the rabbis discussed whether it belonged in their canon of Scripture; although they did not exclude it some early Christians did.[16] Through most of Christian history, however, Esther was given high respect, but in recent years it has tended to be seen as a book in which revenge is an embarrassingly prominent element and Christians have tended just to leave it alone. It has maintained more of its popularity in Judaism because of the continuing observance of the feast of Purim, at which the book is read. For a helpful and sympathetic study of Esther, including the history of its interpretation and an analysis of its major themes, I recommend Elias Bickerman's *Four Strange Books of the Bible*.[17]

We should consider the question of whether this is to be taken as a history book or a short story, since it does deal with the subject matter of history: kings, queens, empires, and the destiny of a people within an empire. Once again, we are not primarily asking how much of it is fact and how much is fiction, but we want to know what kind of literature it is so that we may handle it in an appropriate way. Most scholars today think that the book may be based on a historical incident but they emphasize that the form it takes is that of a historical novel; i.e. it is marked throughout by the artistry of the master story-teller, so what we have been discerning about the effectiveness of stories applies here, no matter what the subject may be. Note especially the use of coincidence and irony as key elements in the development of the plot. The king forgets to reward Mordecai for his service in saving his life (2:19–23) but fortunately a record of the event was kept and at the crucial moment the king was reminded of it. (6:1–3). At the moment when the king desired to reward Mordecai the latter is about to be executed by Haman, who had prepared a gallows for him to take revenge for an earlier insult, but by coincidence Haman is present in the court, not to hear Mordecai's name mentioned but only to be asked what a suitable reward would be for one who pleased the king. So to Haman is given the ironic privilege of choosing Mordecai's reward. Then, when Haman is accused by Esther of plotting against her people and he falls upon her couch to beg for mercy, the king appears at just the wrong moment and thinks he is attacking her. So Haman is executed for a crime he did not commit, but the ironic justice of it is that he dies on the gallows constructed for the unjust execution of Mordecai. It's a well-told story, with suspense and surprises all along the way.

There is another reason for not including this among the history books and that is the absence of any clue that the author intends to write "salvation history." Israel is out there somewhere, it is true, and in jeopardy because of Haman's plotting, but the story reminds us of Daniel and Joseph because it largely deals with the fate of two individuals, and it is they who, by their cleverness, are the saviors of the Jewish people. God is never mentioned in the book; the closest it comes to a reference to anything beyond the human level is in 4:14: "For if you keep silence at such a time as this, relief and deliverance will rise for the Jews *from another quarter.*" To take this as the account of another of the mighty acts of God for the salvation of his people, as both Jews and Christians have done, can still be called theologically legitimate (assuming there is a historical core to the story), but we must be aware that it is something which the *author* did not choose to do.

Here we should mention the differences between the Hebrew text of Esther, on which all Protestant versions are based, and the Septuagint text, the ancient Greek translation which is the basis for the Roman Catholic Old Testament. This Greek version is longer than the Hebrew and includes prayers of Mordecai and Esther, supplying the language of piety which is so conspicuously missing from the original.[18] The theological interpretation of the events which the translator provided would make it easier for us to preach the book, but the evidence strongly suggests that the Hebrew text, with its completely non-religious version of things, is more likely to be the original and thus to be the one with which we need to struggle.

The story contains two intertwined plots with a third, brief story as a prelude. The main plot involves Mordecai, and its theme reminds us of other court tales in which a righteous person is put in jeopardy but eventually receives his just reward. (Cf. Joseph, and in the Apocrypha, Tobit.) The Esther story is more straightforward; it tells of how a queen risks her safety to save her people. The prelude, concerning the deposing of Queen Vashti, tells of what usually happens to those who defy the king, and so it not only sets the stage for Esther's appearance but also adds to the suspense of her story. In addition to the strong importance of coincidence, the motivating force in the story is Esther's love for her people. She is not known to be Jewish by anyone in the court; obviously she is no Daniel in the faithful observance of her religion, but when her people face a pogram her loyalty to them transcends self-interest.

So far, we have no theology at all; only a story about events, loyalties, and emotions which might affect anyone, anywhere!

For our predecessors in the church it was not quite so difficult. Until the Reformation they all used the longer text, for one thing, with its added theological material, and they also used typology extensively. Esther became the type of the church and also of Mary, and the hanged Haman became the *antitype* of Christ.[19] I don't think we are helped by the efforts to find Mary or Christ in this book, but I do want to come back to the question of how the church is related to it a bit later. Luther also could not find Christ in the book, and since he was only interested in what preaches Christ in the Scriptures he judged it to be of little value.[20] During the religious wars which followed the Reformation, however, each group of Christians did find its own branch of the church prefigured there, and so the book was a very popular text, assuring them of their eventual victory. But the danger and illegitimacy of that kind of use of Scripture becomes clear when we find that it is made to promise victory to all sides.

How then shall we make a legitimate and appropriate contact with the Book of Esther? Must it remain only a good story, of doubtful moral value and no theological significance? I have three comments to make:

1. If we consider the type of literature with which we are dealing, Esther may be compared with Daniel, as another example of the exile story.[21] Once again we learn of the occasional precariousness of the lives of Jews in the Gentile world and once again the possibility of great success is presented optimistically. But unlike Daniel, Esther says little about how to be a faithful Jew under the pressures of an alien culture. For all we can tell, Esther and Mordecai may have assimilated quite thoroughly. The Jews are not persecuted for their adherence to their religion, but simply for being a minority group. Chance and wit bring about the happy solution, so although we *might* preach a sermon from Esther similar to what we would preach from Daniel (I have read a good one using 4:14 as its text), we shall be drawing on what is implicit rather than what is explicit in the book.

2. What is explicit is a paradigm of Jewish existence among the nations from that day to this. To be a Jew is to be subject to the whims of the ruling majority, as Mordecai and the nameless Jews in the Persian empire are subject to the will of Haman. Only the final triumph in Esther is atypical. I think I can understand the vital importance for the suffering Jews of the past two millennia and more of *winning*, at least once a year, in the synagogue, on the feast of Purim.[22] And if the Christian is to take the Book of Esther seriously I think we are led to consider what the continuing suffering of the Jews ought to mean for Christian theology. If we approach the book as we have done with other parts of the Old Testament, asking what does this contribute to my history, as a Christian, I suspect that we shall find ourselves in an ambivalent position. Often the church has been responsible for that suffering, and if we know that sorry history we cannot read the book without seeing ourselves in Haman and confessing that corporately we are guilty. One line of continuity between us and the book is that we are Gentiles whose history involves the persecution of the Jews.

3. But we have taken Esther into our canon, and by so doing have somehow identified her cause with our own. Earlier, the church simply substituted herself for the Jews, but I do not think that is acceptable, for the Jews are real people, the people of the covenant, who still exist. They should be important to us as more than just our roots, for they are a living tree, alongside our own, but as a church we have failed to take adequate account of that. It has been easier to call ourselves the "new Israel" (a non-biblical term) and assume the old Israel is out

of the picture.[23] I cannot enter into a discussion of Romans 9–11 here, but refer you to it as the basis for the position taken here, and to remind you that the Apostle Paul did not take such an easy way out as the later church did. The Book of Esther asks us whether we are ready to accept the history of the Jews, that history of pograms and victory over pograms, as part of our own history. We have many collective sins to atone for in the church, not by berating ourselves for past history but by correcting misunderstanding in the present and by preparing our people to make a better history of Jewish-Christian relations in the future. One way that we may use the Book of Esther in our preaching is to let it ask us whether as Christians we are against or with all suffering and threatened Jews, whenever and wherever.

Ruth

From affairs of state and intrigues in the palaces of the great capitals of the world we move to the village of Bethlehem and a story of the fortunes of two poor widows. It is one of the masterpieces of story-telling, showing how the daily events of birth, marriage, and death, without violence, sensation, or high drama, can become the stuff of which great literature is made. Here we encounter the ambiguity of which I spoke at the beginning of this chapter in a way which makes the book somewhat difficult to preach, however.[24] The author simply presents to us a segment of life, apparently without interpretation. The stories in Daniel were very different in this respect; they obviously had a point to make, and the purpose of the various parts of the Joseph story, as well as the way the story fits into the structure of the Pentateuch, is not hard to determine. But what is the purpose of the Book of Ruth?[25]

The story is set in the time of the Judges and it concludes with the family tree of David, so it might seem that we possess here a historical fragment, similar to the units which make up the Book of Judges. That impression is strengthened by the position of the book in Christian versions of the Old Testament, located as it is between Judges and 1 Samuel, but we must be aware that there is another tradition of where it belongs in the arrangement of the canon.[26] The Hebrew Bible includes it in the third section of the canon called Writings, grouped with Song of Songs, Lamentations, Ecclesiastes, and Esther, the five Megilloth (scrolls) which are read in the synagogue on certain holy days. And the book is not really as much like the stories in Judges as it might seem at first; it is not really about the fortunes of Israel and does not tell us of the exploits of its deliverers; it stands on its own merits as a story about two women whose lives are interesting in themselves. It is a surprise to learn, at the end, that Ruth was an ancestress of David so that there is a certain connection made with 1 Samuel, and that information is an extra; it is not essential for the story itself to come to a satisfactory ending. So a good many scholars have concluded that Ruth is a story told just for its own sake, for its value as entertainment. According to this interpretation it was that incidental information about David's ancestry that got it into the canon, but if that is incidental it seems to leave the preacher with nowhere to go!

Since the author has not spelled out explicitly what his point is, or whether he has a point other than telling a good story, his work remains open to us so that we may perhaps find more than one thing being said to us by it. The ambiguity of such a reflection of real life may be frustrating when we are looking for something clear and simple, but it also presents an opportunity, for is it not often possible to discover more than one truth being manifested by a single event in life? So let us not give up, but let us consider some of the themes which scholars have discovered running through the story.

As R.M. Hals studied the references to God which appear in this book he concluded that it expresses the author's conviction that the providence of God is at work even in the small events of life, but that his activity is normally hidden from human sight.[27] It thus contains a theology very similar to what we found in the Joseph story. Other scholars have expressed a similar idea in suggesting that the intent of the story is to show that, in spite of all obstacles, those whom Yahweh has placed under his protection fare well.

The most popular interpretation of Ruth in our day has seen it to be a kind of tract encouraging tolerance and acceptance of foreigners. A pamphlet published in the 1930s called it "An Idyll of International Friendship," and the movie, *The Story of Ruth*, which appeared in the 1950s made tolerance its dominant theme. This interpretation tends to be connected with the post-exilic date which many scholars have assigned to the book. They then take it to be an example of an attitude in Judaism contrary to the exclusivism practiced by Ezra and Nehemiah, who fought against mixed marriages in an attempt to prevent the faith from being corrupted by intermingling with the religious practices of foreign wives.[28] They say this author wants to remind the strict Jews of his community that even David himself had a Moabite ancestress and by making her the heroine of his story to make an appeal for the acceptance of outsiders into the Jewish community.

Certainly there is a surprising openness to foreigners in this book and it is appropriate for us to take that seriously, for it speaks to some of our own present concerns. That an appeal for toleration is the one and only message of the story is another matter, however. For one thing, if that is the author's main purpose, he could have made it much more explicit; the message is presented very gently and without any editorial comment. And there are also many scholars who question the post-exilic dating of the book. If it is earlier than the reforms of Ezra and Nehemiah, dating from the pre-exilic period when mixed marriages were commonplace, then it loses much of its force as a protest against exclusiveness. But even if that was not the author's main intention, and he is not explicit enough that we will ever know for sure, his book does present to us a Moabite heroine of a Hebrew story and contains within it elements which are devastating to any chauvinistic attitude based on national or racial pride, and there are times when that message needs to be heard.

One of the major themes of the book is *hesed*, that almost untranslatable Hebrew word which we render "loving kindness," "steadfast love," and sometimes appropriately "loyalty." It is what Ruth and Orpah showed to Naomi and their dead husbands (1:8). It is what Boaz shows to Ruth in favoring her among the local gleaners (2:20) and what Ruth shows to Boaz in choosing him rather than a young man (3:10). The story may well be read as a message about the triumph of *hesed* over all obstacles, and it is that theme which I have chosen to develop in the sermon presented here as an example of preaching from short stories.

A Sermon on Ruth

Much of what Paul says about *agapē* in 1 Cor. 13 can be taken as a definition of what *hesed* means in the Old Testament, and it seemed natural to me to take verse 7, "Love bears all things, believes all things, hopes all things, endures all things," as a way of summing up the theme I wanted to trace through the story. But I did not want to become analytical in talking about this kind of love, for it seemed that the actions of Naomi, Ruth, and Boaz can get the point across better than descriptive words. So most of the sermon is spent in telling the story. There are various ways of doing this, but the most important thing of all is to find a way which will not turn a good story into a dull one! Whether I have succeeded or not, the reader can decide. Sometimes one may want to become one of the characters, and tell it in the first person. The question then will be whether one has the personality to do that effectively and whether that kind of slant may introduce distortions into the original plot. In this case I decided not to try to become Boaz, let alone take on the personality of Ruth or Naomi, and told the story largely by means of conversation.

One of the aims of *retelling* is, of course, to enable one to explain things which need explaining and to emphasize the major themes. Again, some care has to be taken to avoid letting the explanations dominate, and thus spoil, the story. The big problem with Ruth is the custom of levirate marriage, which we can scarcely expect our congregations to know all about (or even to have heard of), but which must be understood in at least a rudimentary sense in order to appreciate the pathos of Naomi's situation. I took the liberty of assuming that, as a Moabite woman, Ruth would not understand this custom and thus found a way to bring in an explanation in conversation between her and Naomi. I assumed that the custom of gleaning would be better understood and could be described in passing, while the other unfamiliar bit, the procedure for purchasing land, I frankly slurred over somewhat, simplifying it so that it would not delay bringing the story to its conclusion. One tricky place in this story is the scene at the threshing floor. What really happened there, anyway? The author does not tell us, and I finally decided that rather than tip the balance one way or the other in my reconstruction I would tell even less about that scene than the author did, and thus let it remain a private matter.

I decided that an effective place to begin telling the story was with the arrival of the two women in Bethlehem, so used 1:1–18 for the Scripture reading, which in this case served as the prologue to the sermon. I first preached it at the Middlesex United Presbyterian Church, an open country church near Butler, Pa., and have subsequently preached it on three other occasions. The effectiveness of the story form has been verified by the enthusiastic comments which it has elicited from each of these congregations.

Love Never Ends

Ruth 1:1–18   *1 Corinthians 13*

The dogs began to bark and the shouting of the children almost drowned out their barking as they all raced out of the village, for two strange women were coming up the road toward Bethlehem. They walked slowly and the older one staggered a bit—they had come from a distance for their clothes and faces were dusty. The villagers stopped to look at them with suspicion as they approached the well.

Then a woman cried out, "Don't I know you? Aren't you Naomi, the wife of Elimelech, who left here for Moab years ago?" The old woman muttered, "Not Naomi—pleasant; call me Mara—bitter," and she sat down heavily on the well curbing.

"But what in the world has happened? Where is your husband? And who is this woman?"

Naomi told them; how her husband and sons had died, and how this Moabite woman, Ruth, widow of Mahlon, had offered to accompany her back to her old home in Bethlehem.

The two women found Naomi's old house, a one room stone building, now in ruins, and set about trying to make of it a shelter for the night. Evening came, and the neighbor women brought part of their meals, for Isra-elites had been taught the importance of caring for the poor in their midst, and there was no one so destitute as these two.

It was spring, and there were fields which had been Elimelech's but spring is harvest time in Judah, and it would be a whole year before they could hope to raise a crop, and there was a long, dry summer ahead of them. So next morning Naomi sent Ruth out to look for a field where the barley was being harvested. Ruth was afraid and she argued with her mother-in-law a bit. She did not know the country, had never been in Israel before, she knew everyone would spot her as a foreigner by her accent, and didn't know how they would treat her. But Naomi reassured her: "Ruth, it is the law in this country that the poor have the right to go into the fields and follow the harvesters, picking up anything they miss. And our only other choice right now is starvation.''

So Ruth went out, walked up and down timidly until she saw a field of barley being cut and some people scouring the ground for heads and stalks that had been missed, and she began to do the same. She came home in the evening with a quarter of a bushel of barley, a great deal for a gleaner, and one who had never done such work before—and some bread in her hand as well.

''Where have you been? Where did you get all this?''

''It was the field of Boaz. The owner spoke to me, said he appreciated my coming from Moab to live with you, and shared his lunch with me.''

''Boaz! Good old Boaz! He is a relative of my husband. He always was a fine man, but to be so kind to you for my sake—God bless him!''

''He told me to come back tomorrow.''

''By all means, go back. If any two women ever needed a helper and protector, it is we two, and if Boaz is concerned about our welfare, perhaps there is a chance for us after all.''

So it went throughout the harvest season. Ruth went to the fields to glean, and Boaz watched out for her to be sure she was not mistreated because she was young and a stranger and a Moabite. One day Naomi said to her: ''Ruth, you know how despondent I have been since my sons died, but I don't know whether you fully understand what a tragedy this is for an Israelite. As an Israelite woman I believe my chief duty in life is to have and raise children to carry on my husband's name into the next generation. And I thought I had done my duty, I had two fine sons, but when they both died before either you or Orpah could have children, my whole life was shattered. Now my husband's name has been cut off from the land of the living, and your husband's name has been cut off. As a Moabite that may not mean so much to you, but my life is totally without meaning, for I have been unable to do what I was created for.

''But, I have been thinking these past days that there may still be a way. This thing is so important to us in Israel that we have a special provision for serious cases, a law called ''levirate marriage.'' If a man dies without children his brother's duty is to take the widow as a wife and to beget children who will not be his own—by law they will be his dead brother's children, inherit his property and bear his name. Your husband, Mahlon, has no living brother to take on this duty, but Boaz is a near relative; he could do it. Since he's not a brother he is not obligated, but he is a good Israelite, he keeps the law faithfully, and he has been so compassionate to us that perhaps he could be willing to take our part.''

Ruth was a bit stunned at the thought of marrying Boaz. ''Mother, this is very awkward. He is a wealthy man and we are poor. He is an Israelite and I am a Moabite. He is old, must be 35, and I am only 17. How do we dare speak to him about such a thing?''

"Not we, my child. You. I am not your father, I have no legal status in this at all, I cannot arrange a marriage for you as your father should. This is a difficult matter, and we will have to use an irregular procedure. Boaz is winnowing his barley harvest in the evenings, these days, and during winnowing times the men sleep at the threshing floor to guard the crop. Tonight, when it is dark and late enough that no one else will be around, you go down to where he sleeps and speak with him about this."

"No, how can I? I would be too ashamed. Israelite girls do not go wandering about in the dark to where men are sleeping, unless they are prostitutes, and neither do Moabites. What would he think of me? Bad enough even to do such a thing, but then to ask him to marry me! I'm just not that kind of person."

"I understand, Ruth. You are not very outspoken, and you are a little bit timid. Being a foreigner here puts you in an awkward position, too. But, which is more important to you—your honor, your self-respect, avoiding embarrassment, keeping up the standards of ladylike behavior—or Mahlon your husband and Naomi to whom you have pledged your loyalty?"

Silence for a moment. Then, "All that you say I will do."

She returned in the morning. "Boaz is a kind man. He says he will do what he can for us."

Boaz was a staunch and sturdy Israelite. He was determined to rescue Naomi and Ruth from their poverty and from their disgrace of childlessness. But it was not an easy matter to work out and early that morning he was already at the town gate, where every legal and business matter was customarily settled, in order to get the necessary parties together. The problem was that levirate marriage had to be carried out by the next of kin, and there was one relative closer to Elimelech than Boaz. Soon he came by on his way to the fields.

"Cousin, I have some business to talk with you. Come and sit down." Then Boaz gathered ten other men, to be his witnesses, and the negotiations began.

"You have seen Naomi since she came back, haven't you? Did you know that she wants to sell Elimelech's property?"

"No, I hadn't heard."

"Now, of course, you, as next of kin, have the first chance to buy it. Are you interested?"

"Yes, I might be."

"I must remind you, though, that there are two obligations on the next of kin, in this case. This Moabite woman, Ruth, is the widow of Mahlon, and if you buy the land to keep it in the family, by rights you should also marry Ruth and raise children in Mahlon's name."

"Oh! That's another matter. I have children of my own, and if I buy Elimelech's land Ruth's children would inherit it and there is likely to be trouble over the inheritance. No thanks, I have my own family to look out for."

"You're sure? OK, in that case, I'll buy the land and marry Ruth."

And it was done.

Ruth and Boaz have given us one of the most beautiful examples ever of the kind of love Paul described in 1 Cor. 13, of the love which "bears all things, believes all things, hopes all things, endures all things," of love which never ends. Ruth had nothing to gain by going to Judah with her mother-in-law. Self-interest would have kept her in Moab with her family where another husband of her own people could be found. But her love, for her dead husband and for Naomi, was the kind which willingly takes on obligations to others and is glad to do it. Poverty, the difficulties of being a foreigner in a strange land, the embarrassment of asking Boaz to marry her—none of these was an obstacle to doing what love commanded.

And Boaz—a wealthy man, highly esteemed, who had everything already— now he took the risk of being shunned because he married a foreign woman, the risk of creating problems with his inheritance because the children born of Ruth would not be legally his. He didn't need any of that trouble, and yet his heart went out in love to two destitute women and to that branch of his family which would be cut off if he didn't do something about it.

The story of Ruth is often taken as a romantic love story, and maybe there was romance; I'm sure we tend to think of her as a beautiful young girl and of Boaz as both rich and handsome, but try reading it once with a different picture in mind. Try imagining Ruth homely as a mud fence and Boaz as old and decrepit. Will it make one bit of difference in how the story comes out? Not one bit. Oh, I still hope there was some romance there, but the kind of love this story tells us about, the love which motivated Ruth and Boaz to do what they did was the self-giving kind which comes from God, which we know best in Jesus, but which we have also received from our own parents and good friends and neighbors. It is that kind of love which keeps the world going.

Jonah

This is a book which is full of unanswered questions. Why did Jonah run away? Because he was afraid of the Ninevites? Because he hated them and did not want them to repent? Because he was reluctant to make a prophecy which might not come true? Why was he sleeping out cold in the bottom of the ship while the storm raged? Was his request to be thrown overboard a noble gesture, to save the lives of the sailors, or selfish, to escape the will of God by dying? When God decided to spare Nineveh, why did Jonah go out to the east of the city and sit down to wait and see what would happen to it? He is a mystifying character, by all odds the most obstinate creature in the Scriptures, not excluding Balaam's ass, and his book can be interpreted in a great variety of ways. But that is because it, like Ruth, is a work of art; it depicts the same kind of mystifying, aggravating, apparently illogical behavior that we encounter in real people and it does not spell everything out for us neatly any more than real life does. That may make the study of the book frustrating for those who are looking for simple answers, but it is also what has made the book perennially fascinating and a delight to generations of readers.

An early interpretation of Jonah, which continued to be used both in Judaism and in Christianity for many years, is alluded to in Matt. 12:41, when Jesus says, "The men of Nineveh will arise at the judgment with this generation and condemn it; for they repented at the preaching of Jonah, and behold, something greater than Jonah is here." This approach explained Jonah's flight in a way complimentary to him; he did not want to preach to Nineveh, it was said, because he knew that the contrast between converted Gentiles and unrepentant Israel would be a condemnation of the latter, so he fled for Israel's sake.[29] Coming from that same New Testament context is another, specifically Christian use of the book, the "sign of Jonah" (Matt. 12:39–40), i.e. taking Jonah's three days and nights in the belly of the whale as a type of Jesus' three days and nights in the grave. This typological approach thus makes Jonah's experience a prediction of the resurrection, but it then focuses all our attention on two verses of the book (1:17 and 2:10) and tells us nothing about whether the rest of the story means anything.

Another Christian interpretation of the book, which runs contrary to making Jonah a type of Christ, has been widely used since the fourth century.[30] It explains his flight by saying he represents Jewish nationalism and the narrow spirit which begrudged extending the offer of salvation to the Gentiles. This became both the basis for Christian condemnation of the Jews and for many a modern missionary sermon, the burden of which is, don't be like Jonah.[31] It is a theory which modern scholarship has connected with its tendency to give the book a post-exilic date. Like the Book of Ruth, it is said to have been written as a protest against the exclusiveness exemplified by Ezra and Nehemiah. There are some problems with this, however; the two reformers just mentioned directed their activities against syncretism and laxness *within* the Jewish community and said nothing that we know of against the conversion of the nations. Also, Jonah is never said to be a representative of Israel in the book, so we are reading in something when we say that his attitude (assuming we really do understand his attitude!) is intended to represent that of a whole people.

A similar objection can be raised to an allegorical interpretation which has still been proposed in modern works, viz. that Jonah represents Israel and the whale represents Babylon, so that the exile is here allegorically depicted.[32]

Modern studies of the Bible have made two kinds of discoveries which enable us to take a fresh look at this enigmatic character, however. The first has already been mentioned: the frank acknowledgment of the ambiguities of the work as one of its strengths, not a weakness, and I shall come back to this again. The other is the discovery of the humor in the book. The author surprises us in one way or another at every turn, but only recently have scholars acknowledged that he is having a little fun with us.[33] Jonah sets out for Tarshish to flee "from the presence of the Lord." How does he expect to do that? By sea—when he himself will shortly be identifying his God as the one "who made the sea and the dry land" (1:9)? His flight provokes quite a reaction from God, who hurls a great storm upon the sea, but even at this point, Jonah is a contrary soul; instead of reacting as a normal person would he is sound asleep. And this prophet of God has to be urged by pagans to pray. The storm made converts out of the sailors, and perhaps it did lead Jonah to his finest moment, for he suggests they throw him overboard that the storm might be stilled, but we'll never know for sure whether he did it to save the sailors' lives or just to escape God by dying.

Normally, to be swallowed by an animal would be a horrible fate, but not in this book. It's God's none-too-dignified way of saving Jonah's life. And in the fish's stomach he sings a hymn. It is one of the traditional hymns of thanksgiving, using, as many of the psalms do, water imagery and references to the threat of drowning as a vivid way of describing peril of any kind, but for the first time in history such a psalm is actually sung under water. And finally Jonah is vomited out on to dry land.

The story begins again, with the same commission in almost the same words. But this time Jonah goes. He does not call for repentance but delivers a message like that of most of the pre-exilic prophets: an announcement of coming judgment. But the results are the greatest revival of all time! The whole city repented, including even the animals. And the king of Nineveh's theology is not too bad, for a pagan; he only suggests, "Who knows, God may yet repent and turn from his fierce anger, so that we perish not."

And God does change his mind. The city is saved. And Jonah, once again, even when he does what God tells him to, ends up with egg on his face, for by obeying God he has become a false prophet. The author who recently wrote of him under the title, "The Prophet as Shlemiel," may be right.[34] Jonah is angry, not because he didn't want the city to be saved, he says, but because he didn't want to be forced to proclaim judgment when he knew God would probably change his mind and leave Jonah with the reputation of a false prophet (4:2). He is still stubborn and for him there is nothing to do but sit and wait to see whether by any chance his prediction may come true.

At the end God deals with him with the same gentleness as before, giving him an object lesson which leaves him feeling both miserable and foolish. He makes a vine to shade Jonah and then a worm to destroy the vine, and he says, "You are sorry that the plant died; isn't it better to lose your reputation as a prophet, isn't it better for even God himself to change his mind, than that these many people should die?" And at the very end the author surprises us once more: "and also much cattle?"

About midway through the story we begin to discover that Jonah is a bit like one of Chaplin's characters—a comic figure caught up in a very serious situation. This is not burlesque, as we may begin to think about the time we get to the big fish; rather it is an ironic treatment of an issue, or perhaps a group of issues which are of deep theological importance. Here I shall follow an excellent study by J. Magonet, who has spoken of the "polarities" represented in the book.[35] He finds in it tensions between:

1. The knowledge of God and the disobedience of God. Jonah knows God is the maker of land and sea, knows that he is gracious and merciful, but that does not govern his behavior. How can he know the truth about God and yet be so contrary? For that matter, how can we?

2. Particularism and universalism. The author relies on shock effect here by making a klutz of the prophet of God and by making the pagans the good guys. Everyone knew Nineveh wasn't like this, for according to Nahum that city was destroyed for her sins. But in this story even the animals of Nineveh repent, in order to force its readers to re-examine conventional, comfortable views of "insiders and outsiders."

3. Traditional teaching and new experience. These recent studies of Jonah have shown how extensively the author of the book has drawn on familiar language and ideas from the rest of the Old Testament. But they are now used to tell us of surprising things; of a runaway prophet, of a great revival in Nineveh (of all places), and of a God who changes his mind. They force us to reconsider whether God himself is bound by sacred tradition or whether he is still free to do a new thing which may both surprise and shock us.

4. The power of God and the freedom of man. The pagan sailors express one of the dominant themes of the book when they pray: "for thou, O Lord, hast done as it pleased thee" (1:14), and the king of Nineveh is also aware of who is really in charge when he says: "Who knows, God may . . ." (3:9). But Jonah acts out our resistance to the acceptance of limitations on human freedom. It is hard to be comfortable with a God who is so thoroughly sovereign as he is in this story.

We have some things to preach from all this, many things, I believe, but some suggestions about who would produce such a story, and why, may also be helpful. Jonah's own explanation of his anger over God's failure to destroy Nineveh is that it had made a false prophet of him. At this point I think we can have some sympathy for him, for the question of true and false prophecy was a serious one in Israel. The nature of the issue is spelled out for us especially clearly in Jeremiah (23:9–40; 28; 29:15–23), and in Deut. 18:22 a test is given for judging (after the fact, unfortunately) whether a prophet's words are true or false: "When a prophet speaks in the name of the Lord, if the word does not come to pass or come true, that is a word which the Lord has not spoken; the prophet has spoken it presumptuously, you need not be afraid of him." Jonah flunked that test. No wonder he was upset. But why did he fail it? That brings us to the real issue.

Recent form critical studies of the prophets have shown that until the time of the exile *repentance* was not a prominent part of their message.[36] (For more on this see Chapter VI.) They do not so much plead for conversion as announce that the judgment has already been pronounced and that it will soon be executed. That is exactly the kind of message Jonah brought to Nineveh. But Israel had always believed in a God who is "slow to anger, and abounding in steadfast love, and repentest of evil," as Jonah also said, quoting the old formula of Exod. 34:6–7. And at the time of the exile, beginning with Jeremiah and Ezekiel, prophets began to proclaim a message of forgiveness and restoration. But how are justice and mercy to be reconciled? How can a just God forgive? This apparently became a serious issue for those prophets of the sixth century (and perhaps later) who inherited the traditions of judgment prophecy from the past, but who now felt impelled to proclaim restoration.[37] Were they false prophets? In the past that had been the judgment made of those who proclaimed, "Peace, peace."

This book, since it takes a prophet as its central figure and centers on a problem which must have disturbed that type of person more than any other, seems to have been written by a member of a prophetic circle, describing their problem in an ironic fashion, but commenting on a universal theological problem: How can a just God forgive sins? His position is to emphasize the sovereignty of God. He is a God who does as he wishes; in his omnipotence he does not even have to keep his own word, and in his freedom the God of justice chooses to be merciful. – If that bothers us, and well it may, since mercy means breaking the rules, well that shows us the Book of Jonah was struggling with a central theological question, and it may even lead us to think about the Cross in a new light.

CHAPTER IV

Preaching the Law

How—and whether—to preach the laws of the Old Testament presents perhaps the most difficult theological problem we shall encounter in this book, since the place of law in the Christian life has remained one of the perennial issues of our faith since the time of Jesus himself. This is not the place even to summarize that long debate, not to mention pursuing it analytically and critically.[1] As I have done elsewhere, I shall restrict my comments here to the ways in which law has most often been treated homiletically and to the positive statement of a hermeneutic for the normative Christian use of Old Testament law.

The Christian use of the law of the Old Testament has been complicated by two puzzling features of the New Testament:

a)   The New Testament authors reject parts of the Old Testament law as being no longer binding on Christians (at least on Gentile Christians), e.g. circumcision (Gal. 5:2–12) and the observance of the Sabbath and other holy days (Col. 2:16). Yet they reaffirm other laws as still valid (1 Cor. 9:8ff.; Eph. 6:2f.). Christians have normally explained this by differentiating between ritual law, no longer to be observed, and moral law, still binding, but the New Testament nowhere states such a principle explicitly and there are some exceptions, e.g. the edict of the Council of Jerusalem forbade the eating of blood (Acts 15:29).

b)   Both Jesus and Paul make more extreme statements which indicate that the Christian is not bound by law in any way. To the lawyer's quotation of the two-fold "law of love" in Luke 10, Jesus answers, "Do this and you will live"; apparently nothing else is required. Paul, of course, speaks of "dying to the law" (Gal. 2:19; Rom. 7:6), of living not under law but under grace or in the Spirit, and emphasizes Christian freedom. But on the other hand, Jesus is quoted as saying, "Till heaven and earth pass away, not an iota, not a dot, will pass from the law until all is accomplished" (Matt. 5:18; cf. vss. 17–20), and in comparing tithing (a cultic regulation!) with justice, mercy, and faith, "These you ought to have done without neglecting the others" (Matt. 23:23). Paul's comments are even more startling: "Do we then overthrow the law by this faith? By no means! On the contrary, we uphold the law" (Rom. 3:31), and "So the law is holy, and the commandment is holy and just and good" (Rom. 7:12). And so it is that both legalists and antinomians in the church have found it easy to obtain proof texts to support their favorite positions. More difficult has been the effort to take the whole New Testament seriously and to answer the question whether it possesses a unified view of the law, or whether it simply contradicts itself. The position which will be taken in this chapter is that although not all the exegetical problems have been solved it is still possible to discern a coherent view of the relationship between law and liberty for the Christian which is essentially the same (although the accents are different) throughout the New Testament. Then we will be ready to ask about preaching the laws of the Old Testament.

Christians have been remarkably ambivalent in their attitudes toward Old Testament law. Some have tended toward adopting it as if it were as binding upon them as it is for Jews, including such things as food regulations and the observance of the Sabbath (i.e. Saturday). But they stop short of offering sacrifice, so they are still being selective! (I did hear of a minister on Chicago's West Side who killed a sheep on the altar during Holy Week, but I don't know what he meant by it.) Others separate the "moral laws" from the "ritual," but since neither the Old Testament nor the New Testament provides a clear principle for making such a distinction, there are inconsistencies. For example, all agree in general in accepting the Ten Commandments as basic for Christian ethics, but one of those commandments—concerning the Sabbath—is ritual in nature! And there have been Christian groups which have explicitly stated that only the moral law of the Old Testament is binding upon them, but which have nevertheless observed Sunday as the Sabbath in a highly legalistic way. The surprises which the ritual/moral distinction may lead to were recently illustrated by an article claiming that the Old and New Testament statements against homosexual behavior are of no relevance for the modern Christian since they were alluding to *cultic* practices of antiquity.

Another simplistic effort to apply Old Testament law to the Christian life is the attempt to take over laws designed for people long ago, living a relatively simple, agrarian life, and apply them without modification to an entirely different social-cultural system. But fortunately most of the problematic uses of Old Testament law which have been mentioned so far are largely a thing of the past for the major Christian groups, and we encounter them now usually in the legalistic, sectarian groups which do still arise from time to time. The situation in the mainstream of Christianity is better described as libertarian than legalistic. Denominational pronouncements on social and ethical issues tend to take sociology, economics, and psychology as the norm and then to find exegetical devices for making the Bible agree with them. An explicit scriptural directive is never a problem, for it was socially and culturally determined, to begin with, and ultimately we are not under law but under grace, anyway! So the Bible has become almost useless as a normative guide for Christian ethics, since legalists are invariably selective (no one tries to obey the law of the jubilee year, despite—or maybe partly because of—its profound ethical implications) and non-legalists have failed to discover a hermeneutic which will do anything more than enable them to justify doing what they wanted to do in the first place.

In the past the tendencies of the main branches of the church were in the direction of legalism.[2] Complete freedom from law has seldom been taught; the Old and New Testaments have been considered to be the Law of God, binding upon all. Normally the difference made by the New Testament was said to be the abrogation of the ritual law, which was then either ignored or allegorized so as to yield ethical instruction, and the promise of salvation by grace. In the Roman Catholic tradition grace enables one to keep the law so as to be justified by doing it; in the Protestant traditions the emphasis is on justification by grace apart from works of the law. In every communion, however, the Ten Commandments have regularly been called the summation of the whole ethical requirement of God and interpreters from Aquinas on have found it possible to deduce an entire code of behavior from that brief text. The "three uses of the law" with which Christian interpreters have worked are: 1. to convict us of sin by setting God's standard over against our behavior, driving us to fly to God for mercy; 2. to restrain us from evil because of our fear of penalties; 3. to instruct believers in the divine will and to exhort them to do good works as a result of salvation. But today we are faced by the modern emphasis on the New Testament's message of freedom from law in addition to the questions raised about the validity for us of principles which are addressed to agrarian, slave-holding, patriarchal cultures. Merely to announce "The Bible says . . ." is not likely to move the people of many churchs to ethical action in our day, and very probably it should not.

The direction which this chapter will take may lead the reader to think that the author's Calvinist roots are showing, in that Calvin's emphasis on the "third use" of the law may seem to predominate. Luther's emphasis on the first use, on the law as that which places us under judgment, will come in along the way, but it must be made clear that the tendencies of some who followed him, to equate the Old Testament with law and the New Testament with grace, are to be resisted. The condemning aspects of God's law appears in all of God's revelation of himself, since we are not holy as he is holy, and we must not fall into the long-discredited trap of preaching the Old Testament as law = judgment and the

New Testament as gospel = grace. It is this latter concern plus the conviction that the genre "law" in the Old Testament can have real value for us as instruction in what is right for us to do that leads me to develop the following way of preaching the "third use."

In offering a hermeneutic for preaching the Old Testament law as normative for Christian behavior, I must first sketch briefly my position on the relationship of the Christian to law. Fuller descriptions of this position can be found in many other works, so I need not develop it at length. Then, somewhat more carefully, I shall try to show how the history of tradition approach, when applied to the legal materials of both testaments, gives us solid ground on which to stand and from which to say: *This* is what the Bible tells us we ought to do.

Jesus and the Law

First we must affirm that Jesus did not set himself up in opposition to the laws of his people.[3] Normally, he obeyed the law with care, including the ritual laws about pilgrimage to Jerusalem, etc. And in the Sermon on the Mount he cautions, "Think not that I have come to abolish the law and the prophets; I have come not to abolish them but to fulfill them" (Matt. 5:17). Indeed, when, in the same passage he sets his teachings in contrast to the traditional law, it is to set a stricter standard, not to set aside the laws of the past. "You have heard that it was said to the men of old, 'You shall not kill; and whoever kills shall be liable to judgment.' But I say to you that every one who is angry with his brother shall be liable to judgment . . ." (Matt. 5:21-47). But then Jesus deliberately broke the Sabbath law, and defended his disciples when they broke it. The conflict between Jesus and the Pharisees over the observance of the Sabbath, which occupies a large place in the Gospels, reveals to us the true relationship between Jesus' ethical standard and the legalistic understanding of law. I shall not take the space to summarize those well-known stories; they speak of the disciples picking and eating grain on the Sabbath (Mk. 2:23ff.; Matt. 12:1ff.; Lk. 6:1ff.), of Jesus healing the withered hand in the synagogue (Mk. 3:1ff.; Matt. 12:9ff.; Lk. 6:6ff.), and of his healings of the crippled woman and the man with dropsy (Lk. 13:10ff.; 14:1ff.). The stories have, more often than not, been taken as accounts of how Jesus opposed the oral law of the Pharisees, either because it was adding to the *real* law as written in the Old Testament, or because it was unnecessary and inhumane. But it is important to be aware that every effort was made by the Pharisees to be humane in their development of the oral law, and that the intent of their elaboration of interpretations and applications was not to burden anyone but to be helpful by telling people precisely what it was that God wanted them to do.[4] The people Jesus cured had chronic ailments; they and he could have waited until sundown, when the Sabbath would be ended, and then both concerns of the community could have been met—the keeping of the Sabbath and the care for human life and health. The ruler of the synagogue reminded the people of this with respect to the healing of the crippled woman when he said, "There are six days on which work ought to be done; come on those days and be healed, and not on the sabbath day" (Lk. 13:14). Hers was a serious affliction but not a danger to human life, and it wouldn't have hurt her a bit to have waited a few more hours (after living with it eighteen years) and thus all could have kept the law. If she had been in real danger, all the Jews would have applauded Jesus' action in saving her life, for the oral law of the Pharisees clearly specified that to save a life or to alleviate severe pain the Sabbath law *ought* to be broken.[5] And this applied as well as to animals, as Jesus noted; not only were they supposed to save an animal's life if it was in danger on the Sabbath, but they also regularly performed the work of watering their stock, since it would be cruelty not to do so. Hence it is clear that it is not an inhumane law that Jesus is opposing. Rather he is taking an entirely different approach to the law. Judaism expressed concern both for the law, as it is written, and for human needs and life in general. But a faithful Jew stayed as close to observance of the law as possible, even when conscience told him he had to depart from it. What is so radical about Jesus' actions on the Sabbath day is that he set something else above the law, even above one of the Ten Commandments, so that *any* human need, even one such as the disciples' hunger (which they should have taken care of by planning ahead) or an illness which could have waited for a few more hours for healing, can take precedence over the law. What Jesus has done is to reject law as the definition of human righteousness. His substitute for law is clearly stated, although it takes on slightly different forms in the three Synoptic Gospels; in Matthew and Mark Jesus quotes the two "love commandments," while in Luke Jesus asks the question and the lawyer provides the answer. The latter is not an improbable occurrence, for we know the rabbis of the first century had on several occasions summed up the whole law in terms of a few verses.

> And behold, a lawyer stood up to put him to the test, saying, "Teacher, what shall I do to inherit eternal life?" He said to him, "What is written in the law? How do you read?" and he answered, "You shall love the Lord your God with all your heart, and with all your soul, and with all your strength, and with all your mind; and your neighbor as yourself." And he said to him, "You have answered right; do this, and you will live." (Luke 10:25–28)

This is the "two-fold law of love," taken from Deut. 6:5 and Lev. 19:18, but as has often been noted, *love* can scarcely be the subject of *law*. It can scarcely be commanded or enforced. If love is the sole basis for the righteous life, as Jesus seems to be saying here, then law as such is no longer even in the picture.

Yet Jesus himself gave instructions on what to do and what not to do. What is their status, if they are not law, since the Christian lives by another standard than law? We cannot say that the ethical teachings of Jesus have become the

New Law for Christians, supplementing or replacing the law of the Old Testament, for Jesus opposed every legalistic approach to life and he taught and lived a law of love which supercedes all laws, the spirit of which might indeed sometimes be broken if his own teachings were obeyed in a legalistic manner. Let us be guided by C. H. Dodd's description of Jesus' ethical teachings as indicating the "*quality and direction* of action which conforms to the standard set by divine agape."[6] But why isn't love all we need? We shall have more to say about that after considering Paul's teachings, but for now let it be observed that the radical quality of such teachings as turning the other cheek, going the second mile, and the requirements of no-hatred and no-lust can lead to despair if taken as law imposed upon the Christian and expected to be obeyed to the letter. If, on the other hand, they are examples of how far real love is willing to go, they can be of great value in keeping us from compromising too easily, and in holding up the highest possible standard for our motives as well as our actual behavior.

Paul and the Law

Paul's understanding of law can scarcely be treated adequately in a short summary; the bibliography on this subject is a lengthy one.[7] But let us refresh our memories on the way he deals with law in his major theological treatise, the Letter to the Romans; this will remind us of the most important issues.

He begins the argument by showing that all human beings, Jew and Gentile alike, stand under the judgment of God, "for there is no distinction; since all have sinned and fall short of the glory of God" (3:23). Gentiles, who are outside the law, have enough access to the truth of what God requires of them to be held justly accountable for their perversions; and the Jews, who have the great advantage of the law, which is God's revelation of his truth, have not succeeded in keeping it so it declares them guilty. But God shows his righteousness (1:17) by justifying all alike, by his grace as a gift (3:24). This does not set aside the law (3:31), for it was the law which first testified to God's righteousness which has now become manifest in Jesus Christ (3:21f.). Paul's uses of the word *nomos* are multivalent; not always does it refer to the law of the Old Testament, but our concerns will lead us to concentrate on those which do. Already we can see that he speaks of the Old Testament law in two ways; in its juridical function as that which condemns the law-breaker, and in its revelatory function as that which testifies to God's truth.

Paul's offer of free salvation under grace apart from works of the law seemed to leave the door open to antinomianism; the attitude that since we can't be saved by our good works then it really doesn't make any difference what we do, and the more we sin the more opportunity God has to be gracious. He attacks this position in chapter 6, holding that entering into the realm of grace means dying to the very possibility of sinning. Sin could have dominion over them only when they were under the condemnation of the law; having been freed from that judgment they were also to consider themselves free from sin itself. But this does not mean that the law can then be forgotten, and Paul now shows how very complex the matter is when he goes on to describe what it means that the Christian is not saved by the law, yet is forbidden to commit the sins proscribed by the law. He answers that Christians are not only dead to sin but dead to the law; it is no longer binding upon them. Not that the law is evil; it declares to humanity what is right and what is wrong, but by the very fact of doing so, it becomes a temptation to sin. "If it had not been for the law, I should not have known sin. I should not have known what it is to covet if the law had not said, 'You shall not covet.' . . . For sin, finding opportunity in the commandment, deceived me and by it killed me" (7:7, 11). But the source of the problem is not the law itself; "the law is holy, and the commandment is holy and just and good" (7:12), the source is in humanity which cannot obey. Paul goes on to describe the struggle which rages within him between his desire to obey his Lord and the power of evil which so often wins, and concludes again that our only hope is in the power of Jesus Christ (7:24–8:1). He now seems to speak of two kinds of laws: "the law of the Spirit of life in Christ Jesus" and "the law of sin and death" (8:2), but that does not mean that we may automatically identify the latter with the Old Testament, for he immediately goes on to assure us that the work of Christ is "in order that the just requirement of the law might be fulfilled in us" (8:4). This new life in the Spirit, then, enables us who are no longer under the law to live lives of freedom which are in conformity with the law. This made clear by the last five chapters of the letter, for they consist almost entirely of ethical instructions. Paul has been leading up to this ever since chapter 5, in making the point that God not only justifies us—giving us a new status of acceptance before him—but also enables us in this life to live in the Spirit, which means we actually can lead a righteous life. So this letter, which is so strongly opposed to law, as the means of salvation, concludes with rules of conduct; not in a contradictory fashion, replacing the old law with a new one, but acknowledging the human need of help to understand how the principle of love, the inward motivation to do good, is to be applied to daily life. This sort of thing was obviously standard procedure throughout the Christian church of the first century. The preaching of the gospel was followed by teaching concerning how a Christian ought to live. Many of the epistles in the New Testament contain little codes of ethical conduct; e.g., Eph. 5–6; Col. 3; 1 Thess. 5:14–18; Heb. 13; 1 Pet. 2–3, while others such as 1 Corinthians are almost entirely devoted to questions of how a Christian ought to behave. Does this contradict the teachings of Jesus and the theology of Paul concerning freedom from the law and the sufficiency of love as the motive of conduct? Not at all, for those especially who were coming into the church from Gentile communities had need of instruction concerning how one guided by the law of love *normally* behaved. This was not self-evident in every case. The excesses to which an improper understanding of Christian freedom could lead are clearly reflected in 1 Corinthians. So rules of conduct were provided as a guide for those who found that love did not completely take the place of wisdom and experience.

That Jesus' emphasis on the law of love was also taken up by Paul is shown by his expositions of that teaching in 12:14–21 and 13:8–10. Paul's attitude is summed up in 13:10: "Love does no wrong to a neighbor; therefore love is the fulfilling of the law." But how is this to be put into practice? We sometimes need help from others before we understand what kinds of actions may be doing wrong to our neighbor. Proper motivation is not always enough. In 14:1–23 Paul takes up a problem which helps us to understand better what it means to live in freedom from every law but the law of love. It was the issue which faced Christian communities in Gentile cities of whether they could in good conscience eat meat bought in the public markets, knowing as they did that most of it had passed through a pagan ritual, having been offered as a sacrifice to an idol. Some Christians said such meat is forbidden; to eat it would be to acknowledge those false gods. Others said the idol has no power to do anything to that meat; it is like any other and we are free to eat it. Paul said the latter party was correct in its judgment and referred to the former as his weaker brethren, but he went on to show that although Christians do have perfect freedom in such matters, love will constrain them from doing anything which will hurt their brothers or sisters. They will give up some of their freedoms voluntarily, not because any law tells them they must, but because they are concerned enough about their fellow Christians to want to do so. Even when it is something as insignificant as eating meat, Christians will not make an issue of their freedom if it will hurt someone else to do so. This is a far-reaching principle in application of the law of love, and one which can never be legislated into a new law, for it insists on the Christian's freedom from outside constraint of any kind; merely reminding us of how the inner constraint of love moves Christians to behave.

To speak of complete freedom from outside restraint would seem to lead to a situation of considerable disorder within the church, since we know in advance that not everyone is going to behave so admirably as Paul (and he also admits he often does the opposite of what he wants). It will not always be true that the strong will bear with the failings of the weak, each seeking to "please his neighbor for his good, to edify him" (15:2). So there is a necessity for severity at times with one's brethren when they create a clear danger to the faith or to Christian morals, and when no other methods of dealing with them succeed. Paul had to apply his authority as an apostle more than once, and in 16:17–20 we have some advice about how to deal with those who disturb the peace. Love for one's neighbor and the willingness to give up one's freedoms for the benefit of the brothers and sisters is not to be confused with wishy-washiness and spinelessness. It takes a strong character, in the first place, not to insist on one's rights when one has the power to do so, but to give them up voluntarily for the sake of someone else. And it takes a person who not only has love, but also intelligence and common sense, to know when it is best to resist and when best to give in, when to be gentle and when to be severe, when to keep on trying to reform the bad influence among you and when to cut him off because of the harm he is doing to others. Paul faced all these problems in his dealings with the new churches he had founded, and his methods are *illustrations* of how the love of Christ may be applied to specific cases in the form of quite explicit rules and directions.

As negative as he can be when he attacks the belief that one can be saved by works, i.e. by a partial keeping of the law, Paul is never led by this to deny the truth of the standards of righteousness established by the law of the Old Testament, nor does it lead him to leave his pupils without guidance in righteous living, which is understood not to be the means to salvation but the result of it.

The Christian and the Law

First we must qualify the title of this section, for we are not under law but are free persons living in love under the grace of God. But we still use the Hebrew word *torah*, which is usually mistranslated "law." Its basic meaning is "instruction, direction," and we have learned from studying the teachings of Jesus and Paul that we still need that and the Bible provides precisely that for us. That word "direction" will be taken very seriously in the history of tradition approach to the Old Testament which will follow shortly. But let us summarize first:

The "natural man" obeys the law (whether of the Old Testament, the church, or the state) because he believes it is best for him to do so. This may be an enlightened view—that on principle it seems best for all to obey the law for the good of society—or an unenlightened view—that one wants to avoid being caught and punished. In either case obedience is offered because it seems to one's advantage to do it, and when the time comes that it seems to one's advantage to break the law, there is no good reason not to. But those who are redeemed obey the law naturally, without being greatly concerned about it, because their deeds are governed according to the law of love, and actions so governed will normally be in perfect accord with the law. The value and function of the law for them is as a "guide to the perplexed"—as a description of how love *normally* issues in action, as an illustration of the work of love in specific cases. Since they cannot claim divine inspiration for every decision they make in life, and since they do not always have wisdom enough to know what is the loving thing to do in difficult cases, they find the law of God to be a great practical help. They conform to it not because it seems to be to their advantage to do so, nor because they are under constraint or fear, but because they want to do what is best for their neighbors, and such actions are the kind of actions the law describes.

Jesus never commended obedience to the law as law. He said we ought to refrain from murder not because the law forbids it, but because we have no hate in our hearts. If we do not kill because of fear of the law, this may make society better, but it does not make us any better persons than those who kill without fear of the law, for we may find other, legal ways to demonstrate our hatred. One can obey the exterior precepts of the law without being a righteous person, from a great variety of motives, without having a drop of love or mercy in one's heart. But when one has been transformed by the love of Christ, made *free* from any obligation to the law, then one's deeds do normally conform to it, since the law is holy and just and good. However, the redeemed person knows that often love constrains us to go beyond what law would ever command, and is also aware that love sometimes compels us to break the law, for the sake of Him who is above all law.

Preaching the Laws of the Old Testament

Having spoken at some length about law in the New Testament we may now formulate the starting point from which all our work on the legal materials in the Old Testament can begin. First, we now understand that "law" is not even a good word to use for either testament; we continue with it only because it is what we are used to. As Christians we are not under the rule of law but are free and live under grace. The ethical teachings of the New Testament are "directions," guides to help us behave intelligently as well as lovingly. But this does not create a strong contrast between the New Testament and the Old. As already noted, *torah* essentially means "instruction" and the basic meaning of the word is in keeping with the Old Testament message of salvation. As Paul observed (Rom. 4) the promise came first, before the law, and modern scholarship has identified covenants of "divine commitment" in the Old Testament; those with Noah (Gen. 9) and with Abraham (Gen. 15) are the result of grace alone. Nothing is done to merit or earn them. Although the Sinai covenant does have statutes and ordinances attached to it, so that it may be called a covenant of "human obligation," the saving activity of God is by no means earned. It is the God who has already saved Israel from bondage in Egypt who offers to make them his covenant people and, when they agree (Exod. 19) then explains to them how God's people ought to live. Indeed there are blessings and curses attached to the law of Sinai (and the New Testament also speaks of rewards and punishments), but they are not the primary reason for obedience. Deuteronomy, which ends with blessings and curses, begins with, "you shall love the Lord your God with all your heart and all your soul and all your might" (6:5).

Obedience to the law is not, in either testament, the means of salvation. In both, God saves his people by his grace. But to be made a member of the people of God calls for a grateful response, and a part of that is responsible behavior by those who are saved. The essential nature of the kind of behavior which is an appropriate response to the Savior God is summarized in both testaments as love for one's neighbor (Lev. 19:18). But love as a motivation may or may not produce the effects desired by love; i.e. it may not always act intelligently, so is not by itself the infallible guide to the right behavior. Hence the "law" comes in as a guide to instruct God's people in the ways the loving person normally behaves.

Now, human laws cannot remain static if they are to continue to be useful, for societies change. The early copyright laws could not foresee the invention of tape recording and Xeroxing, so they became inadequate when those developments became widely used. On the other hand we no longer need traffic laws which uphold the priority of the horse and buggy as the primary means of conveyance. And something similar must be said for the laws of the Bible, even though they are "divine laws" and God is affirmed to be eternal and unchanging. For the New Testament explicitly and the Old Testament implicitly tell us that the "laws" are not eternal and unchanging statutes which remain the same no matter what happens in human societies. The New Testament does so by making clear that the Christian is free from the law, so that it would be inconsistent to take its rules of conduct as divine law. The Old Testament reveals it by the actual changing of laws over the centuries of history which it records. What law does, then, is to apply to a specific situation the ethical standards which are appropriate for it and to make those general standards concrete. *Human* laws derive their standards from the ethos of the particular society; both the situations and the ethos may change with time. The difference in "divine law" is that the ethos does not change, for it comes from God. But the human situations to which it is applied do change, and so the concrete instructions concerning what one ought to do will also change. No law, not even one from the Bible, can thus be taken as the last word on ethical behavior, for both the needs and the opportunities open to us will change with time. There is a constant element to be discerned in the laws of Scripture, however, and that may be put in spatial terms as their "direction." Earlier it was noted that "direction" in the sense of "instruction" is a possible translation for *torah*; now let us play with that a bit and think of direction both as a synonym for instruction and in its spatial sense as a *pointer*. What we find, both in studying specific laws in the Old Testament and in comparing them with other laws on the same subject, is that in both cases we can determine a constant *direction* toward which they are pushing, and that is our key to knowing what they intend to say to us today.

The Old Testament contains several law codes; the major ones are the Book of the Covenant (Exod. 21:1–23:19), the Deuteronomic Code (Deut. 12–26), and the Holiness Code (Lev. 19–26). The Priestly Code incorporates the last of these and includes the entire Book of Leviticus, to which other, more fragmentary legislation may be added, but in our subsequent discussion we shall confine ourselves to noting the evidence for change from an early period in Israel's history, represented by the Book of the Covenant, through the end of the Monarchy, represented by Deuteronomy, to the post-exilic period, represented by the Holiness Code. One of the motives for every codification of laws is an intent to bring about reform of some sort. Today when a state adopts a new code it is because the old one has become anachronistic and overly complicated; improvement is needed. In antiquity the earliest known law codes were promulgated by kings who depicted themselves as having brought justice and order out of a chaotic situation. That is the nature of the production of a code of laws, including those in the Bible, and so the proper way to understand law is to ascertain what kinds of abuses it is trying to correct and what endangered rights it is trying to preserve. Only against the situation for which it was produced can its effectiveness be appropriately judged and only in terms of its intentions can it be justly compared with codes from other times and places.

I have suggested that the intentions of a law code can be ascertained from the laws themselves as set against a knowledge of the social situation for which they were written. This is true for Old Testament law, with limitations due to the fragmentary information we have about certain aspects of the life of ancient Israel, but our Old Testament codes also provide an even more explicit type of information. They are not written entirely in legal form, but were evidently composed not so much for judges to consult (they probably knew it all by heart) as for public reading—we are back to instruction again! So these Old Testament legal texts contain language which is far removed from the law court, motive clauses to explain why it is best to obey the law (e.g. "You shall not abhor an Edomite, *for he is your brother*; you shall not abhor an Egyptian, *because you were a sojourner in his land*" [Deut. 23:7]), and admonitions and warnings. As form critics have pointed out, in the Old Testament we find the law as it was preached.[8] This is especially noticeable in Deuteronomy, but is true of the other codes as well. This kind of language becomes explicit about the intentions of the law and often reveals the tension between what is aimed for and what can actually be put into practice in the present situation.

Hence our work as interpreters of the law who are trying to learn from it what God wants us to do now will begin by attempting to discover from specific legal provisions for concrete situations in a past society what direction the lawgiver was intending to move. Our conclusions can then be checked in two ways; first, do they correspond with the intention of the more general statements to be found in motive clauses and sermonic materials? And second, do they point in the same direction as the laws for similar cases enacted in other periods? Is there consistency of direction, leading on through the Old Testament and through the New Testament into continuing Christian history? If so, we may be sure that we have ascertained what God's own will is moving *toward*, and our final task is to find out where that "vector" intersects our own time and place and what new options for putting God's intention into practice may be available to us. When we see what they are, I believe we stand under the divine imperative to act accordingly.[9]

Let me offer two examples, one of which would have been controversial one hundred-plus years ago, the other dealing with a subject which is controversial today.

Slavery is nowhere outlawed by the Bible, and the defenders of the institution once made a great deal of that. But what does the Bible actually intend to do with slavery? If we begin with the earliest of the codes, the Book of the Covenant, we find a clear indication of concerns to humanize the institution. It is susceptible to a great many abuses, and all the regulations this code contains are for the purpose of limiting the master's rights over his slaves. Where Hebrew slaves are concerned, slavery is only permitted for a six-year period unless the slave himself chooses that condition for the rest of his life. The slave is still property, but we can discern movement toward the legal recognition of his humanity as well. An interesting (and we would probably say unsuccessful) attempt to find a balance between property rights and human rights appears in Exod. 21:20–21:

> When a man strikes his slave, male or female, with a rod and the slave dies under his hand, he shall be punished. But if the slave survives a day or two, he is not to be punished; for the slave is his money.

Even though the slave is his property, the master may not kill him with impunity, for he is a human being. But what is the appropriate punishment for such an act? Since the slave is property his death represents a substantial loss to the killer, already punishment in itself, and for some reason the lawgiver tries to determine the balance point by reference to how long the slave lives.

But the Covenant Code also contains some motive clauses which refer to the oppression in Egypt and the Exodus:

> You shall not wrong a stranger or oppress him, for you
> were strangers in the land of Egypt. (Exod. 22:21)

> You shall not oppress a stranger; you know the heart of a
> stranger, for you were strangers in the land of Egypt. (Exod. 23:9)

What does it mean to remind a slaveholding community that its God is a God who once set them free from slavery? The full implications of that are not yet worked out in the Covenant Code, but if we were to turn to Deuteronomy, which is probably next in date, we would find an even stronger humanizing element in its references to slaves and a more prominent appeal to the implications of the exodus for ethical action. We shall turn quickly to Leviticus 25, however, to see the confirmation of our decision about the direction in which the Book of the Covenant was pointing. According to Lev. 25:39ff., no Hebrew may be enslaved, but must be treated as a hired servant, not a slave, even when he is working off his debts. Why? "For they are my slaves, whom I brought forth out of the land of Egypt; they shall not be sold as slaves" (Lev. 25:42). In the human realm Israelites are free men, for God has bought them for himself.

Leviticus still permits the owning of foreign slaves, and the New Testament adds no further anti-slavery legislation, but Paul does give instructions which move the church a step further in the same direction. In his letter to Philemon he still respects the law of his day concerning slavery, but he expects that Philemon, of his own free will and not because of any law, will set Onesimus free. And in another of those more general statements he assures us that in Christ there is neither slave nor free (Gal. 3:28). How then could slavery endure? When the laws of the Bible are understood in this way there is nothing to justify it, but it took the church a long time to accept fully those implications, and we may also add that it took the world a long time to reach the point where they could be put into practice. But now no one would try to defend slavery, even on the basis of explicit biblical laws for the regulation of that practice.

The place of women in the church and in society at large is still a debated question, however, so let us try the same procedure again. We shall not find so striking a shift between Exodus and Leviticus as we found in the attitude toward slavery, and the general situation is far more complicated, but we can recognize some evidence of movement and its direction. In Exodus 21 the wife of a Hebrew slave is not to be released after six years if she has borne children, and unmarried female slaves were not set free either. But in Deut. 15:12-15 the law of release is explicitly stated to apply both to men and women. As we have seen, Leviticus goes further and says they are not to be enslaved at all. The Book of the Covenant reveals a tendency to think of women as the property of their fathers in the case of the seduction of a virgin (Exod. 22:16-17). The guilty party is expected to marry the woman and make the usual marriage present to her father, but the father can refuse to permit the marriage and simply accept the present as compensation for the loss of his daughter's virginity. It is likely that the community recognized the inadequacy of this provision from the daughter's point of view, for Deut. 22:28-29 omits the latter provision and requires marriage; furthermore, divorce in such a case is prohibited. Other provisions for the place of women in Israelite society appear in only one of the codes, so cannot be compared with anything, and much was simply assumed as understood by everyone. The whole structure of society was patriarchal, which meant that the father was the economic, judicial, educational, and religious center of life. Any very extensive changes in that would have meant revolution, not reform. With that in mind, we cannot overlook one of the general, non-legal statements of the Old Testament, which this time appears outside the law codes, indicating an understanding of the relationship between man and woman which is truly revolutionary. It is the position taken by Genesis 2-3 that the subordinate relationship of woman to man is not the natural order of things (which was to be side-by-side; Gen. 2:18, 22–24) but the result of a curse.[10] For such an affirmation to come out of a patriarchal society is remarkable indeed.

Jesus offered little instruction in what woman's place in society should be, but by example showed his intention to deal with women as equals. His teaching of Mary was a radical break with the rabbinic custom, for example (Luke 10:38–42). Women obviously played important roles in the early church, without the need for legislation to permit it, and when Paul did refer explicitly to women it was to regulate some of the abuses which had arisen, especially due to the influence of pagan society on the Gentile churches (1 Cor. 11:3–16; 14:34–35). As for the famous "Wives, be subject to your husbands," of Eph. 5:21–33, that dictum follows the sentence, "Be subject to one another out of reverence for Christ," and goes on to put the heavier burden, if possible, on husbands, who are to love their wives as Christ loved the church and gave himself up for her.[11] It is thus not out of step with the Galatians passage we mentioned before, which indicates clearly where God is heading: "There is neither Jew nor Greek, there is neither slave nor free, there is neither male nor female; for you are all one in Christ Jesus" (3:28).

The church learned that this could be realized in ways which were impossible for patriarchal societies, as it moved throughout the urban culture of the Roman world. But the need for women to function primarily as the childbearer and homemaker did not change markedly until this century and so much of the potentially revolutionary import of God's intention for man and woman could not be realized earlier. With reduced infant mortality making it unnecessary for women to bear as many children as possible in order to keep the race alive and with the appearance of machines to do most of the work of homemaking, the slow movement toward equality to which the Bible testifies can now be accelerated greatly, and the biblical laws which were intended to go as far as possible in that direction in a totally different culture should not be taken as fixed statutes to be applied in the same way to every time and place.

This is how the history of the legal traditions of the Bible can show us what to preach from Old Testament law. It assumes (and can then demonstrate it in most cases) that there is something constant, which we may call God's intention for human behavior. But it acknowledges that we live in imperfect and changing environments and that in each of them God's will is lived only imperfectly, and recognizes that the laws and instructions in the Bible show what impact the divine imperative has made on society at a given time and place. We then do not try to archaize ourselves so as to follow those instructions word for word, but rather try to understand where we now stand with reference to the divine intention, to recognize our own potential (and limitations) so as to perceive where and how the divine will must now be put into effect.

My emphasis in this chapter on how Old Testament law may be used as an authoritative basis for ethical preaching should not be taken as suggesting that the preaching of law as that which convicts us of sin and drives us to the gospel is to be ignored.[12] For example, I have preached from Lev. 19:14: "You shall not curse the deaf or put a stumbling block before the blind," as a reminder that we all find it very hard not to do something we know we can get by with and to show that this sentence has already moved beyond legislation to a concern with attitude. The only thing which can preserve us from the kind of meanness described in this verse, from doing those things for which we know we shall never be punished or caught or even accused, is, "You shall love your neighbor as yourself" (vs. 18). But love cannot be commanded; "We love because he first loved us" (1 John 4:19), and the New Testament makes it clear that the introduction to this passage: "You shall be holy, for I the Lord your God am holy," is promise, not law, and in this text both law and gospel are already present.

Two brief comments on other aspects of preaching from the law are appropriate. What do we do with laws of sacrifice and ritual cleanness? The general Christian position is that these laws are not binding upon us, and the inconsistencies of that have been noted earlier. My comment is that indeed it is true that the ritual laws are not binding, because none of the law is binding upon us. We use the law not because we are constrained by it but because it is helpful to us. Now, in what did the ritual law of the Old Testament instruct the people of Israel? At the risk of oversimplifying, I suggest two main functions for it: to provide a means of access to God (via sacrifice and the rules of holiness) and to set apart Israel in the eyes of the nations as a special people (Sabbath, circumcision, food laws). And what does this have to do with Christians? The New Testament has a great deal to say about the former, promising that Gentiles have direct access to God through Jesus Christ. The meaning and value of the old ritual is not denied, but it becomes a type to help us understand the work of Christ on our behalf (see especially the Letter to the Hebrews). So here it seems the typological use of the Old Testament is justified. And the nature of these laws is not violated by it, for their intent is not to tell God's people how to behave in daily life so much as it is to assure them that access to God is possible.

As for the laws which set Israel apart as a chosen people, it is harder for us to know just what to say. We are not Israel, we are the church, so those special marks should not be claimed by us. But what corresponds to them? We do claim to be a part of the Chosen People, but to what extent do we see that as setting us off from "the nations"? We are to be in the world but not of it; does that help or hinder? Are the sacraments the proper correspondences with this part of Old Testament ritual? If so, then typology may again be appropriate. But should there be more to it than that? I think that we have not taken Old Testament law seriously enough in recent history to be able to answer that question with much certainty as yet.

The other comment has to do with the Ten Commandments, the one part of the Old Testament law which still gets preached fairly regularly.[13] My comment is in the way of a cautionary note. We shall not preach them as law, for they are not law in the first place; no penalties are attached, and they are in fact a *description* of what the people of God is like. Grammatically, they could be translated, "You do not kill; you do not commit adultery"; etc. So we shall resist the temptation to make the Christian free of all law *except* the Ten Commandments. These are the briefest possible summaries of a great body of tradition—concerning human life, sexual behavior, property rights, etc., and they must be approached via the most careful exegesis of the wording of the commandments themselves, then by a study of that broad tradition which they represent, and must *not* be preached by making a grand leap from the English words "kill" or "covet" to what concerns us at the moment. To do the latter is to make the error of the pacifist who as a last result pronounces, "But the Ten Commandments say, 'Thou shall not kill,' " or the loophole-hunting legalist who notes that adultery can only occur after marriage, so before marriage anything goes. Instead we shall look for the central concern epitomized in the commandments, then take seriously the ways it was made concrete in the instructions of the Old and New Testaments as guides to the direction God intends human ethical behavior to take before attempting to decide how that direction is now becoming an imperative of us today. Here, as in dealing with other laws, it is the whole legal tradition of the Scriptures on each ethical issue which reveals what is normative for us, and it is not the concrete application to any specific case which is binding upon us as law. It is the revelation of the direction in which God is pushing his people which constrains us, as saved people, acting in gratitude, to apply that knowledge of his will to the fullest extent possible in our own situation.

A Sermon on Leviticus 17:10–14

The sermon which I have chosen as an example for this chapter leaves a good bit to be desired, homiletically; for example, the subject chosen proved to be a bit heavy for its *Sitz im Leben*, a warm July morning, but I include it nevertheless because it does illustrate several aspects of the approach to preaching the law which I have been developing. It takes one of the ritual laws, concerning the treatment of blood, which also may be shown to have both theological and ethical overtones of considerable importance, and emphasizes the latter aspect. It was preached at the Parkwood United Presbyterian Church in Allison Park, Pa., on July 10, 1977.

Life Belongs to God

Leviticus 17:10–14

If you should decide you want a roast for dinner tonight, you'll probably go to the freezer, take one out, put in into the oven, and that will be that. You will have no reason to think about the laws which I have just read from the Book of Leviticus. But there was a time, not too long ago, when the eating of meat involved one quite directly in the killing of an animal. Meat came on the hoof, not in a plastic wrapper. We read this morning about the special care which the Israelites were expected to take when they killed an animal for food, and in order to understand whether that has anything at all to do with our supermarket society, it will be necessary to attend an Israelite banquet.

They didn't eat meat every day; there wasn't enough of it for that, and the ordinary meal was more likely to have been bread and cheese. But on special occasions one of their precious animals would be killed for a feast. Whenever that was done, the animal was killed as a sacrifice to God. There was no ordinary or random or everyday killing of animals for food. When there was to be a feast, the father would take the selected animal to the local sanctuary and in the presence of the priest would approach the altar. He laid his hand on the animal's head, signifying that it was his possession which he was bringing to God. And with a knife he cut its throat. The blood was carefully caught in a bowl and poured out on the altar, then certain parts which were specially prized in those days were burnt as an offering. After the sacrifice the rest of the animal would be cooked and eaten in a joyous feast.

Eventually the time came when sacrifice was only permitted in Jerusalem. This didn't make complete vegetarians of everyone else in Israel, for the law was changed, permitting animals to be killed for food without offering them as a sacrifice. But the blood of every animal still had to be treated in a special way, and it could under no circumstance be eaten.

There was something special about blood. It is never explained at any length in the Bible, probably because everyone instinctively understood it in those days and no need was seen for writing it down, just as we do not have to explain to one another why people still react in special ways to the sight or even the mention of blood. But Leviticus 17 comes about as close as we can get to an explanation of what special meaning blood had for people of Old Testament times.

"For the life of every creature is the blood of it." (vs. 14) A similar statement is made three times. They believed that blood must be handled in a special way because the blood is the life, so when one speaks of blood one speaks of life.

This helps us to understand what was happening when a sacrifice was made in ancient Israel. The Israelites believed that all life belongs to God. No human being had the right arbitarily to take life. So when an animal was killed for food, it had to be done in the presence of God, the giver of life, and the blood which represented the life, or which *was* the life (to the Israelite), had to be given back to God in acknowledgement that it belonged to him alone.

No life could be taken in a random, arbitrary, whimsical, highhanded way.

No human being had the right to treat other lives as if they were his to do anything he pleased with them. Life belonged to God.

But that did not make the Israelite a vegetarian or an opponent of capital
punishment. He ate meat, and people were executed for serious crimes. But
even those things were related to his conviction that all life belongs to God
alone.

1. He killed animals for food because he believed that God had given him
permission to do so. At the conclusion of the Flood story God says to Noah,
"Every moving thing that lives shall be food for you; and as I gave you the
green plants, I give you everything. Only you shall not eat flesh with its life,
that is, its blood." So the eating of meat was a special privilege, not a natural
right. They were reminded that it was a privilege every time an animal was
killed, by the way the blood had to be treated. So everyone remembered that
every meal at which meat was eaten was a very special gift from God.

2. People were executed for serious crimes. In this the Israelites were like
every other society, ancient or modern. We do find, however, that the number
of crimes punished by death tended to be fewer in Israel than in other ancient
nations. Capital punishment was used against crimes which were understood to
be destructive of the very fabric of Israel as the people of God. People were
executed not because Israelites believed that any human being, even the king,
had the *right* to kill any other person, but because through the law God commanded Israel to do it.

These are remarkable facts—this series of data about ancient Israel which I
have been relating to you. Throughout much of history, and in much of the
world today, life—even human life—is taken lightly. People are expendable,
animals don't even count. Yet in that tiny corner of the earth, Palestine,
thousands of years ago, there was a group of people who understood life to be a
precious thing, to be treated with the greatest of care and respect. They did that
not because they worshipped LIFE or because they thought there was something
in and of life itself that was precious, but because they knew that it did not belong to them, that it belonged to God, and was only entrusted to them, to handle
with the greatest care. They might not have agreed with Albert Schweitzer's slo-
gan, "reverence for life"—for their reverence was for God—but "respect for
all life" describes very well their attitude. We find no evidence of wanton killing, of animals or of people, in the Bible. Killing is done by command or by
permission. And that is unusual. Watch a week of average television fare if you
don't believe me.

But that was ancient Israel—3,000 years ago. That was Old Testament law.
And we must ask, "Were they right? Does Old Testament law mean anything to
us?" We do not sacrifice animals, follow kosher food laws, observe the Sabbath, or keep many of the other laws of the Old Testament. Should we then take
Leviticus 17 seriously?

To answer that question, if we take the Bible seriously, we ought to listen for the testimony of the whole Bible. Some things changed; sacrifice for example, which was so important in Old Testament times, was not practiced by Christians at all and was also given up by the Jews after A.D. 70. But other things never change, and are reaffirmed for generation after generation in the Scriptures. The New Testament quotes many of the laws of the Old Testament and reapplies them to the lives of Christians. And as we trace in the pages of Scripture the way the will of God is made known to one generation after another of believers we see that we can discover the direction in which he is moving with us.

We see that the blood of sacrifice, as practiced in Israel, was understood to be a sign of God's work of atonement, of his acceptance of believers despite their sins, and his re-establishment of a right relationship with them.

And we see that the Giver of life himself, in the person of Jesus the Christ, the Son of the Living God, was the only one whose life was ultimately sufficient to make atonement for us.

Life—death—and new life (resurrection) is the whole theme of the New Testament, and nowhere does it deny the Old Testament's message that all of life belongs to God. The New Testament does not spell out all of the consequences of that for the Christian quite so clearly as the law of the Old Testament did for the ancient Israelite, and that means we have some work to do in order to understand what the statement "life belongs to God" means for us. We are not ancient Israelites and their law does not always deal with our problems, but what God wanted them to do can help us find out what he wants us to do.

1. The Old Testament reminds us of something we seldom think of; that to be able to eat meat means to take a life, and that to have meat in our diets is a special privilege, to thank God for.

2. Capital punishment in the Old Testament was used to mark off certain kinds of behavior as destructive to an ordered, healthy society. Already the Israelites had moved toward a limitation of it as compared to other cultures, and within Jewish-Christian history there has been movement toward less use of it. For example, in early Jewish history a court which had executed one man in forty years was called the "bloody Sanhedrin." The question our society faces now is whether we have reached the point where we can or must do without any capital punishment. How can we preserve a healthy society? What crimes must be punished by death in order to keep society healthy? If any? Those questions are not answered outright by the Bible; God *allows* us to use capital punishment, but he gives us the responsibility to decide how and whether it should be used.

3. There is another kind of life-taking which has always been forbidden in our tradition because of the conviction that life belongs to God, and that is sui-

cide. It has been forbidden because to take one's own life is to claim the personal right to end a life, and that right is not our own—it is God's.

4.   The Bible's view of life is and must be one of the important points in all Christian discussions of abortion. Is abortion the taking of a life? That must be decided. If so, then we are responsible to God for that life. He allows us to take life, under certain circumstances; then we must decide whether there are circumstances in which abortion could be acceptable in the sight of God. The Bible, once again, does not spell it all out for us; there is no law on abortion. God made us reasonable and responsible creatures and we must decide. But one thing is clear. Life does not belong to the mother, to do as she pleases, or to anyone else. Life belongs to God, and the reason for an abortion had better be acceptable to God.

I could go on. The next obvious subject is euthanasia, and after that I suppose the efforts to create life by human means. But the principle remains the same. We do possess the power of life and death, over the animals and over our fellow human beings. God has given us that power. But he holds us responsible for how we use it. We cannot take a cop out by refusing ever to kill anything, as the Buddhist may do. But neither can we ignore wanton killing, of anthing, anywhere, for the blood of the innocent cries out before the throne of justice, and God avenges the death of the innocent.

CHAPTER V

Preaching
from Wisdom Literature

The wisdom literature of the Old Testament confronts us with both the largest and smallest possible genres which might be used as a sermon text. The most common form used by the wise men was the proverb, a single sentence. But the wisdom movement also produced the forty-two chapters of the Book of Job, and it may be questioned whether one can legitimately preach from any part of that work without taking the entire book as one's text. Within this body of literature may be found some of the most inspiring, some of the most disturbing, and some of the most soporific materials of the entire Old Testament. One may descend to the deepest anguish of the soul with Job or may be bored to death by the moralizing of some of the proverbs. So the challenges which the wisdom literature presents to the preacher are awesome. We are in danger of turning the drama of Job into bathos, of perverting the intellectual honesty of Ecclesiastes into arid skepticism, and of deriving nothing better than the power of positive thinking from the optimism of Proverbs. But once again, both form criticism and tradition history can help us to find in wisdom the preachable message for our time and the way to preach it.

Both in subject matter and in style wisdom is in a class by itself, and we shall take up both aspects, in that order.

Who Were the Wise Men and What Did They Do?

In the beginning wisdom is the property of the people; it is the human summation of what experience and observation have taught us life in this world is all about and the accumulation of advice on how to live the good life. The typical form it takes is proverbial; a brief, pithy, often humorous, easily remembered distillation of a drop of truth. Proverbial wisdom is apparently to be found

ᗷ ᐁᑊᑋ ᐁ ᗷ

everywhere in human society. Although the biblical proverbs are seldom quoted on the street anymore, we have by no means outgrown that type of folk wisdom; if you doubt me go out and read some bumper stickers. We do not look for authors and dates of this folk wisdom; it belongs to everybody.

But in Israel there were some people especially denoted by the adjective "wise," and it seemed to refer to a function in life and not merely to an attribute. We are still involved in some guesswork about who the wise men were, for they tend to remain anonymous and in the background, but it seems likely that they performed at least two functions in the royal court in Jerusalem: viz. they were advisors to the king and they were the teachers of the royal children to prepare them for life in the bureaucracy of the capitol.[1] Out of their experience as advisors and to help in their work as educators we may imagine that the earliest collections of wisdom materials were formed, such as we now possess in chapters 10–31 of Proverbs. As advisors and teachers they naturally had a strong concern for communication and persuasion and their techniques are worth studying by any teacher or preacher for that reason, although since we live in a very different world we shall not slavishly copy them. The content of their teaching takes us first into a realm which is very near to the hearts of the average congregation, the eminently practical concern about how to live the successful life. But wisdom does not confine itself to a success-philosophy, for the keenness of the intellectual powers of the wise men led them to recognize how the practical concerns of life cannot be settled without coming to grips with theological issues of the most profound kind; such questions as the justices of God and the meaning of human life and death. Hence, despite the previously mentioned pitfalls of preaching from the wisdom literature, it is perhaps harder to be irrelevant when dealing with this material than when using any other kind of text.

But let me expand a bit further on this practical orientation of wisdom teaching.

1.   We find that traditional wisdom is typically addressed to an individual; i.e. it tends to differ from the strongly communal orientation of most of the Old Testament. The destiny of the people Israel is never mentioned; it is the destiny of the individual person that most concerns the wise man. And because of this, most of what is said could apply to anyone, Israelite or not. It is not by accident that the Gideons added first the Book of Psalms and then Proverbs to their edition of the New Testament, for those two books could be read by the salesman in the hotel room or the serviceman in the foxhole without knowing anything about ancient Israel. "He who blesses his neighbor with a loud voice, rising up early in the morning, will be counted as cursing," needs no exegesis (Prov. 27:14).

2.   Traditional wisdom also typically confines itself to human affairs rather than what we might call theological concerns. Wisdom was the key to the successful life, spelling the difference between health, happiness, prosperity, pres-

tige, and long life, on the one hand, and the opposites of all these, on the other. It could be learned, by paying attention to one's teacher, by experience, and observation on one's own. This does not mean the wise men were secularists, for God is mentioned regularly in the proverbs and is the ultimate source of all wisdom and blessing; rather it means that their normal subjects were business, the family and other personal relationships, not things we usually call "theology" or "religion." As wisdom thinking develops, however, it does move in the direction of systematic thought about God and the meaning of life. In passages such as Proverbs 8 and the books of Job and Ecclesiastes they took up profound theological questions, but never forgot the practical issues which had produced those questions in the first place.

3.   Outside of Job and Ecclesiastes wisdom teaching tends to be strongly optimistic; the wise man believed he had found the key to the good life and that he could pass it on to others. It was when God was brought into the picture, as the bestower of wisdom then of the rewards of wisdom, and as the one who brings misfortune upon the fool, that questions of justice began to be raised which led the two books just mentioned to question the traditional optimism of the wise man. These books share most of the beliefs and techniques of the more orthodox writers, but for them wisdom had become transcendentalized, i.e. it belongs to God alone, and what human beings need to make sense out of this life seems to be inaccessible. As these writers struggled to make sense of life they provided for us some of the most profound treatments of certain existential problems to be found anywhere; of the goodness of God, his accessibility, of the meaning of suffering and the purpose of human life.[2]

Conclusion: Although parts of this material deal with profound theological issues, much of wisdom literature deals with rather "ordinary" stuff, the affairs of daily life, rather than what we usually think of as properly "religious." There is little or nothing explicitly Christian or Jewish in much of this literature, and so if we think that our preaching must always have something distinctively Christian in it, we may decide to omit most of wisdom literature from our lectionary. But is that the right conclusion? Does not Christianity comprehend all of life? If our theology has no place in it for wisdom's concerns, then perhaps it is not wisdom, but our theology which is askew with reference to the witness of the whole Bible.[3] There is a danger in what I am saying, of course. Those of us who are dedicated to biblical preaching see the kind of moralizing, topical, success or issue-oriented preaching which is so common in America as one of the great weaknesses of the church, and Old Testament wisdom may seem to encourage the very abuses we deplore.[4] But this is a case where balance and discretion are needed. In my theology one can't do without the Incarnation and justification by faith, but there's more than that in the Bible. It also talks about getting along with your spouse and your employer, and I think that also needs to be a part of what we preach.

The Techniques of Wisdom

The proverb has already been mentioned as the basic form of traditional wisdom. In addition, form criticism has identified fables, riddles, parables, numerical sayings, and a kind of "sermonette" as genres which were regularly used for wisdom teaching.[5] Fables appear in the Old Testament only within popular wisdom, not in the collections made by the wise men themselves. One of the best examples is Jotham's fable, in which he creates a story about animated plants in order to make a point about politics (Judg. 9:7–21). Riddles also appear most often in popular literature, such as the Samson cycle (Judg. 14:12–18), but a type of riddling saying which was used for teaching purposes, rather than entertainment, occurs in Proverbs and elsewhere (Prov. 30:4, 15b–16). Parables, such as Isaiah's story of the vineyard (Isa. 5:1–7) probably also formed a part of the wise man's repertoire. The numerical saying is best known from Prov. 30:15–31, and was used both to create interest and to aid the memory. It may remind us of the traditional preacher's technique of announcing how many points his sermon has, in order to help the congregation to follow him. The "sermonette" is to be found in Proverbs 1–9 and Ecclesiastes, and it appears in an expanded form also in the dialogues of Job. In the former books it takes the form of a short paragraph, expounding a wisdom theme at greater length than the proverb could do, using admonition and argumentation, even to the extent of having personified Wisdom herself become the speaker (Prov. 1:20ff., 8:1ff., etc.).

The wise men clearly chose or developed genres primarily for their pedagogical usefulness. The effective proverb gets its point across as much by the combination of words which is chosen as it does from the logic of the case it makes; indeed, sometimes the verbal effect is stronger than the logic. It has an apodictic quality which does not leave room for argumentation or qualification. In this is both its usefulnes and its danger. As an example, let us take a modern proverb from a bumper sticker: "When guns are outlawed, only outlaws will have guns." Taken as a logical statement, it is a truism; obviously if it is a crime to possess something, those who possess it are criminals, and that is hardly worth repeating. But that is not what the proverb intends to say at all. It is playing on the emotive force of the word "outlaw" and really wants to say that "outlaws" will still have their guns when they are taken away from "law-abiding citizens" who will thus be left defenseless. It is a neatly balanced statement which leaves no room for discussion; no place for the inclusion of an armed police force, for example, or for questions about whether private citizens' guns really provide them with much protection against "outlaws." But it has grasped a fragment of truth, even though we may think it is presented in a distorted form.

Biblical proverbs also present fragments of truth, of necessity because of their brevity, but their apodictic form tends to make their message sound like the whole truth. For example, not everything that needs to be said about wealth and poverty can be summed up in one proverb, and so the observation,

> The poor is disliked even by his neighbor, but the rich has many friends. (Prov. 14:20)

needs to be qualified by

> He who despises his neighbor is a sinner, but happy is he who is kind to the poor (Prov. 14:21)

and

> A rich man's wealth is his strong city; the poverty of the poor is their ruin (Prov. 10:15)

by

> Better is a little with righteousness than great revenues with injustice (Prov. 16:8).

Some poverbs seem to contradict one another, but we don't ask which is true, "Out of sight, out of mind," or "Absence makes the heart grow fonder," for in fact each of them is true sometimes, and neither of them is the whole truth. The proverb is thus a potent means of conveying and making it possible to remember nuggets of truth, but it is easily subject to misuse.

Of what use can the Old Testament proverbs be to the preacher? Their very nature suggests they ought not to be taken as texts to be expounded in a sermon. What needs to be said, they have already said in the most effective way. They are like the punch line of a joke; if they have to be explained, better not to bother with it in the first place. I have a copy of a sermon on Prov. 13:20 which begins with a kind of apology to the congregation, pointing out how difficult it is to do more than gild the lily when preaching from Proverbs, since once you have read the text you have already said it all. The sermon which follows then demonstrates the truth of what the preacher said in his apology. When one preaches on wisdom themes the best way to use the proverbs may be as the writers of those sermonettes did, to intersperse them along the way to drive home a point and to serve as memorable summaries of what has been developed (cf. Prov. 6:20–7:5, note vs. 26; Eccles. 5:1–7, note vs. 5; Job 11:1–20, note vs. 12).

The use of fable, riddle, and parable by the wise men show us how effective communication can often best be attained by inducing one's hearers to think along with you or even to try by their own wits to get ahead of you, rather than just trying to lead them along through a logical progression or hammering away repetitively at a single point. In this, Old Testament wisdom has an important insight to offer modern preachers concerning human psychology and the techniques of persuasion, even though they may not always use those same genres in order to bring the congregation into sharing their thinking process.[6] The sermon-ette already shows us how wisdom themes began to be "preached" and one of my examples in this chapter will be based on such a text. One comment should be added here on the techniques of the wisdom teacher. Earlier I noted that ex-perience and observation provided the raw materials for the wise man's work. This means that the autobiographical element will sometimes be an essential part of their message; what I have seen, done, and experienced plays a promi-nent role in this literature and especially in Job and Ecclesiastes. This requires us to consider whether it should not be true that when we preach on wisdom topics we are claiming to be "wise men" or women, who are carrying on the old tradition of using all our powers to discern the truth about life, adding what we have learned to what the Bible teaches in order to "confirm" it and to help make it convincing. That is to say, the nature of the biblical material itself sug-gests that the autobiographical element (used with due humility, of course) is quite appropriately present in a sermon based on Old Testament wisdom.

What to Preach from Wisdom Literature

Wisdom is an area in which the orthodoxy of Proverbs and some of the wis-dom psalms tends to be difficult for us, while the challenges to orthodoxy in Job and Ecclesiastes seem to speak to us more directly and with more realism. How can one preach orthodox wisdom, i.e. advice to cultivate the virtues and eschew the vices with the promise that the good life will result, without producing either a moralizing sermon which will leave the people nodding—in assent and in slumber—or a sermon which makes assertions equating goodness with prosper-ity which simply are not true?[7] Do we avoid those pitfalls by simply avoiding orthodox wisdom? I hope not, for people need "wisdom," help in learning how to lead a good life, as much now as they ever did. That is the first subject for preaching for which the wise men offer us something to say. *How* we say it, I shall come to in a moment. A second subject is to be found in their strong testi-monies to God's justice and providence (e.g. Ps. 37; Prov. 15:3–11; 30:5–6). Sometimes they overstated their case, as Job and Ecclesiastes discovered, so we need to be careful not to be misled by such texts as Ps. 37:25: "I have been young, and now am old; yet I have not seen the righteous forsaken or his chil-dren begging bread." We must preach the message of the whole Bible on such subjects, not that of isolated texts, but there are times when the affirmation of God's justice desperately needs to be heard.

A third subject appears in their thinking about Wisdom itself, which led to a tendency to transcendentalize it, making it an attribute of God and almost a hy-postasis.[8] This is of great importance for the development of New Testament Christology, for the exalted place ascribed to Wisdom (especially in Prov. 8:22–36) was reaffirmed in the literature of the intertestamental period (Sirac 24; Wisd. of Sol. 6–7), and this concept clearly forms the background of John's equation of Christ with the Logos in the first chapter of his Gospel.[9] Elsewhere in the New Testament Christ is also spoken of as the Wisdom of God (1 Cor. 1:24; cf. vs. 30) and we can see that as the first Christians searched for a way to speak about the whole truth of their experiences with Jesus they found in Jewish wisdom theology a way of talking about such difficult concepts as pre-existence and about identity with God without giving up their essential monotheism. So wisdom theology became the key to the development of the doctrine of the Trinity.

Orthodox Wisdom: Psalm 1

Let me now offer an example of what one might do with one of the completely orthodox wisdom passages from the Old Testament which may attract those who enjoy platitudes and moralizing, and repel all others. It is the first Psalm, one of the psalms appropriately identified as part of the wisdom literature, a neat, well-known statement of the basic tenets of orthodox wisdom. I recall reading a sermon on this text submitted as a part of ordination trials several years ago and thinking, "It's a moralizing sermon, but I can't fault him too much for that, since it's a moralizing text." But now the question is whether there is anything more to it than that. Does it say anything beyond, "It's nice to be nice," and "Smilers never lose and frowners never win"? Is it all generalities? We hear of only the righteous and the wicked, with no middle ground. It is assumed we know who belongs to which group, and once again cynicism raises its head as we recall the saying, "There are two kinds of people in the world; the good and the bad. The good decide which is which."

And there are other problems as well. The psalm tells us God rewards the righteous and punishes the wicked *in this life*, and who of us doesn't then immediately begin adding up the exceptions? But let us not then give up in disgust and tear that page out, for as a matter of fact, in our problem with the perceived exceptions to "they succeed in everything they do" (vs. 3), we may have found an opening. Let us ask ourselves and our congregation, in spite of the exceptions, do we believe that for some reason or other it is still better to do good than to do evil? It is likely that everyone who comes to church is ready to answer yes, and then we are ready for another question. Why do we believe it is better to do good than to do evil? We could find a spectrum of reasons, no doubt, from desire for rewards to enlightened self-interest to pure altruism. But we aren't really interested in a statistical sample, now, for our text mentions only one reason; it speaks of rewards. It says in a very simple and straightforward way that it makes a difference to God and to us whether we do good or evil, and that God shows that it makes a difference to him by enabling the righteous to prosper in everything. As long as we stick with the text, we cannot move away from concentration on this—worldly reward and retribution.

If we look to the recent history of interpretation for help, we shall find that most of our resources (commentaries, sermon helps) just use the psalm as traditional, orthodox wisdom said it, without acknowledging the problems that may cause. Two variations on that may be noted. The *Interpreter's Bible* says Psalm 1 means for us less the rewards of the good life than the manner of living the good life and its sources.[10] The German *Biblischer Kommentar* tends toward typology, emphasizing that in the light of the New Testament no one is "righteous" except Christ, so that the psalm points to him.[11] But cannot the history of the wisdom tradition in the Bible help us more than this? It first of all warns us not to try to use such a text apart from its full history, which means that to preach from orthodox wisdom requires reading it along with Job, Ecclesiastes, Sirac, the Wisdom of Solomon, plus the Christology of the New Testament. Neither the optimism of Psalm 1 nor the pessimism of Ecclesiastes is the whole story. Each needs the other and each gains new and deeper meaning from Christ, the Wisdom of God.

From the whole wisdom tradition we can indeed learn some things about the abiding value of Psalm 1:

a) Nowhere is anything said to recommend the way of the scoffer, and much could be added to the psalm's brief comparison of them with the chaff which the wind blows away to remind us that, in spite of our tendency to concentrate on the "prosperity of the wicked," there is much evidence to be observed in this life that those whom the Bible identifies as fools do suffer a great deal for their folly.

b) Ecclesiastes reminds us that the other side of it is not quite so straightforward as Psalm 1 seems to indicate: the righteous cannot expect prosperity as an automatic reward. But even the questioning of that book does not lead it to argue against going on to do what is right anyhow, and *in this life* he finds the reasons to justify it.

c) The New Testament questions whether anyone can honestly put himself in the group called "righteous," for One alone is righteous. Hence all grounds for boasting and all claims for rewards, which might otherwise be thought justified by Psalm 1, are undercut. But the New Testament does not go on to deny that God rewards those who please him, so it is not an outright contradiction of the psalm. What it does add to the psalm is the reminder that the desire for reward ought not to be the main motive for obeying God, and so once again something illegitimate, which is not in the psalm but which we might be tempted to add to it, is ruled out.

d) Left unmodified by the whole wisdom tradition are these elements of Psalm 1: the warnings based on the way of the scoffer, already mentioned, and the attractive picture of the person of faith as one whose *delight* is in doing God's will—a picture of one who flourishes and is fruitful. Now, isn't that subject worth talking about, and developing along precisely the lines found in this psalm? Can we, in a sermon, help others to picture the attractiveness of good people as wisdom sees them? Can we help them to understand the delight with which those who are committed to God seek to serve him? We can, of course, use Jesus as the classic example of how true and unselfish righteousness makes one a joy to be near, but there are innumerable other examples of such attractive saints to be found in our own experience. Goodness is too often yoked with unattractiveness, but that is a caricature; it needs a better press. And in the light of the picture of the really good person who delights in pleasing God all the lesser motives over which we stumbled at first—rewards and punishments—are seen to be not so important after all.

A Sermon on Proverbs 4:1–9

For a sermon on traditional wisdom I have chosen a short unit from the first part of Proverbs, in which we find several of those one-paragraph developments of wisdom themes, earlier called "sermonettes." The unit is Prov. 4:1–9, marked off from what precedes it by the address, "Hear, O sons," in vs. 1, and from what follows it by another address in vs. 10. I found it to be a very difficult sermon to prepare and was by no means satisfied with it, but was taught something about the potential usefulness of preaching from this kind of material by the number and type of comments which came to me after the service. It does have its value, but the difficulty of doing a good job of preaching it should not be underestimated. I tried to let the text itself help me as much as possible. A teacher is speaking, one who has learned about life first from his father, and then from his own experience which has confirmed his father's lessons. I decided that as a minister I ought to accept the role of wise man for myself, immodest as that may seem, and ought to follow the lead of the Scriptures by giving a personal testimony to the truth of what the Bible says about wisdom. Furthermore, I was fortunate in being able to refer to my own father as the ancient sage referred to his. This meant that the first part of the sermon tended to parallel the text, without citing it explicitly, but the latter part takes up and comments on the imagery of personified wisdom. It was preached in the First United Presbyterian Church of New Cumberland, West Virginia, on April 25, 1976.

Get Wisdom!

Proverbs 4:1–9

I have come to you today to talk about success: How to get it, and how to know when you have it. The Book of Proverbs, from which I read this morning, might have been called "How to Succeed *by* Really Trying," and it is the way to success, which the wise men who produced this book had found, about which I want to talk with you today.

Success is measured in different ways; by how much money we have acquired, by the excellence of the skills we have developed, or by the reputation we enjoy. Some aim for success as money-makers, some at getting promotions, some at getting good grades, some at making the team, some at getting nominated and winning elections, some at raising good children, some at acquiring new abilities.

But what do we want to do all that for? What's the point of all that work, and when do we reach the plateau where finally we can say, "I am a success"? I think we do it because we want to feel satisfied with ourselves. It's self-satisfaction which makes it possible to say, I have succeeded. And so that long list of measurements—money, promotions and the rest—turns out not to be the real goal we are striving for after all; it's the means to our real end, which is satisfaction and contentment. So if you're uneasy, if you're discontented, if you're unsatisfied with life, it is very unlikely that you can think of yourself as a success, no matter what you have done or what others think.

Satisfaction—contentment—the real measures of success. And it takes great wisdom to know where that true success is to be found. It is not always where we think.

The Apostle Paul was a wise man, and he once commented on this subject: "Not that I complain of want; for I have learned, in whatever state I am, to be content. I know how to be abased, and I know how to abound; in any and all circumstances I have learned the secret of facing plenty and hunger, abundance and want. I can do all things in him who strengthens me" (Phil. 4:11-13). He said he was a contented man. Not like Borden's contented cows, placidly put out to pasture, for he was always on the go, always pressing on to do the work of Christ, in the thick of controversy, not always winning every battle, yet content.

Paul's secret was that he did not feel constantly miserable because ; something he wanted was still out of his reach. He was a success because he had found out what he was good for, because he knew that he was doing a good work for Christ, and he was satisfied to be doing that. He was a wise man.

My father was a wise man. He wasn't a learned man; he had an eighth grade education. But he knew what he could and couldn't do, and he didn't fret about it. He had plenty of native intelligence, he had good character, he had common sense, he had the desire to do good for the people around him, and he was satisfied with who he was and what he could do. With his eighth grade education he was accepted as a leader in the church, in the school, in the community affairs of our small town, and he was universally respected because he was honest and fair, he did the job that needed to be done, he didn't push himself on anybody and he never let an honor go to his head.

He passed on some of that wisdom to me. Not all of it, unfortunately. I went a different way, spent years in school just preparing to contribute something to this world. I haven't made much money and never will; I'll never have fame or power. But I can contribute some things of value to the church, to my family and to others, and that makes me content. Certainly, I'm not satisfied with everything around me; there are things every day which cause regret and disappointment and frustration. But I don't let any of those things cripple me or stop me from doing what I *can* do. I am content.

The kind of success I've been talking about won't make sense to everyone—a success which doesn't necessarily involve money or prestige. They are the people the Bible calls "fools." But if that kind of success does make sense to you, how can you get it?

It takes wisdom. Wisdom to tell the difference between the things that are very attractive but don't satisfy, and the things that are really worth working for.

Money is important, no question about it. Good reputation is important. Sex appeal is important. Talents and skills are important. Social life is important. All of these things can do us a lot of good. They are the gifts of God, to be enjoyed.

But there's a catch. Nobody ever gets enough of any of them to be really satisfied. And none of them lasts forever; all of them are things we hold on to precariously; we could lose them any minute. And with death, all of them are gone.

Is that all there is? Some will say yes, and that's all right. These are the only things that matter and they are worth devoting one's whole life to. They are the people the Bible calls "fools."

There is a wisdom that says a human life ought not just to be snuffed out at death and that's the end. There ought to be something that lasts. Our text says wisdom gives life, that wisdom keeps you, guards you, exalts you, and honors you. But who can do all that except God himself? What is there that really lasts but God himself? If you are wise enough to know that there should be something more to your life than eating and drinking and going to work and having kids, then you know that you need God.

The answer is that my dad was more than a small businessman, a husband, father, and taxpayer, because he was a Christian. His life, what he did and didn't do, what he said and stood for, was adding a little something every day to the Kingdom of our Lord Jesus Christ, who does not die, who is eternal, who lasts.

And the answer is that inadequate as my work may be, and despite the many things that are missing from my life that I wish were there, I am content. Because as a Christian my life has been taken up into a bigger life—Christ lives in me, and what I do is worth something because he can make it worth something —that makes me a success—that and nothing else.

Our text ends in a somewhat surprising way. The teacher has been praising wisdom and describing it as a woman—since "wisdom" is a feminine noun in Hebrew—speaking of the good gifts which wisdom brings. Wisdom is a royal figure, almost, able to guard and honor, and even to bestow a crown upon the young person who seeks her. Maybe that's appropriate, for true wisdom leads us into the service of the Kingdom. Now, it may sound a little strange to talk of any of us wearing a crown, and it is. But that strange language represents the surprising truth that we ordinary people can be a part of something quite extraordinary, part of something that will never end, never die.

Some of us may get the money, the prestige, and the power, too. Good enough. Use them well and enjoy them (with wisdom). But they will all go, some day, and so will you. If you are wise, that won't be the end of it because your wisdom will have led you to join your life with Christ's, and you will have become a part of the greatest success story of all time.

Questioning Wisdom: Job and Ecclesiastes

The cheerful optimism of orthodox wisdom does not adequately account for all of life's experiences. Although traditional wisdom did readily acknowledge that parts of life were beyond human understanding and control ("A man's mind plans his way, but the LORD directs his steps" Prov. 16:9), there was regularly expressed a confidence in the observable justice of the Lord's governance of the world ("The LORD has made everything for its purpose, even the wicked for the day of trouble" Prov. 16:4). More than one Israelite found this unacceptable in the face of quite obvious inequities in human affairs. There had always been a place in the worship of Yahweh for the expression of one's complaints, doubts, and pleas for justice, and we have many examples of how that was done in the psalms of lament. Closely associated with them are texts which are heavily influenced by wisdom vocabulary and theology. Psalms 49 and 73 take up complaints which are familiar from the laments and show by their treatment of them that their authors are deeply influenced by the wisdom movement, but that in traditional wisdom there is something missing. Each psalm achieves a resolution which remains somewhat vague to us:

> But God will ransom my life from the power of Sheol,
>   for he will take me (Ps. 49:15, author's translation)

> But I am continually with you; you hold my right hand.
> You lead me by your council; and afterward you will
>   take me (to) glory. (Ps. 73:23–24, author's translation)

The psalmist is not explicit about it, but appears to affirm some sort of continuing existence in God's presence as reward enough for his sufferings. Nevertheless, each psalm falls back on the teachings of traditional wisdom at the end, asserting that eventually God will punish the wicked.

This melding of materials from the cult and from the teachings of the wise men can also be found in a prophetic book, Habakkuk, which also takes up the problem of the suffering of the innocent and the prosperity of the wicked.[12] The prophet hears a response from God: "Behold, he whose soul is not upright in him shall fail, but the righteous shall live by his faith" (2:4), and as this verse suggests, the resolution of the problem occurs in the realm of faith rather than reason (cf. 3:17–19). The same kinds of materials are used in a much more elaborate way in the poem of Job, and that poem is encased in a short story which sets the stage (1:1–2:13; 42:7–17).[13] The complexities of this master-work of world literature can only be suggested in the paragraphs which follow. But first we mention the final work of this type in the Old Testament, the Book of Ecclesiastes. Unlike the others, it does not make use of the lament genre as a way of dealing with the issues raised by the inability of orthodox wisdom to sat-isfy Israel's keenest minds with its defense of God's justice. This book is com-posed of short discourses on wisdom, interspersed with collections of proverbs. Frequently the author quotes a proverb only to repudiate it from his own experi-ence and reasoning (e.g. 2:14).[14] In other cases, he quotes two contradictory proverbs and leaves us to ponder what the truth may be (e.g., 4:5 and 6). His quandary is that adequate wisdom to understand the world and to achieve satis-faction from life is not accessible to human beings, as orthodoxy has taught. Only God has it; we cannot acquire it. This does not lead him to utter despair, for he has wisdom enough to be able to choose what is good and to make the best of life, but death will bring all of that to an end and that leads him to speak of an ultimate futility about life. He longs for something that will last beyond the grave. Some Christians have had problems with this book, seeing nothing in it but pessimistic skepticism, but I find it to be a very helpful one and my second sermon in this chapter will be based on it.[15]

First, however, some comments on preaching from the Book of Job. The greatness of the work presents the main problem for us. It contains so many levels of meaning that scholars can debate without end what the primary subject of the book really is.[16] Also its unity, with the presentation of a problem at the beginning, followed by a long debate over it and concluding with a resolution, forces us to consider whether it is legitimate to take anything smaller than the entire forty-two chapters as our text. And how does one condense this complex argument over life's deepest questions into a twenty-minute sermon? An addi-tional unique characteristic which Job shares with Ecclesiastes is their position as "outliers" in the history of the wisdom tradition, so that we cannot appeal to later forms of the same tradition to help us understand them, as we have done elsewhere.[17] The cultic form of raising questions about God's justice does have an ongoing history; laments continued to be written, but the type of questioning found in these two biblical books does not reappear again. What happened as the wisdom tradition moved on is that orthodoxy triumphed. To the assertions of Job and Ecclesiastes that wisdom is transcendental, the possession of God alone, and thus inaccessible to human beings (cf. Job 28:1–27), the mainstream of the wisdom school answered yes, it is the possession of God, and cannot be obtained by purely rational processes, but by his grace he bestows it on the righteous as a gift. So we need not despair of finding wisdom; indeed, Israel has it in the book of the law of Moses (Sirac 24:23).[18] To the objection that justice manifestly does not always triumph in this life, orthodoxy reasserted the old explanations of suffering as testing, as discipline, or as a sign of unacknowledged sinfulness and added to it the message that there is a life after death in which the ultimate justice of God's dealings with humanity becomes clear (Wisd. of Sol. 1:16–3:11).[19] Many commentaries have been written on Job and Ecclesiastes, but they did not create their own, alternate wisdom tradition and thus they represent a special kind of problem for the preacher. Because their way of dealing with things was not well-integrated into the later tradition, it is easier here to stay close to the text and yet to be led away from the ongoing Judeo-Christian tradition than in any other part of the Bible.

What is Job's real problem? The answers which have been suggested are many, for the book itself raises more than one of the issues which deeply trouble those who see beyond the surface of the biblical religion. Here I shall simply describe five suggestions which have been made as to the central problem of the book, then will offer some comments on what such a challenging work can be helped to say to a congregation through a sermon.

1. The oldest and most frequently suggested central problem for Job is the meaning of suffering.[20] Undoubtedly the prose introduction creates a setting in which intense, undeserved human misery is inflicted on a man without a word of explanation to him. The matter is *not* a problem for us, however, since we have been given a glimpse of the heavenly court and know the reason for it—it is a test of Job's faithfulness. This means that although Job and his friends, who are ignorant of what has happened in heaven, try out several possible explanations for his suffering, the whole book does not really present the suffering of the righteous as a problem to the reader, nor does it offer a general solution to the problem.

2. Other interpreters focus their attention on God rather than Job and maintain that the central problem of the book is theodicy—the justice of God's dealings with the world.[21] Again, there is no question that this is one of the issues dealt with at some length in the dialogue, but the prologue does not prepare us to expect that to be the main subject, and if a rational answer is ever given to the question of God's justice, it could be maintained that it is a negative one: God is not just and there is nothing we can do about it but humble ourselves before the tyrant.[22]

3. It has been suggested that human access to God is the main problem of the book, since what happens to Job is not explained to him and one of his most persistent cries is for some means of confronting God face to face.[23] The resolution of the book then occurs in the speeches of Yahweh, for although Job does not obtain the knowlege of why he suffers or how God manages the world, he does attain a knowledge of God himself.

4. Instead of knowledge, faith has been called the central concept of the book, since Job in all his speeches strives to know, but at the end, without hav-

ing received answers to any of his questions he has reached a new state of existence, the level of faith from which he no longer needs to ask those questions.[24]

5. Finally, it has been suggested that the book really focuses on the problem of whether disinterested righteousness is possible.[25] Satan says of course Job is good; he's well rewarded for it, and the contest centers on what Job will do without all his rewards. Throughout the dialogue both Job and his friends assume that the righteous should be rewarded, and while they hold on to that assumption there is no resolution of his problem. But in spite of all his questions and accusations, Job maintains his own integrity; he does not give in to the tempter (his wife) who says that when everything has been lost you might as well curse God and die. God appears to him, answering none of his questions, for they are beside the point, and Job is both humbled for his insistence on his own righteousness and justified for his faithfulness.

I think that all of these themes are to be found in the book and obviously all of them are related, so that it is hard to develop one without touching on others. Certainly the preacher will attempt to focus as closely as possible on one theme in order to avoid trying to crowd too much into a single sermon. And the portion of the book which one reads as the text can be chosen in order to highlight that theme. The sermon will certainly be based on a knowledge of the entire book, but it is more likely to be successful if most of what is to be said can be taken directly from one reasonably short passage.

What will we aim to do in preaching from a book which takes the form of dialogue, long speeches which sometimes involve fierce debate over Job's righteousness, sometimes exalted statements about wisdom and the creative activity of God? Its dramatic form is surely intended to draw the reader/listener into the anguish of Job's situation and to lead one to wrestle with the issues as the speakers try out every human possibility.[26] The sermon ought to strive to enable the congregation to feel what Job feels and to appreciate his position, as one who doesn't know what's going on up in heaven, as a reflection of our own situation at times when no answers come. Then we would be unfaithful to the book if we wound up with a pat answer; the book is more faithful to reality than that. Job does maintain his faithfulness and by the grace of God comes to a position of faith, however, and thus we need to end on a note of assurance based on faith in a sovereign God, and not to leave a congregation wondering what is left that they really can believe in.

A final comment on preaching Job. I once heard a lecturer point out that the general pattern of this book reflects a type of complaint literature which was common in ancient Mesopotamia: prosperity, followed by misfortune, a dialogue, and restitution.[27] The Mesopotamian works seem to have been used as scribal exercises, since a series of similar but not identical texts following this pattern have been discovered, as if, the lecturer said, the master of the scribal school had made an assignment: "Write your own Book of Job." Maybe that is what the preacher will have to do in order to get across a part of the wisdom of this book, within the confines of a sermon, so that a congregation can grasp at least some of it: Write your own Book of Job.

A Sermon on Ecclesiastes 9:1–12; 5:18–20

My second sermon example is taken from Ecclesiastes rather than Job because I wanted to show that the negativism of the book does not make it unpreachable. The sermon was prepared for a different sort of group from the others in this book; it was preached in the chapel of Pittsburgh Theological Seminary on February 17, 1977. Since scholars and students made up most of the congregation I could use the author's own designation of himself—Koheleth —without causing problems, and could speak without the barrier which being a guest preacher has created for most of the other sermons. The situation to which the sermon is addressed is adequately described at the beginning, I believe. I chose two texts which expressed most clearly the relationship between Koheleth's predicament and our own, but like most sermons on this book it draws freely from the entire work. The author's preoccupation with time (one of his major themes) is reflected in my description of the month of February in a litany which is never likely to rival Eccles. 3:1–9 in popularity, and the atmosphere which I attempted to create also reflects the remarkable perseverance of the faith of this "gentle cynic" which permitted forms of the word "joy" to appear a surprising number of times in a book so filled with questioning. The New Testament lesson was read by the liturgist at the conclusion of the sermon and it made a very appropriate concluding paragraph; not, it will be noted, as a corrective to Koheleth but as a reaffirmation of the intention to make the best of what God has given us. The title was borrowed from a poem by Ogden Nash.

Is Tomorrow Really Another Day?
Ecclesiastes 9:1–12; 5:18–20

That mysterious person who called himself Koheleth and wrote the Book of Ecclesiastes continues to fascinate us. In the effort to understand this strangely pessimistic book, it has been compared with the Pensees of Pascal, with the Rubaiyat of Omar Khayyam, with the sayings of Confucious, the essays of Montaigne or Voltaire, and with the works of Epicurus, Horace, or Spinoza. His book has been called the "musings of the old professor," and he has been labeled a "gentle cynic" and a hardened skeptic.

But one explanation for the tone of his work has occurred to me which has not been mentioned by anyone else.

Maybe the book was written in February.

Now, you know I don't mean that as a serious historical suggestion, for Koheleth was not subject to the North American climate or to the North American academic calendar. But the idea does create a certain point of contact with him, for I have long since discovered that, for the North American academic, February is without doubt the low point in the year. I have diagnosed a mild form of mental illness in myself, which I have unimaginatively named "Februaryitis," and as I endeavor to describe it to you it will be interesting to see whether there are any other sufferers from that disease in the congregation this morning.

This is the time when the mornings and evenings have been dark for a long time, and they show no signs of getting lighter.

It is the time when it has been cold for so long that the sight of blooming tulips in a grocery store this week was like the memory of something from childhood.

It is the time when the snow turns to black, icy slush, and more snow continues to fall, and we discover that the spots that black slush makes on our clothes don't come out.

It is the time when the car is so filthy we are ashamed to drive it, but we are afraid to get washed lest it be true that it is only the grime and the rust that are holding it together.

It is the time when it is no longer possible to remember the beginning of this school year, and not yet possible to foresee the end of it.

It is February—the only month with "rue" built right into it.

This, ah this is the month when we might almost be ready to agree with the gambler in one of Damon Runyan's stories who was told that someone was offering 3 to 1 odds on the Harvard-Yale boat race and who answered, "I do not know anything about boat races and the Yales may figure as you say, but nothing between human beings is 1 to 3. In fact, I long ago came to the conclusion that all of life is 6 to 5—against."

February makes us feel a little like the bear I once saw sitting by the roadside high up in Glacier National Park, obviously having just emerged from hibernation, gaunt, weak, with matted fur, yawning, without much interest in anything around him, his resources used up. We don't hibernate; we keep going in winter, but as academic types that makes a heavy drain on our resources. And we feel it especially when we appeal to those things which usually keep our morale up, to our dreams, our ideals, yes, our illusions. In February the dreams become stale and we understand how thin the illusions are.

Then why, of all times, should we read Ecclesiastes?

And the answer is that he, more than any other author, takes as his subject the struggle to live without depending on dreams and illusions. His work has been interpreted in many ways, but no one has ever accused him of wishful thinking. He was a realist of the most brutally honest kind. He sought to do what most of us simply cannot do, without losing our mental health—that is, to live without illusions. He scrutinized the values others affirm and devote their lives to, looking for something which is worth the dedication of this life which

God has given us. He was not deceived by the attractions of wealth, or fame, or work, or sex, or wine. He understood what they are worth, and he assured us that they are all worth something—but none of them is enough.

None of them lasts. And none of them is completely under our control. He was a man not satisfied with little goals. And that created his problem, for what lasts belongs to God, not man.

> That which is, is far off,
>> and deep,
>>> very deep;
> who can find it out?'' (Eccles. 7:24)

We may and do read his book as a preparation for the gospel, as a most effective way of stripping away the illusions by which all of us tend to live in order to reveal to us our need for something which lasts, a need we find that God has met for us in Jesus Christ. But even so, February does come around, and we learn that Christians, also, have their days when they live where Koheleth lived.

Let me share with you one of my stranger fantasies. Once I noticed, on the map of Pennsylvania, two little towns up by Punxsutawney, named Panic and Desire. And I thought one might someday be moved to carry out a symbolic act, like the prophets of old, representing in oneself the experiences of one's people, by purchasing a plot of land along the road up there, and building a cabin and living out the rest of one's life "between Desire and Panic."

I don't know what Isaiah would have thought of that, but I think Koheleth would have understood.

But all that is the negative side, and we look for something to help us. It seemed to me acceptable for today's message, based as it is on a book which takes "emptiness" (traditionally translated "vanity") as its main theme, to draw some conclusions from what Koheleth does *not* say. There are some very important omissions in the conclusions which Koheleth draws about life. He finds no real satisfaction from life, that is true; the answers he seeks evade him, and yet he does not conclude:

that we might as well commit suicide.

He does not conclude:

that there is no God.

He does not conclude:

that nihilism or existential anxiety is the best we can do.

He does not conclude:

that an antinomian kind of epicurianism is the way—live it up and the devil take the hindmost, for nothing really matters.

If ever he alludes to any such ideas, he calls them folly, and wisdom is still better than folly.

If at times he does come close to despair, he had learned to despair faithfully. His brutal honesty and that unreachable ideal for life which he insisted on were united in him with a strength, indeed a faith which enabled him to go on affirming what is good and right and beautiful and joy-bringing—even in a life which, for him, faced ultimate frustration.

Who was he; some kind of super-stoic?

He was no hero; not of the Greek tragic model, nor of the noble, humanistic kind, nor of the despairing, existentialist ilk. He was an example of life lived under grace. This is a book which speaks remarkably often about what God *gives*: our work—sometimes an unhappy business, that's true; our lives—vain lives to be sure, because ultimately frustrated; but also wealth, possessions, human relationships, and the power to enjoy them. And to the ascetic type who protests that all of this is passing away, he answers: Sure it is, but it is also the gift of God; don't knock it. And to the discouraged who ask, what's the use? he answers: But life is the gift of God, don't despise it, make the best of it, for God intends us to find joy in it.

Monday night this week we learned as we sat down at the table that it had been a hard day for all four members of the family, and it promised to be an unpleasant meal. In desperation, I insisted we talk about nothing but good things which had happened to us. It was a struggle, and I had to keep changing the subject to accomplish it, but eventually each of us searched the day and found some small, good things to report, and the meal ended with us in good spirits. It's not often things are so bad that I have to use that "positive thinking" approach, but sometimes those days come.

And it may take more than those human techniques, for human hope may fail us. People keep telling me, "Spring is coming," but every time someone says that I recall a Paul Bunyan story I read as a boy, entitled "The Year of the Two Winters," about the time when spring was so late it was already next fall by the time it came, and there was no summer. Human hope may fail. Yet we hold on to our human hopes, dreams, and illusions, and the day will come when it will be warmer and we will be nearer the end of the academic year, and they will look brighter and will be full of power for us again.

But Koheleth reminds us, and in February we may be inclined to listen to him, that we need more than that. The impressive thing about his book is that, as troubled as he was, he never gave up on God, and that meant he never gave up on life.

The testimony of the bubblingly cheerful is great, but can be a bit wearing at times. And the testimony of the perennially triumphant may become suspect. But the testimony of the *defeated*, who yet affirm that all is not lost, that God puts good, beauty, and joy into life, is to be taken with the utmost seriousness.

I believe it.

(Read Philippians 4:4–9.)

CHAPTER VI

Preaching from the Prophets

The interpretation of the prophetic books in the Old Testament is more akin to that of history than of the other types of literature we have considered. We have observed the universalism of wisdom thought, have seen how the saga is recapitulated in the lives of believers over and over again, and have noted that law deals with repeated human problems, even though the social and political setting in which they occur does change. But history is unique, particular, and non-repeatable. It is "back there" and not contemporary, and its effects upon us (which are profound) are brought about in and through time. So it is also with the work of the prophets. Despite statements to the contrary they are not our contemporaries,[1] for as interpreters of history they are time-bound, and indeed if their messages are loosed from the particular events to which they refer, the heart of Old Testament prophecy is lost.

The preceding statements are based on an understanding of the canonical prophets[2] which has grown out of form critical research. But before developing it further it will be helpful to recall alternate approaches to the interpretation of these books.

Who Were the Prophets?

1. The prophets as predictors of the coming of the Messiah: The earliest Christian use of the Old Testament found in it many passages which seemed to have been fulfilled with the coming of Jesus. Consequently, it came to be thought of as a book of "prophecies," i.e. predictions, of the Messiah and of the imminent end of history.[3] This way of using the whole Old Testament has had a continuing effect on the church's understanding of the prophetic books to this day. The first time I taught a course on the prophets in college I discovered

that my students were interested at first in only one question: did everything the prophets predict come true? But such an approach to this large portion of the Old Testament corpus scarcely does justice to it. At the beginning, it leaves out great sections which can in no way be taken as predictions of Christ's coming, or of the last days. And it falls into the trap of coming to a part of the Bible with a preconceived idea of what it should contain without asking it to tell us what it wants to say. More careful study shows that there are indeed predictions in the prophetic books, but that to think of the prophets as essentially fortune tellers, forerunners of Nostradamus and Jeane Dixon, is a great error.

2.   The prophets as social reformers: In the latter part of the nineteenth century many scholars found in the prophetic books words which seemed especially appropriate for societies which were being radically changed by the Industrial Revolution. The addresses of the prophets to their contemporaries in which they castigated them for their sins contained such stirring calls for social justice that "prophetic religion" came to be equated with attacks on the evils of society and insistence on reform.[4] In the heyday of religious liberalism, when so much that was traditional in Christianity was questioned or abandoned completely, social justice could still be affirmed with enthusiasm, and so the prophets (or selected parts of them) became a favorite part of the Bible. But these books contain much more than the concern for social justice and the newer studies of prophecy have revealed that the prophets were quite different from the protestant preachers of the social gospel which they had been made to appear to be.

3.   The prophets as ecstatic personalities: The rise of psychological studies led to an interest in the personalities of the prophets. They had been pictured as great religious geniuses, lone voices calling for worship of the one God and adherence to principles of justice and mercy; they had been made over in the image of the ideal nineteenth century religious leader. This inevitably involved ignoring such embarrassing things as their visions, auditions, and symbolic actions which included much that was bizarre and of a compulsive nature. Some efforts to psychoanalyze the prophets led to the conclusion that they must have been psychopaths, but more serious studies suggested there was no good evidence that they were mentally ill. There was, however, a strong case developed for concluding that they possessed a peculiar kind of personality, which we may call visionary or ecstatic.[5] All of this may be cheering news to modern charismatics, but it provided little help for those who were striving to know how best to preach the prophetic books. Its main result was negative, in that it raised questions about aspects of the familiar portrayal of them as social reformers.

4.   The prophets as bearers of tradition: A more recent emphasis in the study of the prophets has been to move away from the conception of them as great isolated individuals of either kind—reformers of mystics—and to look instead at how much they had in common with the rest of the Israelite people. For example, although they criticized the cult severely, it could be shown that they

used a great many cultic forms for their own purposes.[6] History of tradition studies showed that in many respects what the prophets were doing was to preserve what was best in the religion of their forefathers, and to take as their responsibility the teaching of the essentials of the ancestral faith.[7] So instead of the familiar emphasis on their individualism, we began to hear of the "office" of prophet, of people whose regular role it was to "preach" in this way. Such an emphasis on the traditional elements in the prophetic books tended to de-emphasize the personal factor, and questions began to be raised about all the previous efforts to write biographies of the prophets, to reconstruct their personal experiences as the basis for understanding their messages. Now it is being said we may have only fragments of authentic information about the lives of the prophets and that is really of no great importance, because what is truly important is not their own religious experiences but their faithfulness in carrying on the prophetic tradition. There is a good deal to be said for this position, but we need to be aware of one potential danger; if we overstress their role as the preservers of the faith of the fathers, we begin to overlook the fact that they also did something that was radically new and previously unheard of. It is this aspect of their work which tends to dominate my own approach, which I am now ready to describe.

New Light on the Prophets from Form Criticism

If you can remember the first time you read through one of the prophetic books you may have a memory of the very confusing impression it made on you, for that is the usual effect which these great conglomerations of different kinds of materials, without either logical or chronological order, make upon the unprepared reader. Some kind of literary analysis is obviously called for if one is to understand more than just a few isolated passages of these works. Form criticism has proved to be a tremendous help in understanding the prophetic books. It enables us to appreciate both the prophets' relationship to Israel's traditions and their astonishing originality. A brief survey of some of the results of this research will be provided here as the background for some conclusions about the essence of the prophetic message.[8]

At the first level, three quite different kinds of speech may be discerned in these books: a) Narratives about the prophets: e.g. the so-called biographical material about Jeremiah; b) Prophetic speeches: almost the entire contents of books such as Amos, Joel, and Micah, and the major part of all the canonical prophetic books except for Jonah; c) Words addressed from man to God, such as prayers, laments and hymns: e.g. the doxologies in Amos (4:13; 5:8–9; 9:5–6) and the "confessions" of Jeremiah (15:15–18, 17:14–18, etc.). The narratives concerning the activities of various prophets seem to go back to an early period; we find many examples of them in Samuel and Kings, and they will not be our major focus of interest in this chapter, since a good deal has already been said about preaching from various kinds of narratives. Within these stories are quotations of brief prophetic speeches, but most of them tend to concern themselves to a great extent with the activities of the prophets. In the eighth century something new appeared in the prophetic movement; extensive collections of the *words* of certain prophets were made, the earliest of which are the speeches of Amos and Hosea, uttered in the Northern Kingdom. From that time on, for a period of three to four hundred years, such collections continued to be made, then this kind of literary activity died out—prophecy, in that peculiar Old Testament sense, had come to an end. One of the questions which will concern us a bit later will be whether we can suggest a reason why this kind of activity had a beginning and an end.

These collections of words from and about the prophets are composed of a great variety of literary types. There are funeral songs (Amos 5:1) and parodies of the same (Isa. 14:4–21). There are series of "woes" (Isa. 5:8ff.) which probably also had their origin in funeral customs. There are speeches reminiscent of legal procedure (Mic. 6:1ff.). There are parables (Isa. 5:1–7), wisdom sayings (Amos 3:3ff.), and quotations of torah (Isa. 1:16–17). We could add many others, such as Jeremiah's use of the lament-form so well known from the Psalter (e.g. 18:19ff.) in his complaints to the Lord. But we shall not attempt to make a complete list here. The main points to be observed are the freedom which the prophets exercised in drawing material from every aspect of life in order to convey their messages in the most effective possible way and their originality in putting old forms to work for new purposes. Each of these genres now has more than one *Sitz im Leben,* more than one function; its original place and meaning and a new one, created by the prophet who put it to another use. For example, the dirge was sung on the day when someone died and was buried, its form and its typical wording fit the needs of that occasion perfectly. But then Amos sang a dirge over Israel, a nation, not a person, and sang it while Israel was still alive and vigorous (5:1)! It thus became in part a prediction of coming doom which had a force and pathos which could not be produced in any other way. The same form could be transformed further, as we can see from Isa. 14:4–21, in which it becomes a taunt-song expressing joy rather than grief, since the singers are those who suffer under a tyrant whose death they anticipate. Again, no more forceful way of pronouncing judgment against tyranny could be imagined than the creation of a mock funeral song.[9] So we can learn much about the effective use of the traditional forms of language (our own as well as Israel's) from what form criticism has discovered in the prophetic books.

There is one form of speech which is especially important for our understanding of who the canonical prophets were and what they were up to, since it is a form which is typically prophetic. They did not borrow it from any other area of life, and so it seems to tell us most directly what they wanted to say to their people. It is a two-part speech, an announcement accompanied by a reason, and it occurs hundreds of times in the prophetic books.[10] Let me cite just one example:

> Therefore because you trample upon the poor   (REASON)
>   and take from him exactions of wheat,
> you have built houses of hewn stone,   (ANNOUNCEMENT)
>   but you shall not dwell in them;
> you have planted pleasant vineyards,
>   but you shall not drink their wine.
> (Amos 5:11)

Occasionally the announcement promises a blessing (cf. Jer. 35:18–19), but normally it contains the message that God is about to bring doom upon Israel, and the reason which is given explains why that is going to happen by reciting Israel's sins. Because of the predominance of this genre in the prophetic books, form critics have emphasized that the prophets were essentially "messengers," sent by God simply to *announce* what he was about to do, and to explain why. This is a more striking conclusion than it may seem to be at first, for it essentially rules out that favorite image of recent years of the prophet as a reformer, come to preach repentance. As a matter of fact, although there are a few admonitions (appeals for change connected with a promise) in the prophetic books, they are far from the dominant feature. There is one only in Amos, and the promise attached to it is a very "iffy" one: ". . . *it may be* that the Lord, the God of hosts, will be gracious *to the remnant* of Joseph" (5:15b). Although the faint possibility of the preservation of a remnant is held out there is no suggestion that the nation as a whole has a chance of averting the doom Amos had announced. In Hosea there are more admonitions, but in the other prophets very few can be found. And this leads us to a disturbing (and for most preachers, discouraging) conclusion about the canonical prophets.

These prophets were messengers sent by God to Israel to announce to them that he was about to bring an era to an end, to do with them a radically new thing. They announced that the relationship between God and Israel which had existed for many centuries was to be drastically changed. God had made a covenant with Israel at Sinai, and because of that had given them a land and helped them to maintain themselves in it. But the time had come when this relationship was no longer valid, and because of that the nation of Israel would come to an end and her land would be taken away. If there was to be any Israel as a people of God in the future, that would have to depend on a new act of God's mercy, the introduction of a new age.[11]

This understanding of the nature of the prophets' work has grown out of the form critical analysis of their words, as we have seen, but it may be supported by other considerations. We may begin to understand the reason for the limited span of time during which canonical prophecy existed, once this point of view is adopted. This "prophetic era" began just before the fall of the Northern Kingdom (722 B.C.) and most of the prophetic books cluster around that event and the fall of Jerusalem in 587 B.C. More exactly, a look at the chronology of the prophets suggests that they cluster around three events: the fall of Samaria, the fall of Jerusalem, and the restoration of Jerusalem. Four prophets are dated in the eighth century; Amos and Hosea in the Northern Kingdom, Isaiah and Micah in Judah. Around the fall of Jerusalem we find Zephaniah, Nahum, Habakkuk, Jeremiah, Ezekiel, and Obadiah. Around the restoration we find Second Isaiah, Haggai, and Zechariah, with Malachi coming a bit later. The date of Joel is very uncertain, and there are parts of Zechariah and perhaps some of the other prophetic books which are to be dated at least as late as Malachi, and perhaps later. But it may be seen that prophecy thins down and dies out very soon after the restoration of Jerusalem.

What does this suggest, in the light of the character of the prophetic words as announcements? It is clear. God was about to do a new thing in history, to make a radical change in his relationship to his people.[12] It first took the form of judgment, of bringing something old to an end, and so the downfall of Israel and then of Judah was proclaimed and explained by a series of men sent for that specific purpose. When the end did come God also sent men with the message that the new era was about to begin, and when the restoration did occur there was no further need for that kind of messenger.

But now, something suggests itself to Christians. Perhaps there was one more time in history when God planned to do a new thing, in sending his Son to earth in order to bring all humanity to him. This allows us to add another prophet, in the Old Testament sense, to the series, John the Baptist, not because of his preaching of repentance but because he announced the imminent appearance of the Messiah. The prophetic aspects of Jesus' ministry also fit this definition, in that he announced the coming of the Kingdom and seems to have emphasized that with his advent on earth God was doing something radically new.

In my understanding of things there have been no more true prophets of that kind since Jesus.[13] There have been prophets, yes; Muhammed and Joseph Smith fit the Old Testament definition, but the question still remains whether they are *true* or *false* prophets. The unique character of canonical prophecy can be emphasized, however, if we imagine what it would be like if another figure should arise in our time who really functioned the way Amos or Jeremiah did. Such a prophet would say to us: "Your religion as you practice it can no longer save you. Your nation is no longer going to be able to provide security or any kind of prosperity—and this is because God has given up on you. God has repudiated the church and Jesus Christ is no longer your Savior, for that means of creating a faithful people of God on earth simply has not worked. Now God is going to erase it and start over."

This is exactly what the Old Testament prophets said to Israel. Is it any wonder that their words are filled with anguish, that they tried every conceivable means to make the message understandable, and that they were not believed? How could anyone believe them? That a few people did is surely due only to the grace of God, and subsequent generations of believers have benefited from their memory of what the prophets said. Soon enough their words came true, and then people recalled, "This is what Amos (and the others) told us. Now we understand that these disasters are not some terrible accident or proof of the superiority of the gods of Assyria or Babylon but the work of Yahweh the God of Israel." And so those words were collected and studied and became the basis for a new seriousness of dedication to that same God who had taken everything away from them. Then out of nothing he created a new people, explaining again through his prophets what he was about to do and why. But before the eighth century, and after the fifth century, when there existed an ongoing relationship which could be the source of blessing for God's people, he worked through that, and there was no need for prophets of that kind.

Now, I know you are wanting to protest, as have members of every class to which I have presented these ideas. Does not the Bible itself say that God raised up his prophets to preach repentance, to give his people a chance to change and to avert disaster? Indeed it does, and we must take such statements seriously. But where do they occur? For the most part, in the work of the Deuteronomistic Historian, not in the prophetic books! For example, in 2 Kings 17:13 we find a typical statement:

> Yet the LORD warned Israel and Judah by every prophet and every seer, saying, "turn from your evil ways and keep my commandments and my statutes, in accordance with all the law which I commanded your fathers, and which I sent to you by my servants the prophets."

But the strange thing is that in the books of the prophets we can find few passages which fit this summary of the prophetic message. As I have pointed out, such calls to repentance occur only rarely. So what shall we conclude? My suggestion is this: There may have been a type of prophetic office in Israel which had a very long history, and a part of the work of those prophets was the preaching of repentance based on reminders of the requirements of God's law. Such prophets are alluded to frequently in the historical books. But at a given time in Israel's history a new kind of message began to be heard from certain men who were in other respects like all the other prophets. What distinguished them from the rest was this unconditional threat of coming doom, and it was the fact that such unbelievable messages actually did come true that led to the collection of their words and no others into books which provided an explanation for the otherwise unacceptable disasters which had befallen people, land, city, and temple. So there may have been two kinds of prophets during that period of Israel's history, with a great deal of continuity between them but with one thing marking a certain group as special: the content of their message, which was tied to the occurrence of the destruction and restoration of God's people.

What Can We Preach from the Prophetic Books?

The much-loved expression "Prophetic preaching" needs some qualification if it is to be used with any faithfulness to what we now know about the prophets of the Old Testament. Certainly we do have a work to do comparable to that of institutional prophets in Israel, viz. calling for repentance. But we can do the same work as a Hosea or a Micah only if we become convinced that God is about to begin another revolution and that he has given us the authority to announce that to our people.

What, then, can we preach from Hosea or Micah? It should be becoming clear that I will not recommend making a direct application to the church or to America of the threats or promises which they addressed to Israel. We are not Israel. What they spoke of is now past history and unless we can claim some new, direct inspiration from God, what right do we have to say that the same things which once happened to Israel are now about to happen to us? The most dubious move of all is to apply to America what was once spoken to Israel, as if America were the new convenant nation. America is, in fact, one of the "gentile" nations, to use biblical terminology, and the prophetic speeches concerning the great nations of the earth are more directly applicable to our country than any other part of their work. So I recommend some caution in deciding how the words of the prophets are to be applied to us.

But this does not leave them stranded in the past, without any point of contact with us, as it might seem at first, for we have found it possible to preach from the historical books of the Old Testament, and the same principles apply here. From them we learn what God was doing with and for his people and from that we have our only access to a knowledge of who God is and how he treats his people. The prophets are of special importance to us because they speak of those times in history when God intervened with power to do a new thing, and because in their explanations of what was happening we can see what is most important to God in the behavior of his people and we can be assured of the intention and direction of his acts of judgment and redemption. Both of my sermon examples draw lessons of this sort from the texts which have been chosen. But this does not mean that religious liberalism, which preached for social justice from the prophetic books, was completely wrong.

The prophets did not call for reform, for they knew it was too late; the end of the present order was near and could not be averted. The best they could hope for was that there might be a few who would hear, change, and be saved to become the nucleus of a new people created by the grace of God. They were right; the old order of Israel did soon come to an end. But, during and after the exile, those who remained alive were taught by the prophetic word to take God's requirements with a new seriousness; the opportunity for reform did exist and a new people was produced with a dedication to the law and the one God which was never again shaken. Now, if we believe that no prophet has arisen in our day to announce that God is once again about to intervene in human history to change things radically, as he has done a few times in the past, then we ought to conclude that we live in one of those times where reform is both possible and necessary. As long as there is still time, God calls upon men and women to change things—to change themselves and to change society—and so we ought to be evangelists, preaching repentance, and reformers, preaching social justice. And even though I emphasize the uniqueness of the canonical prophets, that their message is specifically connected with the falls of Jerusalem and Samaria and the return from exile, this in no way means that their work is irrelevant for us who are called to be evangelists and reformers. As post-exilic Judaism was led by the prophets to re-examine its life, so the basis for reform is present in their messages for us. The content of that reform is not distinctively prophetic at all, for they got it from the Law and from Wisdom, but the *form* in which they expressed it and the historical circumstances with which their words were connected (which became a revelation of God's purpose) give to the old teachings a new bite and a new urgency which remain vivid for every generation.

So, although it may break our hearts to be told that we are not really supposed to be Amoses or Isaiahs, let us be of good cheer, for that means it still isn't too late to do something to help ourselves and these people truly to become the people of God. And those old prophets tell us more sharply and clearly than any other what it is that we had better be doing, while we still have time.

Preaching Judgment and Promise from the Prophets

Let me now offer two exercises in moving from exegesis to the development of a sermon idea and two examples of sermons. The first exercise will take up a typical example of the reason-announcement form which speaks of coming doom; the second will treat one of the most famous Old Testament promises. Because of the great variety of material in the prophetic books, there are many different kinds of sermons which can be preached from them, and I do not want to leave the impression that there is only one preachable subject—the exile and restoration. For example, I have preached on what the promises, "And I will put my spirit within you . . . and I will summon the grain and make it abundant and lay no famine upon you," of Ezek. 36:27, 29 can be taken to mean to twentieth century Christians, using the history of the eschatological traditions of the Bible to show that God's promises are fulfilled again and again, but are never exhausted. I have used Joel's threats against the nations in chapter 3 as a basis for speaking of a God who is involved in international politics, who needs to be spoken of at times as a God of war because war is the way of the nations. I have used Ezekiel's individualization of responsibility in 33:10–20 as a way of dealing with the power of memories over us and of God's power to free us from past guilt. The hymns and prayers and prophetic narratives may be preached in the ways which are appropriate to them. But one of my exercises and one of my sermon examples will concentrate on the principal new message which the prophets brought to the world: the death and resurrection of the people of God.

Amos 2:6–16

This is a reason-announcement oracle in an expanded form. In context it follows a series of seven such oracles which are addressed to the nations surrounding the Northern Kingdom, each of which is constructed in the same way:

Thus says the LORD: "For three transgressions of
. . . , and for four, I will not revoke the
punishment;
    because they have . . .   (REASON)
    So I will . . .   (ANNOUNCEMENT)

The eighth oracle has expanded the reason by listing transgressions at greater length (vss. 7–8, 12) and by inserting a recollection of the sacred history (vss. 9–10). The announcement of coming judgment is also longer, but this can be explained by the fact that the whole passage is addressed to the Northern Kingdom, so that it would be only normal for this final and climactic unit to be longer than the others. The purpose of the whole passage, 1:3–2:16, must thus be kept in mind when interpreting a part of it.

In this oracle Amos has made extensive use of the earlier traditions of his people. Verses 6–8 do not quote the law verbatim but they clearly allude to it, and parallels can be found in the wisdom literature as well. The law's efforts to humanize slavery have been thwarted (6b; cf. Deut. 24:7, etc.): justice has been denied the poor (7a; cf. Exod. 23:6–8): cult prostitution (probably, since this relationship is not explicitly condemned as incestuous in the law) has become commonplace (7b): and the garments of the poor are taken as security for their debts (8a; cf. Exod. 22:26, etc.). There is nothing in the law to explain, "in the house of their God they drink the wine of those who have been fined" (8b), so we can only assume it also refers to the results of unjust court proceedings. This is the indictment of Israel. They have been found guilty of all these crimes and Amos announces them before pronouncing sentence.

But in order to preclude any defense which Israel might offer, the prophet expands the typical, two-part form by reminding them of all that God has done for them in the past. Verses 9–10 recall the conquest, the exodus and the wilderness, in that order. And as another of God's gifts to Israel, the presence of prophets and Nazirites among them is pointed out, providing for Amos a way of concluding the indictment by tying together that gift with their ingratitude: "but you made the Nazirites drink wine, and commanded the prophets, saying, 'You shall not prophesy.' "

The announcement makes use of imagery from war, for the most part (vss. 14–16), speaking of a disastrous defeat which will come upon them, and it is here that an understanding of the traditions which lie behind the entire section become helpful. Earlier prophets had been regularly consulted in wartime, for no king dared to go out to battle without the assurance that God was with him (cf. 1 Kings 22). Often the oracle of assurance which a prophet might give would take the two-part form. Because of the sins of the enemy, God will intervene to save Israel (cf. 1 Kings 20:28). Thus prophets were involved in the promulgation of the idea of *holy war*,[14] in which God did battle on behalf of his people. In this section we see Amos doing a new thing with an old tradition. Using the familiar form he announces that God is once again going out to war against his enemy. But this is not a time in which Israel is endangered; the country is strong and at peace, so the *Sitz im Leben* of Amos' holy war oracles is different. Furthermore, unlike any real situation in the past, the prophet pronounces a long series of holy war oracles, including every neighboring country. And he concludes with the home country itself—Israel, the people God ought to be saving, has now become the object of his holy war. It is world judgment which Amos announces. This interpretation is confirmed by his use of another holy war tradition in the same way in 5:18–20, for when he makes the coming of the Day of the Lord a threat he has reversed its original meaning, since "Day of the Lord" originally meant the day of Yahweh's victory over his enemies.[15]

Form criticism and tradition history have thus shown us how Amos depended on the past but made use of it to bring a disturbing new message. In a time of peace and prosperity he announces the coming of a sweeping defeat in battle, using materials so familiar to everybody that its bite could not be avoided, despite the unbelievable nature of what he said. "You have violated the basic rights of humanity and in doing so have sinned against the God who saved you. Now he has given you up and there is no hope for you." From the rest of his book we can add very little to that message; only a faint hope that a tiny remnant may be preserved (3:12; 5:4–6, 14–15). The promises at the end (9:11–15) in no way mitigate the disaster, even if they are the work of Amos and not a later prophet, for they speak of what will come *after* the disaster, not *instead of* it.

That is as far as Amos goes, but it is not the end of the history of his words. What was their effect? First we must say that they came true. Not long after Amos' time the Northern Kingdom was destroyed, and one might think that should be the end of it. But Judah, to the south, was so closely tied to Israel in thought, though a rival politically, that they found Amos' words to be indispensable, for they offered an explanation of something that *needed* to be explained, of how this part of God's people could be apparently given up by their God.

And the words of Amos were preserved in Judah. A century and a half later, however, Judah also was destroyed, and that really should have been the end. But the words of the prophet played their part in God's work of raising a new people out of the grave of the exile.

Preaching from Amos (or from any of the rest of the judgment passages in the prophets) must then emphasize the dark side of human existence, but without ever forgetting that it is still existence under grace. a) This text deals with the pervasiveness of sin as it contrasts the good that God has done for his people with their hardened refusal to take seriously his requirements of them. It does not quite yet teach total depravity, but it forces us to ask whether we are really any more faithful than those Israelites. b) It insists that God is not mocked, that despite his patience and long-suffering we dare not think we shall not be held accountable in some way for our faithlessness, any more than Israel could escape the coming disaster. c) But the end of Israel was not really the end, or there would be no Book of Amos preserved for us. The gospel in such a book is its very existence, the proof that God's purpose is not thwarted, no matter how we fail him. d) And we thank God that Amos' words are not addressed to us directly, for that would mean it was too late for the church. But if God has not yet determined that we must die in order that he may bring new life out of death, then we had better be about the work of the people of God with vigor.

A Sermon on Isaiah 1:2–9

I have used this passage for homiletical purposes in much the same way as the Amos text. In form it is different, as it contains a combination of genres. The first unit (vss. 2–3) is now called the "covenant lawsuit" form; i.e. it is reminiscent of presumed legal procedure in ancient Israel, which began with a call to the witnesses to appear, then proceeded with a charge against the accused.[16] Form-critical research has led to the hypothesis that the prophets used this familiar genre to speak of a suit which God has brought against Israel over the latter's breach of the covenant. It is significant for our understanding of the prophets' work that no defense is ever quoted. Israel *has* no defense and the outcome of the lawsuit is not in doubt, for the prophets' task is only to announce the verdict: Guilty![17] Only a fragment of the lawsuit is present in this passage; it is followed by a "woe-oracle" (vss. 4ff.). It has been shown that the interjection *hoi!* (traditionally translated "woe," but also sometimes "alas" and here, "Ah" in the RSV, "O" in the NEB and in the TEV paraphrased "You are doomed") was originally a cry of mourning,[18] and that fits the context very well, since most of what follows takes the form of a lament over the desolation of Judah. The contents strongly suggest that it should be dated in 701 B.C., after Sennacherib's army had occupied all of Judah except Jerusalem (cf. vs. 8), and so the entire passage speaks of a fulfillment of the kind of destiny which Amos had predicted for the Northern Kingdom. Like Amos, Isaiah accounts for the disaster by citing the rebellious nature of God's people, but he does not spell out their sins in detail. The funeral tone of other passages in Amos is also dominant here and is more to be emphasized than the words of condemnation. As in Amos, Isaiah has no word of comfort to offer; he knows only of a pitiful remnant of survivors (vs. 9). So the entire passage is a very depressing one. It stands in some contrast to the narratives elsewhere in Isaiah which depict this prophet as a bringer of salvation oracles—chapter 7, where he promises deliverance from Rezin of Syria and Pekah of Israel, and chapters 36–37, where Jerusalem's delivery from Sennacherib is the subject. For our purpose in preaching from chapter 1 we need not worry about whether both pictures of the prophet are accurate and need not spend time reconstructing all the events of 701 B.C., for the evidence is clear from all sources that 1:7–8 provides a true picture of the fate of Judah in that year. That fact that Jerusalem did not fall to the Assyrians became of great theological importance in later years (cf. Ps. 48; Isa. 29; Jer. 7; 26; Zech. 12–14, etc.) but at the time our text was written that was small enough comfort for those who had only one city left untouched in their whole country.

Now the question is whether taking that disaster as seriously as the forms and content of this passage ask of us can lead to anything which should be preached to a twentieth century congregation. As you will see, I begin the sermon by raising just such a question with the people, then proceed in much the same way as I outlined for Amos 2:6–16. The point of the sermon was to try to understand what place this lament over the destruction of a land and a people has in the redeeming work of God. In order to show that it is *redemption* which God is up to, I had to go beyond this passage and to speak of the later facts of the exile and restoration, but that move did not lead me away from the real concern of this text, for I conclude with the question over which Isaiah is lamenting: Can we really be *that* bad? The sermon was preached in the Wayside United Presbyterian Church in Erie, Pa. on Nov. 17, 1968.

Life Out of Death

Isaiah 1:2–9

Last fall I was teaching a course in Isaiah at the Seminary, and during one of our classes we worked through the Hebrew text of this passage. After we had translated the passage, discussed the meaning of certain words and the historical setting in which these words originated, I asked my students, "Now, could you preach on this text?" One of them answered, "That's just what we were going to ask you."

What can we make of a passage such as this? It was produced 2,700 years ago, was addressed to Israel, and concerns one specific event in the history of Israel. These words are not addressed to us. Shall we then consider them to be just a fragment of ancient history, and not a very interesting fragment at that?

That would be all we could say, were it not that the Christian faith believes in a God of history. We believe that our God gets involved in human affairs, that he interferes in our history, that it is God who is responsible for certain events. More than that, everything that Christians believe they know about God is based on certain events of the past which we believe are God's work.

Isaiah was talking about an event which had just occurred in the life of his people, which he believed had been caused by God—by the same God we're worshipping here this morning. That was important to Isaiah, and to the people who believed him then. The question is whether there's anything in this that's important to us, 2,700 years later. It's the same God, the same one whom we love and to whom we are responsible. But does *this* text tell us anything that we need to know about that God?

To answer that question we must understand what Isaiah was doing when he spoke these gloomy words. Israel had been divided into two parts for 200 years, with the capital of the north at Samaria and the capital of the south at Jerusalem. In Isaiah's lifetime the armies of Assyria swept into the Northern Kingdom, destroyed Samaria, and made that part of Israel an Assyrian province. He also saw the same armies invade his own homeland, the Southern Kingdom, take all the smaller cities, and threaten Jerusalem itself. It must be that invasion and its consequences which the lamentation I read this morning describes. To put it briefly, Isaiah lived at a turning point, when the history of his people took a turn for the worse.

We tend to think of the prophets as men who called for reform and pleaded for repentance. Isaiah did not do that. It was too late for reform. The first words of our text (vss. 2–3) are put in the form of an ancient lawsuit. Isaiah says God has a case against Israel, it has already been tried, and Israel has been found guilty. All that Isaiah can do is to announce the verdict, the reason for it, and the sentence. But he was a human being, a man who loved his country, his people, his religion; and what God had called him to do was a terrible thing. It is as if one among us who truly loved his country and his church were to come to the conviction that the history of the United States will very shortly come to a dreadful end, with the few Americans left alive to be scattered among the other countries of the world, and without even a church to go with them to guide and comfort them. What could such a man do but lament? So Isaiah does in vss. 4–9 of our text. He expresses in the form of a lamentation his dismay over the terrible fate that has overtaken his people and at the stubbornness and wickedness that has caused it and prolongs it.

There is something else which Isaiah might have done, which others in the same circumstances have done, and that is, to cry out against God, "Why have you brought this upon us? Why must a God who says he loves us be so severe?" Isaiah doesn't ask this question because he knows why. As a prophet of God he understands that at this point in history there is no other way for God's purpose to be accomplished. God had been patient for a long time. He had given Israel a covenant so that they might live with the assurance of his love for them, a law to guide them in what is right, a temple and sacrifice and a priesthood, kings and prophets—but all had failed. Worship, ethics, politics, and economics had gone from corruption to corruption. Now God is about to destroy his people. Why? In anger at them? To revenge himself for their spitefulness? To punish them by making them suffer? None of these is the answer.

At present there is one city left—Jerusalem—and there are a few survivors. But the day will come, one hundred years after Isaiah's time, when even Jerusalem will lie in ruins and most of the people who still call themselves Judeans will be in exile in Babylonia. There is worse to come. And yet out of that sweeping disaster came something unbelievable—a new people. Out of the exilic community of Jews came a people who for the first time took Isaiah and the other prophets seriously, who dedicated themselves to the service of the one God to the extent that they were willing to die for him, who took as the mandate for their existence the keeping of God's law. What the prophets had pleaded for in vain finally came true—but only as a result of the death of a nation.

God had in the exile accomplished something of great good for mankind, but it was a terrible thing he had to do to bring it about. He could not produce a people after his own heart through covenant or law or king or priest or prophet; he had to do it by devastating a land, by leaving children fatherless, by making refugees of a whole people. He had to kill, and to bring back from the dead.

And it was not just ancient Israel that was so obstinate. The sixth century B.C. is not the only time God has had to deal so drastically with mankind. The exile did succeed—it produced a tiny nucleus of people dedicated to him, the Jews—but to break out of that nucleus and bring all of mankind to himself he came to earth in human form in the person of Jesus Christ. And the pattern was repeated. Just as priest and king and prophet failed by teaching and example to make Israel faithful to their God, so even Jesus' teaching and example failed. People showed how well they understood the message of love by ridiculing him and torturing him to death. Once again God's efforts to bring humanity to himself led to death. But once again God was not defeated by death, but by resurrection created a new community of faith, the Church.

This is how God works with human beings. None of us knows how God's mind works, all we know is what he does, but I assume he has not chosen to do these things because it is his favorite way. He is so patient, and he has tried so many ways to reconcile us to himself—but because we are so obstinate, so set in our rebellion against God, it seems that finally there is no other way but to kill us and remake us. He killed Israel, and brought from the dead a new people. He killed mankind in Jesus Christ, and brought again from the dead a people who could believe him and be faithful to him. So it is true, hard as it is to believe, that Isaiah's lament over a desolate land and a despairing people is a part of the redeeming work of God.

Now we must ask something about ourselves and the rest of humanity: Can we really be *that* bad? Oh, I suppose it is not so hard to believe that ancient Israel and the Jews of Jesus' day were that bad—but we can hardly believe it about *Presbyterians!* Can what history reveals to us about the way God has to work with humanity be true—that, far from cooperating with God and seeking the best, we have inevitably sought the worst, and have worked against him so persistently and effectively that the best thing God could do for us is to kill us?

Can that be the truth about me?

That's the question I leave for you to answer, reminding you that Paul said Christians have *died and risen* with Christ.

Does that help explain why the world is in the mess it's in?

Does that account for the failure, even of people supposedly of good will, to agree on plans which could bring peace, health, freedom, and equality to their brethren?

Does it help us to understand why even in the Church there is rivalry and self-seeking and apathy toward the work of Christ?

Does it warn us not to count too much on what we and our fellowmen may be able to accomplish that is good—knowing what we are?

But, on the other hand, does it also keep us from despairing, despite all this, because we know that although we fail again and again there is a God who *has*, in history, brought the dead to life?

I don't think God will have to kill the church in order to bring to life a community which will obey him. I may be wrong, that may come, but as yet I hear no authentic prophets among us announcing that God is about to treat us in so radical a way. And that must mean that we still have time—time individually to die with Christ that through the death of our own self-centeredness we might be able to be God's new, resurrected people, time to breathe new life into the church that it may truly be the people of God and a source of blessing to the world.

If we fail, I am convinced that God will not fail, for he can bring life out of death. But it is our job to live *now*, to bring the word of life to the world *now*, and then to trust God, that he will not fail, no matter what comes.

Jeremiah 31:31–34

My first two examples, judgment passages, are probably not used as sermon texts very often. In contrast, the two promise passages to be discussed are among the Christian's favorite Old Testament texts, the New Convenant prophecy in Jeremiah and the Immanuel prophecy in Isaiah. Once again I shall offer some notes on how to move from exegesis to the development of a sermon on the first text, then will present a sermon on the second.

Since Jer. 31:31–34 is obviously a convenant text, some background study on the convenants of the Old Testament will be a logical place to begin our work. We have noted earlier that there are two types of covenants between God and human beings in the Old Testament: a convenant of "divine commitment" which involves promise without stipulations placed on the human recipient, and a convenant of "human obligation" which requires an obedient response if it is to be kept in force.[19] The covenants with Noah (Gen. 9:8–17), with Abraham (Gen. 15; 17) and with David (2 Sam. 7; Ps. 89; Jer. 33:14–26) belong to the first type; they are given by God to man, they involve blessings and promises of future blessings, and there is no indication that anything a human being can do would have the effect of anulling the covenant. Certainly Genesis 17 indicates that an uncircumcised individual will be cut off from the covenant people, but that does not affect God's relationship with the people, and 2 Samuel 7 warns that the king who disobeys God will be punished for it, but it also goes on to reaffirm that the covenant with David will never be abrogated under any circumstances.

At Sinai, however, a relationship was established with Israel which required obedient human participation in order for it to be effective. At the very beginning of the "negotiations" we find an "if-clause": "Now therefore, if you will obey my voice and keep my covenant, you shall be my own possession . . ." and the people's response is, "All that the LORD has spoken we will do" (Exod. 19:5, 8). It is the Sinai covenant to which the law is attached, and the conditional nature of that covenant is further emphasized by the concluding blessings and curses which we find in Leviticus 26 and Deuteronomy 28. It is clearly this covenant to which Jer. 31:31ff. refers, since it is dated, "when I took them by the hand to bring them out of the land of Egypt," it refers to law (vs. 33), and it is identified as "my covenant which they broke" (vs. 32).

Jeremiah's promise is that God will, sometime in the future ("the days are coming"), make with his people a covenant which is different from the one made at Sinai ("not like the covenant which I made with their fathers"). The reason for the promise of a new covenant is that the old one has not been kept, on the human side. Now, one of the crucial questions which faces us is whether this means that on God's side the Sinai covenant has now been abrogated. Recent scholarship has tended to find indications that this is the understanding held by the canonical prophets and that this accounts for their threats that the possession of the land and all else which the Sinai covenant promised has been revoked.[20] This is certainly the type of disaster predicted by Jeremiah elsewhere in his book. But it is a terrible judgment to make, for it means that in the interim between the abrogation of the Sinai covenant and the giving of the new covenant Israel stands outside that special relationship with God which had once prevailed.

Jeremiah's ministry bridged the period when the threats of the pre-exilic prophets came true, the time of the fall of Jerusalem, destruction of the temple, and exile of the upper classes of Judah, and so it is that we find in his book the move from announcement of judgment—predicting and explaining the fall of Jerusalem—to announcement of promise—assuring those who had lost everything that with God there was still a future.[21] Chapters 30–31 contain a lengthy series of such promises, not all of which are ascribed to Jeremiah himself by every scholar. But for homiletical purposes authorship is not of crucial importance here, since some prophet, at some time, obviously did promise all these things. This broader context is important to us, since we need to see how the promise of a new convenant is associated with those other promises.

The passage is addressed to both Israel and Judah and asserts that God intends to overcome all the disasters which have befallen them because of their rebelliousness. They will be restored to their land (30:3, 10; 31:7–11; 16–17), their oppressors will be punished (30:11, 16, 20), they will no longer be in servitude (30:8), their city will be rebuilt (30:18), their numbers will be multiplied (30:19–20), they will have their own king (30:21), their land will become fertile again (31:12) and they will rejoice (30:19; 31:4, 7, 13) in the God who will once again pronounce over them the covenant formula: "you shall be my people, and I will be your God" (30:22; 31:1). But more than that is needed. God must not only overcome the disaster but must overcome the reasons for it if the future is to be any different from the past, and so the prophet promises forgiveness for sin (31:34) and the establishment of a covenant which they will be able to keep (31:33–34). If, however, we ask what will be *new* about the new covenant we discover that nothing is said about a difference in content, i.e. no criticism is made of the Sinai covenant itself, for what needs to be changed is not the content of the covenant but the nature of its recipients. The new gift from God is the "internalizing" of the covenant. As Jeremiah puts it: "I will put my law within them, and I will write it upon their hearts." Ezekiel also spoke in similar terms, although he did not use the word "covenant" in the immediate context, when he promised: "A new heart I will give you, and a new spirit I will put within you; and I will take out of your flesh the heart of stone and give you a heart of flesh. And I will put my spirit within you, and cause you to walk in my statutes and be careful to observe my ordinances" (36:26–27). There was, then, nothing wrong with the Sinai covenant but there was something wrong with one of the covenant partners, so that to make the relationship right an anthropological change is called for, and this God promises to do—one day. In Jeremiah it is still just a promise, not a reality. Israel and Judah, it seems, still exist in that interim period.

Now the question of fulfillment becomes a crucial one. Christians believe that Jeremiah's prophecy was fulfilled at the Last Supper, for when Jesus said, "This cup is the new covenant in my blood," there is no other Old Testament passage to which he could have been referring, and Hebrews quotes this passage twice (8:8–12; 10:16–17) in comparing the work of Christ with the Sinai covenant. The Last Supper is thus to be understood as a covenant meal, and from this passage the whole New Testament got its name: "The New Covenant of our Lord and Savior Jesus Christ" (see the title page of the KJV or RSV).

But what of all the other promises in chapters 30–31? Did they also come true? Do we care about them? If we refuse to make that grand leap from the exile to Christ which Christians have so often done, and instead take seriously all the intervening years of God's working with his people, then the rest of the passage will concern us also, and we shall be led to some important insights about the New Covenant and about promise and fulfillment in general.

It can honestly be said that *parts* of this prophecy were fulfilled in the post-exilic period. Some of the exiles returned to Judah, Jerusalem was rebuilt, the worship of Yahweh was re-established in a new temple, and in the second and first centuries B.C. they even had their own king, although he was not of the house of David. But parts of it have not been fulfilled to this day. The exiles from the Northern Kingdom have never made a triumphal return, and the rejoicing which is described here has had a short life-span for any who have made Palestine their home. Because of the unfulfilled parts of this and all similar passages in the Old Testament there has been a tendency among Christians to think of them as having had *no* fulfillment at all among the Jews; it has been an all or nothing approach. But how does that apply to the New Covenant promise and our belief that it became effective with the coming of Christ? Jeremiah says, "And no longer shall each man teach his neighbor and each his brother, saying, 'Know the LORD,' for they shall all know me, from the least of them to the greatest." Has that come true, and if it has why am I writing a book about preaching? Why do we still seem to find it necessary to teach and preach and exhort and admonish? As a matter of fact, it is not yet true that "they shall all know me, from the least of them to the greatest." Have we then misunderstood the meaning of the Last Supper in saying that it represented the establishment of the New Covenant?

Our answer has to do with promise and fulfillment in general in the Scriptures, for we may see that the New Covenant is in this respect just like all the other promises of God. The covenant with Abraham was fulfilled; he was given an heir, out of whom came a great people who were given a land. And yet over and over again the existence of that people was jeopardized and indeed the land itself was lost to them. The promise was fulfilled, but not finally and completely. Hope for the future was still necessary. The Sinai covenant was fulfilled. Yahweh became the God of Israel and they became his people; a nation was constituted on the basis of redemption from slavery with redemption from idolatry as its watchword. And something new came into the world: a worship of one God alone and the refusal to identify him with anything in the created world. Yet to this day idolatry and polytheism still exist in this world and we await the culmination of God's purpose to redeem all his children. The covenant with David was also fulfilled for a time, but for all the centuries since 587 B.C. it has remained only an object of hope.

So too with the New Covenant. God's promise of redemption was extended to the Gentiles through the work of Jesus Christ, and thus the Sinai covenant's message found a far broader constituency than ever before. We believe Jesus Christ has redeemed us from slavery to fulfill the promise of that covenant for us. And we believe that something has happened to us to make new people of us, something which is the fulfillment of Jer. 31:33 (author's translation): "I will put my law within them and write it on their hearts." Yet we still sin, and we still need those exhortations which Jer. 31:34 says will no longer be necessary under the New Covenant. What do we say to this? We answer that until the eschaton comes God's work in all of these things is not yet finished, that all of his promises remain partly unfulfilled. But he does not leave us without an earnest on every one of his promises. God has fulfilled them in the past, he continues to fulfill them, and he will one day fulfill them. We have been made new creatures in Jesus Christ, but we are not yet perfect. Something really has happened to us because of our faith in him which we can legitimately call the fulfillment of Jeremiah's promise of the New Covenant, but God is still at work in us and for us, and the eschaton has not yet come.

So we may also dare to agree with those Jews who say that the promise of the New Covenant was already fulfilled early in the post-exilic period, in the internalization of the law of God which really did take place in Judaism at that time.[22] We need not rule out Judaism as a recipient of that "new heart and new spirit," as Ezekiel called it, in order to claim that promise for ourselves. The new things that came out of the exile experience included God's partial fulfillment of all his promises. And thus the full tradition of promise and fulfillment in the Bible, making no leaps from Old to New Testament, but including the whole history, involving all of that Judaism which is our heritage, eliminates some of the old problems about whether certain prophecies have been fulfilled or not. The truth is that God is *always* fulfilling his promises.

A Sermon on Isaiah 7:1–17

This passage has been discussed many times and at great length and there is an extensive scholarly literature on it. I do not propose to delve into the formidable exegetical problems of the text, which would take us far beyond the scope of this book, but will only indicate how certain exegetical conclusions which I have drawn, plus my emphasis on tradition history, have led to the preaching of a certain kind of sermon.

The genre is a prophetic narrative, with strong emphasis in this case on the words of the prophet. Since my sermon is based on vs. 14 I shall comment only on the exegetical issues which concern that verse, thus eliminating the lengthy discussions of other parts of the passage which could ensue. In this case, one verse presents us with problems enough.[23]

a)   The *sign* which the Lord will give Ahaz, must it be miraculous to be a sign?[24] (A study of word usage suggests a negative answer.) If Isaiah was consciously predicting the birth of Jesus many years hence, how could that be called a sign to Ahaz? He would see nothing in his own lifetime.

b)   "Behold, *the virgin*"; or is it "the young woman"?[25] Word studies of the Hebrew *'almah* do not suggest that the term conveys any certain information about the woman's virginity. It denotes a young woman of marriageable age, but would not be used of her after she was married. The traditional English rendering "virgin" comes from the Septuagint's used of *parthenos* here, and it is the Septuagint which Matthew quoted in 1:23. Why is the definite article used with the word? Does it indicate that she was present so that Isaiah could point to her: "Behold, the young woman . . .? Or is he seeing *the* Virgin in a vision?

c)   There is no verb in this part of the sentence, but only a predicate adjective, so our first impulse would be to translate it, "Behold, the young woman is pregnant." There is nothing to indicate it should be future tense. Furthermore, the prophet continues to keep us guessing about the time reference by using a participial form for the next verb: "to give birth." "Behold, the young woman is pregnant and bears (or is bearing) a son," then finally a finite verb form: "and you (addressed to the woman) will call his name Immanuel." Isaiah could be witnessing the birth of Jesus in a vision, or could be speaking of an event to occur very soon in his own time.

d)   How important is the name, Immanuel, which means "God is with us"? Isaiah gave his sons symbolic names: Shear-yashub was with him that day, and Maher-shalal-hash-baz appears in chapter 8. So when he mentions the child's name he may have intended that to be taken seriously, and perhaps it is the sign. Indeed, some scholars think the young woman was Isaiah's wife and Immanuel his own son.[26]

e)   Finally, we must return to the question of the sign: What is it? Is it virgin birth—a miracle? Is it the symbolic name of the child? Or is it (as seems most likely) the fact promised in the next two verses, the truth of Isaiah's warning that help against Pekah and Rezin should not be sought will be verified within the time it takes for a child to grow old enough to know the difference between good and evil?

These are the major exegetical issues raised by this single verse. I have tended to indicate already the direction my exegesis has taken me in the way I have formulated the questions. Probably the discussion of them will never end, but in the meantime, the history of tradition sheds some helpful light on how best to preach the text. There are three important strands of pre-history to be noted:

a)   The setting takes us back to the old tradition of the holy war. Judah is beset by enemies more powerful than she, and a prophet appears to announce (using the familiar two-part form, as in 1 Kings 20:28) that God has the victory in his hands (7:5–9). But Ahaz refuses to believe the message, so Isaiah offers a sign that it is true. Now, a confirmatory sign may appear either before or after the fact, but since in this case it seems impossible to think the sign occurred just then, he must have been referring to something in the future.

b)   The sign takes the form of a conception and birth announcement, a standard genre which occurs in numerous other places in the Old Testament. Note especially the announcements to Hagar (Gen. 16:11) and to Samson's mother (Judg. 13:3–5), and compare also other birth announcements such as that of Samuel (1 Sam. 1:20).

c)   The name "God is with us" repeats an old promise, to be found many times in the Bible. I shall not cite them here, since the sermon refers to many of them.

This is the pre-history of our text, the traditional materials which came together here to say something unique to that situation. And now we look for its subsequent history, to see what it continued to mean to later generations. Let us ask some important questions of the tradition:

a)   Is this text taken as a prediction of a miraculous event, the birth of a child to a virgin? The answer is that nowhere in the literature between Isaiah and Matthew (over 700 years) is such an idea mentioned. It did not mean that to the Jews who preserved it.[27]

b)   Was this text taken as a prediction of the birth of the Messiah? The answer again is that in the messianic literature which precedes the New Testament, Isa. 7:14 is not one of the Old Testament passages which is used. Neither is "Immanuel" ever referred to as a messianic title.

It seems that our conclusion must be that Matthew used Isa. 7:14 in a new way, that we have here a certain discontinuity in tradition. But that is not so bad as it may seem, for it has been suggested that the belief that Jesus was born of a virgin came about in this way: "Isaiah predicted the Messiah would be born of a virgin; we believe that Jesus is the Messiah; therefore he must have been born of a virgin." But there is no evidence that the first part of this syllogism is true. From what we know it is more logical to say that from some source or other Matthew obtained the information that Jesus was born of a virgin, he then happened upon *parthenos* in the Septuagint and, given his delight in quoting Old Testament texts as prophecies wherever possible, he concluded this must be another reference to the Christ.

So, do we preach the Virgin Birth from Isa. 7:14? Tradition, again, should guide us. Certainly the doctrine eventually took on great importance in the Church, and that might lead us to a positive answer, but it was not a prominent idea at first. In the New Testament it appears only in Matthew and Luke, so it obviously was not considered one of the most important parts of the faith. We must ask, is there anything in our text which is more central to the mainstream of belief, and the positive answer which comes also shows us that in Matthew's new use of it there was also a strong element of continuity with the past. The central feature is the promise, "God is with us": further explanation of that appears in the sermon. It was preached on Dec. 21, 1975 in the Middlesex United Presbyterian Church, near Butler, Pa.

God Is With Us

Isaiah 7: 1–17
Matthew 1: 18–25

I'd like to tell you about the quietest Christmas I ever spent. Then I'll explain why I'm telling you this. It was 1951, my first year out of college. I was working in Richland, Washington, at one of the Atomic Energy Commission plants run by the General Electric Company. The plant and the town we lived in had been built by the army during the war and in 1951 the only housing available for single employees was in dormitories, so I lived in one room on the second floor in a dorm across the street from the plant where I worked. As Christmas approached some of my friends planned a trip into the mountains and asked if I would like to go along, but for some reason which I don't remember I decided not to. Perhaps it was because I was in the choir at church and they were giving a concert on Christmas eve. At any rate I went to that midnight service and to refreshments for the choir afterwards, then back to my room to open the presents my folks had sent from Iowa. Next morning I got up late and walked down to a nearby restaurant for dinner, ate supper at the same place, and spent the rest of the day in my room. There was no one around the dorm, as most people who had anywhere at all to go had cleared out. By evening I realized that I had gone through an entire Christmas day without seeing one person that I knew.

But it was not a bad Christmas. I remember doing two things: writing a letter home, and spending a lot of time thinking about what Christmas really meant to me. I didn't know any theology then and not very much about the Bible, but I did know that a Christian is never really alone, anywhere or anytime, and I was fully convinced that day that a Christian especially cannot feel alone on Christmas day.

Now, why tell you this story? To make you feel sorry for me? Not at all, for there was nothing to be sorry for. I tell it as a small illustration of what Matthew says is the meaning of Christmas: that with the coming of Jesus, God was with us, in human flesh. I consider this sentence to be the Bible's best promise: God is with us. It is a promise which God has repeated consistently throughout the history of his dealings with humanity.

Moses was tending his father-in-law's sheep in the wilderness of Midian when he saw a burning bush and turned aside to investigate. A voice stopped him, and from the bush God spoke to him, appointing him to be the leader who would bring the people of Israel out of slavery in Egypt. Moses was appalled. He was a fugitive from Egypt, for he had killed a man there. To go back would be to take his life into his hands. He had made one effort to help his people long ago and had failed miserably. He was a stammerer and could not face a crowd of people and talk coherently. He answered in protest, "Who am I that I should go to Pharaoh and bring the sons of Israel out of Egypt?" God said, "But I will be with you."

Gideon was quietly trying to thresh out some wheat down in a wine press on his father's farm. It had to be done in secret, for the country was overrun with bands of nomads who were making sudden, surprise raids, stealing everything of value they could lay their hands on. A messenger appeared to him as he worked, with a word from God: "Go and deliver Israel from the hand of Midian. I am sending you." Gideon couldn't believe it. "How can I deliver Israel?" he answered. "My clan is the weakest in our tribe, and I am the young-est in my family." God said, "But I will be with you."

Jeremiah was a young teenager, living in the village of Anathoth, a few miles north of Jerusalem. And one day he heard a voice: "Before I formed you in the womb I knew you, and before you were born I consecrated you. I ap-pointed you a prophet to the nations." Jeremiah's heart sank. Prophets were men of power who uttered harsh words against the sins of their people and who took abuse and ostracism because of it. He was timid, kind-hearted, and just wanted to be left alone. He answered, "Ah, Lord God, behold I do not know how to speak, for I am only a youth." God said, "Do not say, I am only a youth, for to all to whom I send you you shall go, and whatever I command you you shall speak. Be not afraid of them for I am with you to deliver you."

Jerusalem was facing a war. A coalition made up of the Northern Kingdom of Israel and the kingdom of Syria was about to attack Judah. The king, Ahaz, was preparing to withstand a seige and was out inspecting the water supply of the city when Isaiah met him. "Do not be afraid of those northern kings," Isaiah said, "for the danger is not as serious as you think. Above all do not do anything rash," for he knew Ahaz was thinking of sending to ask Assyria for help (like the mouse asking the fox to save him from the cat). But Ahaz had made up his mind and was not about to have it changed by any prophet, not even by a sign from heaven itself.

Isaiah had his commission from God, a message to get across somehow, and he responded that Ahaz would receive a sign, whether he wanted one or not: "A young woman shall conceive and bear a son and you shall call his name God-Is-With-Us . . . For before the child knows how to refuse the evil and choose the good the land before whose two kings you are in dread will be deserted." There is a young, pregnant woman among us. Her child will be given a symbolic name which is God's own message to you, Ahaz: Immanuel—God is with us. And before that child is old enough to know the difference between good and evil, this danger which has you in such a panic will have passed.

The promise came true. Ahaz didn't believe it and sold his freedom to Assyria, but there was no need for that. Syria and the Northern Kingdom of Israel were rebels against Assyria already and would have been smashed anyway. And that is what happened. Within seven or eight years they were no threat to anyone any more.

But God's promise is never exhausted. It comes true, and yet still remains a new promise for the future. Long after Isaiah's day a child was born in a mysterious way in Bethlehem of Judea, only a few miles south of the spot where Isaiah had once spoken. That child became the teacher Jesus of Nazareth, who was crucified and who rose from the dead, whose followers then came to believe that he was the Son of God, their Savior. As they sought to learn and remember all they could about his earthly ministry, they came across a family secret, that his mother had still been a virgin when he was conceived. It was one of those things Mary had kept and pondered in her heart, but now it seemed to take on some meaning for Jesus' followers. Those who could read Greek found in the Greek translation of the Book of Isaiah not "a young woman shall conceive" as in the Hebrew, but "a virgin shall conceive," and they said, "This is a prophecy of the birth of Jesus!" So Matthew quoted it in his Gospel. But he did not stop there. He went on to quote the name of the child born in Isaiah's time, even though that name was not given to the Savior, who was called Jesus. He quotes, "and his name shall be called Emmanuel," and then translates it for his Greek readers: "which means God with us." Why did he do this? Surely because in Jesus God's old promise had come true again. It had come true in a way far surpassing all the fulfillments of the past. God was with Moses, with Gideon, with Jeremiah, giving them the words to speak, the power to lead, the courage to face opposition. But when Jesus came God was with us in human flesh, one of us, to share this life we lead and to leave us without any doubt that the promise is true.

The promise continues. Jesus said, "Lo, I am with you always, to the end of the age," and when God restores all things at the end of time, the Book of Revelation says, "and God himself will be with them." But we need not wait. It is true now.

It was true for me that Christmas day long ago. It was true for me three years later when I felt as unqualified as Jeremiah when a call to the ministry came, and I went into it with one assurance, that God would be with me. It was true for me as a seminary student when I had to make my first sick call, on a man dying of leukemia. I had no experience in calling, no personal knowledge of sickness, and I didn't know what I would do. But constant prayer to the Lord Jesus, who was there with us, got me through it. It was true when my wife lay in agony in a hospital room, her body smashed in a car accident so that no drugs would help, yet our prayer to the suffering Jesus, who was there with us, gave her rest.

It's what makes the good times great and the bad times bearable. It's what makes us sing, for that same promise occurs over and over again in the Scriptures. Once again God said to Israel:

> Fear not, for I am with you,
>   be not dismayed, for I am your God:
> I will strengthen you, I will help you,
>   I will uphold you with my victorious right hand. (Isa. 41:10)

And we still sing it, for one of our greatest hymns was written, back in the eighteenth century, on that text:

> Fear not, I am with thee, O be not dismayed,
> For I am thy God, I will still give thee aid;
> I'll strengthen thee, help thee, and cause thee to stand,
> Upheld by my righteous, omnipotent hand.
> ("How Firm a Foundation")

Epilogue

Form criticism has revealed both the variety of literary types in the Old Testament and the possibilities of using the Scriptures for homiletical purposes in new and different ways, corresponding to these various forms. Six of the major types have been discussed at some length; what remains now is to comment briefly on some genres which have been omitted, then to conclude by suggesting some questions which may help the preacher who now wishes to begin trying to apply the methods which have been developed in the preceding chapters.

A. 1. The *songs* of the Old Testament have been omitted from any serious discussion in this book. This includes, most obviously, the books of Psalms, Lamentations, and the Song of Songs, plus scattered chapters such as Exodus 15, Deuteronomy 32, Judges 5, and 1 Samuel 2. A few negative remarks will be offered here, in justification of the omission of so important a book as the Psalter, but some positive suggestions will also be added. Although form criticism has proved to be helpful in a variety of ways in preaching from different parts of the Old Testament, when we turn to the Psalter it produces somewhat peculiar and surprising results. Modern studies have emphasized that most of the psalms were used in worship; they are human language addressed to God. But if we follow our principle of being as faithful as possible to the character of the original form, concerning its choice of the appropriate language to preform a certain function in a given life-situation, where will that lead us? Can we produce a sermon which performs the same function as a biblical hymn or lament? Not impossible, perhaps, but not easy and not the sort of thing a sermon usually tries to do. Indeed, we already have, in the service surrounding the sermon, places for that sort of thing, do we not? And the psalms have had, throughout the history of the church, a temendous influence on the prayers and hymnody used in our worship.[1] They have maintained their place in their original life-setting.

It must be admitted, however, that many a sermon has been preached from the Psalter. David was considered to be a prophet (Acts 2:30) and the psalms were taken to be oracles direct from God, to be interpreted the same as every other part of Scripture. This attitude appears as early as the New Testament itself, but nonetheless it must be questioned on form critical principles which say that language is not all alike and that each text should be interpreted in accordance with the way the authors of Scripture chose their language and shaped it in order to fulfill a certain function. That suggests that the integrity of the psalmists' words addressed to God in praise or lamentation ought to be preserved and that ordinarily they ought not to be considered as texts to be expounded to a congregation.² We ought to use them, certainly, but in their appropriate place; we ought to pray them and sing them rather than preach them.

However, not all of the psalms are addressed exclusively to God, and when they contain testimony addressed to fellow worshipers such language ought to be fully appropriate material for preaching, and the same could be said for some of the other biblical songs. Indeed, some of the psalms are didactic in purpose and are addressed to human beings throughout (e.g. Pss. 1, 37, 49), and form criticism would suggest that a sermon is a fully appropriate way to use these poems in worship. As for the other major psalm types: *hymns* contain recitals of God's saving acts in history (e.g. Pss. 103, 135) and descriptions of his work as creator and sustainer of the world (e.g. Pss. 8, 29), *thanksgivings* sometimes recount God's acts of deliverance at length (e.g. Ps. 107), while the psalms of *trust* or *confidence* contain humanity's finest expressions of certainty in God's help (Pss. 4, 11, 16, 23, 27:1–6, 62, 131).³ There are, then, subjects such as praise for the God of creation, expressions of confidence in the God who delivers us, and thanksgiving for what God has done for us, which can appropriately be preached from the Psalter. The lyrical form of the psalms remains a challenge for us, however; unless preachers have special lyrical gifts of their own, how can a sermon avoid sounding very pedestrian and dull in comparison with its text? If form criticism does nothing else for preachers, in its concern for the appropriate use of language, it may at least inspire them to be challenged by the beauty, pathos, and power of the Psalter and all the rest of Hebrew poetry, to find new ways of bringing some of that into the words of their sermons.

2.   Many of the same comments could be made about the *prayers* of the Old Testament. Obviously they are addressed to God and have their counterparts in our own worship; however, like some of our own prayers they may also contain a good deal of material intended to remind the congregation of who it is and what it believes. So, prayers such as those in Nehemiah 9 and Daniel 9 may contain material which it is appropriate to preach.

3.   *Genealogies* and *itineraries, instructions* and *descriptions* (such as how to build the tabernacle and what the temple looked like) have been omitted simply because, despite their value for other purposes, it is seldom that they will be found helpful for preaching. I admit that I have preached from the genealogy of

Jesus in Matthew 1:1–17, which contains some interesting material for homiletical purposes (even though it makes for a rather dull Scripture reading), but I
haven't found anything of this type in the Old Testament which is quite as
useful.

4. The *oracles against the nations* make up a large portion of the words of
the prophets (e.g. Isa. 13–23, Jer. 46–51, Ezek. 25–32) but they have been
largely neglected in biblical theology and in preaching. There is more of value
in this material than appears at first, but I did not think that space should be devoted to them in this setting.[4]

5. The *apocalyptic visions* in Daniel 7–12 are a unique type of material for
the Old Testament; a type which is regularly misused in certain Christian cir-
cles, as they combine it with the apocalyptic parts of the New Testament. It has
been omitted here because the problems created by those misinterpretations
would require a treatment all out of proportion to the amount of material contained in those six Old Testament chapters.

Other genres could be listed here, but this selection should suffice to remind
the reader of the variety to be found in the Old Testament beyond the types dealt
with in this book.

B. Now for a final word about the six major types of Old Testament literature. How should one begin to work on each of them in order to seek out a sermon which is faithful to Scripture and relevant to one's congregation? Form
criticism suggests that different questions ought to be asked of each type, and in
conclusion it might be helpful to remind you of some of those questions:

History and *Prophecy* should in several respects be approached in the same
way. Among the questions to be asked are: What did God do then that affects
who I am now? How did God's people react to their crises in ways that may
help us meet our crises faithfully?

Sagas suggest questions such as these: What recurring issue of faith and life
is presented here in dramatic form? How does this same issue repeat itself in my
life?

Stories are told to entertain while making a point and so, much the way the
parables of the New Testament are preached, one may ask what point or points
the author wants to make and then how we can best reinforce that point by
means of a sermon which takes advantage of the natural strengths of the story
form.

The *Laws* of the Old Testament challenge us not to stumble over the theological problems they pose for Christians so as to be able to use them for guidance in faithful living. We ask of them: In what direction is the divine ethical
instruction pointing? Where does the divine direction strike the matrix in which
we live; i.e. Where are we now, with reference to the biblical settings of law
and ethical instruction and how fully can we now obey the spirit of the law?

Wisdom also asks about faithful living. Of the fully orthodox materials we inquire: How can this moralizing, rationalistic advice keep company with the radical words of the gospel, with its message of our total depravity and of salvation by grace alone? Why are the Old Testament proverbs still needed? Of the skeptical wisdom writers we ask: How can the Christian use these deep probings of life's most critical questions without either giving cheap answers or leaving people with no answer?

Preaching is an art, and as with any art some take to it naturally and have it as a gift, some learn to be proficient at it by means of good teaching, hard work and years of experience, while others just never quite catch on. My aim in this book has been to try to explain how modern scholarship may aid the Old Testament itself to teach us to be better preachers. Form criticism is just one way of looking and listening, and the more we do of that the more likely it is that we will learn something from the Bible. But since form criticism looks and listens in order to understand and appreciate the selection of appropriate *language*, and since we who preach are attempting to create something new and effective with language, it is an approach to the Scriptures which can be especially useful in aiding them to teach us how to speak. As for the task of tracing the history of traditions in order to learn how we are connected with our past, its greatest drawback also holds its greatest potential for enriching our preaching. The drawback is that it can be used only with great difficulty by novices; to use it effectively one needs to know the contents of the Bible very thoroughly, so that the major occurrences of a given theme can be traced immediately in one's head. But surely it is still the Christian minister's business to know the Bible that well, so that we are not asking the impossible. And let it be said with certainty, the more thoroughly and extensively the relevant biblical material is recognized and used in the preparation of sermons, the richer, the more varied, the more interesting and the more convincing our preaching will be.

Abbreviations

AB	*The Anchor Bible*
AJSL	*American Journal of Semitic Languages*
BET	*Beiträge zur Biblischen Exegese und Theologie*
BKAT	*Biblischer Kommentar, Altes Testament*
BZAW	*Beiheft, Zeitschrift für die alttestamentliche Wissenschaft*
CBQ	*Catholic Biblical Quarterly*
CBQMS	*Catholic Biblical Quarterly Monograph Series*
HKAT	*Handkommentar Zum Alten Testament*
HUCA	*Hebrew Union College Annual*
IB	*The Interpreter's Bible*
ICC	*International Critical Commentary*
IDB	*The Interpreter's Dictionary of the Bible*
JBL	*Journal of Biblical Literature*
JQR	*Jewish Quarterly Review*
JSS	*Journal of Semitic Studies*
OTL	*The Old Testament Library*
PTMS	*Pittsburgh Theological Monograph Series*
SBT	*Studies in Biblical Theology*
SJT	*Scottish Journal of Theology*
SNTS	*Supplement, New Testament Studies*
TDOT	*Theological Dictionary of the Old Testament*
VT	*Vetus Testamentum*
VTS	*Supplement, Vetus Testamentum*
ZAW	*Zeitschrift für die alttestamentliche Wissenschaft*

Notes

Introduction

1. E. Achtemeier, *The Old Testament and the Proclamation of the Gospel* (Westminster, 1973), pp. 13–44; J. Bright, *The Authority of the Old Testament* (Abingdon, 1967), pp. 15–109; F. R. McCurley, Jr., *Proclaiming the Promise: Christian Preaching from the Old Testament* (Fortress, 1974), pp. 3–11.

2. For a good introduction to early Christian use of the Old Testament, see R. P. C. Hanson, "Biblical Exegesis in the Early Church" in *Cambridge History of the Bible*, ed. P. R. Ackroyd & C. F. Evans (Cambridge, 1970), Vol. I, chap. 13, pp. 412–454.

3. E. Best, in *From Text to Sermon: Responsible Use of the New Testament in Preaching* (John Knox, 1978) has devoted an entire chapter (chap. 2) to the cultural differences between us and the New Testament and in the chapter which follows it he discusses at length nine ways in which the gulf is usually bridged. A treatment of the *sociological* differences between our times and the biblical periods, with a homiletical concern, appears in R. L. Rohrbaugh, *The Biblical Interpreter: An Agrarian Bible in an Industrial Age* (Fortress, 1978).

4. So I do not share the necessity discussed by Achtemeier, *The Old Testament and the Proclamation of the Gospel*, pp. 142–144, of "Pairing an Old Testament Text with a New."

5. J. Smart describes this problem in terms of a hiatus between the biblical and practical departments in our seminaries in *The Strange Silence of the Bible in the Church: A Study in Hermeneutics* (Westminster, 1970), pp. 28–38. M. Noth speaks of the "fatal chasm" between historico-critical exegesis and the concern for contemporary proclamation, in "The 'Re-presentation' of the O.T. in Proclamation" in *Essays on Old Testament Hermeneutics*, ed. J. L. Mays (John Knox, 1963), p. 77.

6. Note G. Ebling's article: "Church History is the History of the Exposition of Scripture" in his *The Word of God and Tradition: Historical Studies Interpreting the Divisions of Christianity*, tr. S. H. Hooke (Fortress, 1968), pp. 11–31. On p. 29f.

he writes, "Church history is that which lies between us and the revelation of God in Jesus Christ. It separates and unites, obscures and illuminates, accuses and enriches. Through it alone has the witness to Jesus Christ come down to us. To that extent it belongs to the event of revelation." Compare also the comments of B. S. Childs, *Biblical Theology in Crisis* (Westminster, 1970), chap. 8, "Recovering an Exegetical Tradition."

7. W. E. Rast, *Tradition History and the Old Testament* (Fortress, 1972), offers a useful, brief introduction to the subject.

8. E.g. H. W. Hertzberg, "Die Nachgeschichte alttestamentlicher Texte innerhalb des Alten Testaments" in his *Beiträge des Alten Testaments* (Vandenhoeck & Ruprecht, 1962), pp. 69–80. Cf. Rast, *Tradition History*, pp. 72–77. Brief but important comments on this aspect of tradition history are offered by K. Koch in *The Growth of the Biblical Tradition* (Scribners, 1969), pp. 100–106.

9. "For the Bible is a dialogue: God and man are the partners in a conversation which is meant to be overheard." M. Barth, *Conversation With the Bible* (Holt, Rinehart & Winston, 1964), p. 4, and see the entire Introduction, pp. 3–10.

10. Smart has suggested a similar method in *Strange Silence of the Bible*, pp. 152–155. See also D. Ritschl, "A Plea for the Maxim: 'Scripture *and* Tradition,' " *Interpretation* 25 (1971), 113–128. Childs' "exegesis within the context of the canon," as demonstrated in his examples in *Biblical Theology in Crisis*, pp. 149–219, is similar to what I am proposing, but tends to devote less attention to the whole tradition within the Old Testament and to move rather quickly to the New Testament. J. A. Sanders also speaks of "inner biblical hermeneutics" in *God Has a Story Too: Sermons in Context* (Fortress, 1979), p. 10f.

11. R. S. Paul *The Church in Search of Its Self* (Eerdmans, 1972), p. 50.

12. Cf. D. M. Beegle, *Scripture, Tradition, and Infallibility* (Eerdmans, 1973), pp. 91–123.

13. E. Best, in *From Text to Sermon*, pp. 14–17, uses a different set of metaphors to say something similar. Speaking specifically of the New Testament he alludes to the tradition as a fluid and calls each document a "freezing" or a precipitation of crystals. When he comes to the question of what that *tradition* is that is frozen at various points (pp. 25–29), he concludes that we cannot capture it apart from those individual crystalization, much as I said the "theme" is God's alone.

14. G. Ebeling, *Word of God and Tradition*, p. 31.

15. G. M. Tucker, *Form Criticism of the Old Testament* (Fortress, 1971); J. H. Hayes, ed., *Old Testament Form Criticism* (San Antonio: Trinity University Press, 1974); Koch, *Growth of the Biblical Tradition*. A popularly written, but accurate treatment of the subject appears in G. Lohfink, *The Bible: Now I Get It! A Form-Criticism Handbook* (Doubleday, 1979).

16. A helpful application of this truth to the interpretation of the New Testament may be found in A. N. Wilder, *The Language of the Gospel: Early Christian Rhetoric* (Harper & Row, 1964).

17. Some obvious omissions are the apocalyptic parts of Daniel (chaps. 7–12) and lyric poetry such as the Song of Songs, but these involve only a few chapters of the Old Testament. Perhaps in the future more thorough treatments of the way to preach the various genres of Scripture may be forthcoming.

Chapter I

1. E.g. G. von Rad, *Old Testament Theology*, tr. D. G. M. Stalker (Harper & Row, 1962), Vol. I, pp. 334–347; and "The Deuteronomistic Theology of History in I & II Kings" in his *The Problem of the Hexateuch and Other Essays*, tr. E. W. T. Dicken (McGraw-Hill, 1966), pp. 205–221; W. Brueggemann, "The Kerygma of the Deuteronomistic Historian," *Interpretation* 22 (1968), 387–402. Aimed at the preacher is the volume by W. E. Rast, *Joshua, Judges, Samuel, Kings* in the "Proclamation Commentaries" (Fortress, 1978).

2. Although it must be admitted that O. Eissfeldt does describe it in just that way in *The Old Testament: An Introduction*, tr. P. R. Ackroyd (Blackwell, 1965), p. 48.

3. Cf. this definition of "historiography proper": "literary compositions devoted to a specific period, which link the materials both internally and externally and form them into a unified whole by means of an imposed structure." G. Fohrer, *Introduction to the Old Testament*, tr. D. Green (Abingdon, 1968), p. 98.

4. Koch, *Growth of the Biblical Tradition*, pp. 132–148.

5. Cf. note 1 and H. W. Wolff, "Das Kerygma des deuteronomistischen Geschichtswerks," *ZAW* 73 (1961), 171–186.

6. E. Vermeule, "The Promise of Thera: A Bronze Age Pompeii," *Atlantic Monthly* (Dec. 1967), pp. 83–94.

7. L. S. Hay, "What Really Happened at the Sea of Reeds?" *JBL* 83 (1964), 397–403; but cf. D. Patrick, "Traditio-history of the Reed Sea Account," *VT* 26 (1976), 248f.

8. B. S. Childs, *The Book of Exodus: A Critical, Theological Commentary* (Westminster, 1973), p. 220.

9. Koch, *Growth of the Biblical Tradition*, seems to raise an unnecessary question when he takes up the important subject of "The Relevance of Transmission History for the Church" (pp. 100–108). He writes, "If the preacher or catechist wishes to translate a text with a long tradition into modern terms he is faced with the decision as to which stage of transmission must be considered the binding, and therefore the canonical one" (p. 101). But on the same page he answers himself, as I would answer, "Of course the ideal is to trace the entire transmission history of a tradition in a sermon or bible class, and thereby bring out the vitality of the text." Or better, one should *use* the entire tradition in preparation, but not necessarily inflict it all on the congregation.

10. G. A. F. Knight, *Theology as Narration: A Commentary on the Book of Exodus* (Eerdmans, 1976), p. 107.

11. Fohrer, *Introduction*, p. 163.

12. Childs, *Exodus*, p. 231f.

13. M. Buber, *Moses, The Revelation and the Covenant* (Harper & Row, 1958), p. 74.

14. Buber, *Moses*, p. 75.

Chapter II

1. H. Gunkel, *Genesis*, 3. Auflage (*HKAT* 1: Vandehoeck & Ruprecht, 1910). The introduction was translated into English as *The Legends of Genesis*, tr. W. H. Carruth (1901; repr. Schocken, 1964). Other scholars have agreed with Carruth that

the proper word to be used in English should be legend rather than saga, since the Nordic sagas were lengthy, written family histories, not short, oral forms such as appear in Genesis. Cf. P. Gibert, "Legende ou Saga" *VT* 24 (1974) 411–420. However, the alternative word "legend" appears to be an even worse choice because of the inability of form critics to find a suitably exact description of it. On the vagueness of "legend" as a form-critical term, see R. M. Hals, "Legend: A Case Study of Old Testament Form-Critical Terminology," *CBQ* 34 (1972), 166–176. Since the standard English texts on Old Testament form criticism in use today have chosen "saga," I have used it here as the lesser of two terminological evils.

2. Fohrer, *Introduction*, p. 86; S. Thompson, "Myths and Folktales" in *Myth: A Symposium*, ed. T. A. Sebeok (Indiana University Press, 1955, 1958), pp. 104–110.
3. Fohrer, *Introduction*, p. 90; cf. G. von Rad, *Genesis* rev. ed. (Westminster, 1973), p. 347f.
4. This chapter is identified as a short story rather than saga by E. F. Campbell, Jr., in his careful description of the Hebrew short story in *Ruth* (*AB*; Doubleday, 1975), pp. 10–18. As such it also lacks a close connection with the surrounding units.
5. H. W. Robinson, *Corporate Personality in Ancient Israel* (Fortress, 1964).
6. R. C. Culley, "An Approach to the Problem of Oral Tradition," *VT* 13 (1963), 113–125; B. O. Long, "Recent Field Studies in Oral Literature and Their Bearing on OT Criticism," *VT* 26 (1976), 187–198.
7. Koch, *Growth of the Biblical Tradition*, p. 156.
8. E.g. J. Bright, *A History of Israel*, 2nd ed. (Westminster, 1972), pp. 67–102.
9. Koch, *Growth of the Biblical Tradition*, p. 154.
10. J. G. Frazer, *Folk-Lore in the Old Testament*, abridged ed. (Macmillan, 1927), pp. 46–143.
11. C. Westermann, *Genesis* (*BKAT* 1; Neukirchener Verlag, 1972), p. 531.
12. J. A. Fitzmeyer, *The Genesis Apocryphon of Qumran Cave I*, 2nd rev. ed. (*Biblia et Orientalia* 18A; Pontifical Biblical Institute, 1971), p. 63.
13. Midrash Rabba, *Bereshith* XLI.2 (Soncino, 1939), p. 333f.
14. For the distinction between the Sinai covenant with its accompanying law and the covenant of unconditional promise given to Abraham see especially D. N. Freedman, "Divine Commitment and Human Obligation: The Covenant Theme," *Interpretation* 18 (1964), 419–431.

Chapter III

1. J. M. Myers, *The World of the Restoration* (Prentice-Hall, 1968), p. 92
2. On the Hebrew short story, see Campbell, *Ruth*, pp. 10–18. Campbell's list of examples of the genre is as follows: Gen. 24, 38, the Joseph story, Judg. 3:15–29; 4; and other parts of the same book, Ruth, the prose parts of Job, Judith, Esther, Susanna, and perhaps Tobit.
3. One of the most readily accessible of these is in the introduction to Campbell's commentary on Ruth, but see also E. M. Good, *Irony in the Old Testament* (Westminster, 1965); D. F. Rauber, "Literary Values in the Bible: The Book of Ruth," *JBL* 89 (1970), 27–37.

4. J. Magonet, *Form and Meaning: Studies in Literary Techniques in the Book of Jonah* (*BET* 2; 1976), p. 87f.

5. The understanding of Christians as a "cognitive minority" in contemporary culture is developed by P. Berger in *A Rumor of Angels* (Doubleday, 1969), Chap. I.

6. Two quite different approaches to Christian life in such a society may be found in W. Stringfellow, *An Ethic for Christians and Other Aliens in a Strange Land* (Word, 1973) and K. Rahner, "The Teaching of Vatican II on the Church and the Future Reality of Christian Life" in *The Christian of the Future* (Herder & Herder, 1967), pp. 77–101.

7. 1 Macc. 1; 2 Macc. 5–7; described in more detail in D. Gowan, *Bridge Between the Testaments: A Reappraisal of Judaism from the Exile to the Birth of Christianity* (*PTMS* 14; Pickwick, 1976), pp. 89–100; W. Foerster, *From the Exile to Christ* (Fortress, 1964), pp. 31–40; E. Lohse, *The New Testament Environment* (Abingdon, 1976), pp. 23–30.

8. Cf. the comments on this verse by N. Porteous, *Daniel, A Commentary* (*OTL*, Westminster, 1965), pp. 55–62.

9. F. C. Conybeare, J. R. Harris and A. S. Lewis, *The Story of Ahikar* (Cambridge, 1913).

10. Cf. G. von Rad, "The Joseph Narrative and Ancient Wisdom" in *The Problem of the Hexateuch*, pp. 292–300.

11. Cf. W. Brueggemann's application of this type of Old Testament wisdom to his evaluation of modern ministry in *In Man We Trust: The Neglected Side of Biblical Faith* (John Knox, 1972), chap. 6.

12. G. von Rad. *Old Testament Theology*, Vol. 2, p. 369f.

13. G. W. Coats, *From Canaan to Egypt: Structural and Theological Context for the Joseph Story* (*CBQMS* 4; 1976), pp. 82–86.

14. G. von Rad, *Genesis*, pp. 381–400.

15. A useful survey of the ongoing tradition was made by A. W. Argyle, "Joseph the Patriarch in Patristic Teaching," *Expository Times* 67 (1955/56), 199–201.

16. C. Moore, *Esther* (*AB*; Doubleday, 1971), pp. xxi–xxx.

17. E. Bickerman, *Four Strange Books of the Bible: Jonah, Daniel, Koheleth, Esther* (Schocken, 1968), pp. 171–240.

18. A helpful setting of the Greek and Hebrew parts of Esther, using different type faces, may be found in the Apocrypha of the *Common Bible, Revised Standard Version* (1973).

19. Bickerman, *Four Strange Books*, p. 211f.

20. Bickerman, *Four Strange Books*, p. 212f.

21. W. L. Humphreys, "A Life-style for Diaspora: A Study of the Tales of Esther and Daniel," *JBL* 92 (1973), 211–223.

22. For a helpful description of how the feast of Purim is celebrated, see H. Schauss, *The Jewish Festivals, History and Observances* (Schocken, 1974), chapters 25–28.

23. G. A. F. Knight comments on "Israel" in this respect in the Epilogue to his *Law and Grace: Must a Christian Keep the Law of Moses?* (Westminster, 1962), pp. 121–124.

24. H. H. Rowley's article, "The Marriage of Ruth" in *The Servant of the Lord and*

Other Essays on the Old Testament (Lutterworth, 1952), pp. 169–194, contains a list of the unanswered questions which the story raises.

25. For various theories, see Campbell, *Ruth*, pp. 3–10.
26. Campbell, *Ruth*, pp. 32–36.
27. R. M. Hals, *The Theology of the Book of Ruth* (Fortress, 1969).
28. L. P. Smith, "Ruth, Exegesis" (*IB*; Abingdon, 1953), Vol. 2, p. 831.
29. Bickerman, *Four Strange Books*, p. 15f.
30. Bickerman, *Four Strange Books*, p. 17f.
31. Cf. D. W. Cleverley Ford, *New Preaching from the Old Testament* (Mowbrays, 1976), pp. 98–102.
32. J. Smart, "Jonah, Exegesis" (*IB*; Abingdon, 1956), Vol. 6, p. 874.
33. Good, *Irony in the Old Testament*, pp. 39–55; M. Burrows, "The Literary Category of the Book of Jonah" in H. T. Frank and W. L. Reed, eds., *Translating and Understanding the Old Testament* (Abingdon, 1970), pp. 80–107; J. A. Miles, Jr., "Laughing at the Bible: Jonah as Parody," *JQR* 65 (1974/75), 168–181.
34. D. F. Rauber, "Jonah—the Prophet as Shlemiel," *Bible Today* 49 (1970), 29–37.
35. Magonet, *Form and Meaning*, pp. 89–112.
36. T. Raitt, *A Theology of Exile: Judgment/Deliverance in Jeremiah and Ezekiel* (Fortress, 1977), pp. 35–58.
37. R. E. Clements, "The Purpose of the Book of Jonah," *VTS* 28 (1975), 16–28.
38. Bickerman, *Four Strange Books*, pp. 45–48.

Chapter IV

1. See, among others, C. H. Dodd, *Gospel and Law, the Relation of Faith and Ethics in Early Christianity* (Columbia University Press, 1951); G. A. F. Knight, *Law and Grace: Must a Christian Obey the Law of Moses?* (Westminster, 1962); J. M. Myers, *Grace and Torah* (Fortress, 1975); G. S. Sloyan, *Is Christ the End of the Law?* (Westminster, 1978).
2. For a convenient survey, see G. F. Thomas, *Christian Ethics and Moral Philosophy* (Scribner's, 1955), chap. 6, "Law and Liberty in Christian Thought."
3. See, for example, J. Knox, *The Ethic of Jesus in the Teaching of the Church* (Abingdon, 1961); P. Ramsay, *Basic Christian Ethics* (Scribner's, 1950), chaps. 1–3.
4. A fuller description of the law in Judaism during the first century A.D. may be found in Gowan, *Bridge Between the Testaments*, chaps. 12, 24.
5. Mishnah, *Shabbath* 16, 18, 24.
6. Dodd, *Gospel and Law*, p. 73.
7. C. E. B. Cranfield, "St. Paul and the Law," *SJT* 17 (1964), 43–68; W. D. Davies, *Paul and Rabbinic Judaism. Some Rabbinic Elements in Pauline Theology* (SPCK, 1948), chap. 6; V. P. Furnish, *Theology and Ethics in Paul* (Abingdon, 1968), pp. 135–161, 207–241; R. N. Longenecker, *Paul Apostle of Liberty* (Harper & Row, 1964), chaps. 4—8.
8. G. von Rad, *Studies in Deuteronomy* (SBT 9; 1953).
9. It may legitimately be asked at this point whether this is not a form of the liberal theory of "progressive revelation," but I believe that term is not an appropriate designation of the approach recommended here. It does not intend to downgrade or

apologize for the earlier parts of Scripture, but on the contrary takes them with the utmost seriousness. Some of the most useful material in the Bible on human rights can be drawn from the early legislation in the Old Testament, for example. It does not suggest that God has revealed different things at different times or that he began with parts of his truth and gradually moved toward the fullness of revelation represented by Christ, but speaks only of the extent to which human societies were able to *apply ethical* insights to a given situation. Over the years there has been some improvement in matters of social justice, as the two examples which follow will illustrate, and in that sense we can speak of progress. But this is in no way to be thought of as social evolution; every generation has to relearn the same lessons, is in danger of losing what has been gained, and stands under the judgment of the same divine imperative which has been addressed to every generation which has preceded it.

10. P. Trible, "Eve and Adam: Genesis 2–3 Reread," *Andover Newton Quarterly* 13 (1973), 251–258.
11. M. Barth, *Ephesians: Translation and Commentary on Chapters 4–6* (AB; Doubleday, 1974), pp. 607–650, 655–662, 700–738.
12. For a recent exposition of the Lutheran position, see H. G. Stuempfle, Jr., *Preaching Law and Gospel* (Fortress, 1978).
13. For helpful exegetical material, see J. J. Stamm & M. E. Andrew, *The Ten Commandments in Recent Research* (SBT : 1967). For recent expositions, see B. A. Haggerty, *Out of the House of Slavery: On the Meaning of the Ten Commandments* (Paulist, 1978); W. Harrelson, *The Ten Commandments and Human Rights* (Fortress, 1978).

Chapter V

1. R. Murphy, "Assumptions and Problems in Old Testament Wisdom Research," *CBQ* 29 (1967), 411ff.
2. An excellent treatment of wisdom theology may be found in J. C. Rylaarsdam, *Revelation in Jewish Wisdom Literature* (University of Chicago Press, 1946). For a briefer outline of these developments, Gowan, *Bridge Between the Testaments*, pp. 397–411.
3. The downgrading of wisdom in biblical theology is quite common. E.g. Achtemeier, *Old Testament and the Proclamation of the Gospel*, p. 48, is so strongly influenced by the emphasis on history in von Rad's theology that she relegates the wisdom literature to a minor position in her treatment of preaching the Old Testament.
4. See the diagnosis of the church's illness in Smart, *Strange Silence of the Bible*, and the sharp criticism of moralizing sermons in L. E. Keck, *The Bible in the Pulpit: The Renewal of Biblical Preaching* (Abingdon, 1978), pp. 100–104.
5. On the form criticism of the wisdom literature, see the chapter by J. L. Crenshaw in *Old Testament Form Criticism*, ed. J. H. Hayes, pp. 225–264.
6. Compare the methods recommended by F. B. Craddock, *As One Without Authority* (Enid, Oklahoma: Phillips University Press, 1974) in chap. 3: "The Inductive Movement in Preaching."

7. A classic example appears in the famous sermon "Acres of Diamonds" by Russell Conwell: "Let me say here clearly, and say it briefly, though subject to discussion which I have not time for here, ninety-eight out of one hundred of the rich men of America are honest. That is why they are rich." (Harper & Brothers, 1915), p. 19.

8. H. Ringgren, *Word and Wisdom: Hypostatization of Divine Qualities and Functions in the Ancient Near East* (Lund: Ohlssons, 1947), but compare the corrective to any overemphasis on hypostatization in G. von Rad, *Wisdom in Israel* (Abingdon, 1973), chap. 9.

9. On wisdom in the New Testament see R. G. Hamerton-Kelly, *Pre-existence, Wisdom and the Son of Man* (SNTS Monograph 21; Cambridge, 1973) and M. J. Suggs, *Wisdom, Christology, and Law in Matthew's Gospel* (Harvard University Press, 1970).

10. Vol. 4 (Abingdon, 1955), p. 21.

11. H.-J. Krauss, *Psalmen* I (*BKAT*; Neukirchener Verlag, 1966), p. 9f.

12. D. E. Gowan, *The Triumph of Faith in Habakkuk* (John Knox, 1976), chapters 2 and 3.

13. For the relationship between the prose and poetic parts see R. Gordis, *The Book of God and Man: A Study of Job* (University of Chicago Press, 1965), chap. 6; E. Dhorme, *A Commentary on the Book of Job* (Nelson, 1967), pp. 1xi–1xxxv.

14. R. Gordis, *Koheleth: the Man and His World* (Schocken, 1968, revised ed.), chap. 12.

15. The approach I do not espouse may be found in the sermon, "No, Mr Preacher" by D. E. Cleverley Ford, in his *New Preaching from the Old Testament* (Mowbrays, 1976), pp. 81–85. Opinions of Ecclesiastes, pro and con, have been listed in an intriguing way as the "Advertisement" at the beginning of the commentary by A. D. Power, *Ecclesiastes or the Preacher* (Longmans, Green & Co., 1952), p. ii.

16. Recent commentaries on Job: R. Gordis, *The Book of Job: Commentary, New Translation, and Special Studies* (Jewish Theological Seminary of America, 1978); M. Pope, *Job* (AB; Doubleday, 1965); S. Terrien, "Job: Exegesis" (IB 3; Abingdon, 1954).

17. G. von Rad, *Wisdom in Israel*, p. 206.

18. See especially the discussion of this line of thought by Rylaarsdam, *Revelation in Jewish Wisdom Literature*, chap. 4.

19. O. S. Rankin, *Israel's Wisdom Literature* (T. & T. Clark, 1954), chaps. 5–8.

20. E. Kissane, *The Book of Job* (Dublin: Browne & Nolan, 1939).

21. S. R. Driver & G. B. Gray, *Critical and Exegetical Commentary on the Book of Job* (ICC; Scribner's, 1921); E. G. Kraeling, *The Book of the Ways of God* (Scribner's, 1939).

22. J. G. Williams, " 'You have not spoken Truth of Me.' Mystery and Irony in Job," *ZAW* 83 (1971), 231–255.

23. O. Baab, "The Book of Job," *Interpretation* 5 (1951), 329–343.

24. S. Terrien, *IB* 3 (1954), p. 898.

25. Gordis, *The Book of God and Man*, p. 153f.

26. L. Alonso Schökel, "Toward a Dramatic Reading of the Book of Job," *Semeia* 7 (1977), 45–61; with a response by J. L. Crenshaw, pp. 63–69.

27. S. N. Kramer, " 'Man and His God.' A Sumerian Variation on the 'Job' Motif,"
     VTS 3 (1955), 170–182.

Chapter VI

1. As, for example, in the rewriting of the prophets' message by J. E. Corbett, *The Prophets on Main Street* (John Knox, 1965).
2. I use the term "canonical prophets" to refer to those who have books attributed to them, i.e. Isaiah through Malachi. The older expression, "writing prophets," is scarcely appropriate any more, now that we understand the prominence of oral proclamation in the work of the prophets.
3. Cf. Acts 2:25–31; 8:32–35; Heb. 1.
4. Examples of the continuing use of the term in this way: O. J. Baab, *Prophetic Preaching: A New Approach* (Abingdon, 1958); R. Q. Leavell, *Prophetic Preaching: Then and Now* (Baker, 1963); H. E. Quinley, *The Prophetic Clergy: Social Activism Among Protestant Ministers* (John Wiley & Sons, 1974).
5. The best description of this aspect of prophecy is to be found in J. Lindblom, *Prophecy in Ancient Israel* (Fortress, 1962), Chaps. II and III.
6. R. E. Clements, *Prophecy and Covenant* (*SBT* 43; 1965), chap. 5.
7. R. E. Clements, *Prophecy and Tradition* (John Knox, 1975).
8. For more detail see any of the recent introductions to the Old Testament, or the chapter on Prophecy by W. E. March in J. H. Hayes, ed., *Old Testament Form Criticism*, pp. 141–178.
9. On the similar reuse of the "woes," see Gowan, *The Triumph of Faith in Habakkuk*, chap. 3.
10. Described most fully by C. Westermann, *Basic Forms of Prophetic Speech* (Westminster, 1967), pp. 129–188.
11. The radical nature of this break with the past is emphasized by T. M. Raitt, *A Theology of Exile*, chap. 6.
12. J. Lindblom, *Prophecy in Ancient Israel*, p. 311ff.
13. Cf. the discussion of such a question by W. S. Towner, "On Calling People 'Prophets' in 1970," *Interpretation* 24 (1970), 492–509.
14. L. E. Toombs, "War, Ideas of," *IDB* 4 (Abingdon, 1962), 797–800.
15. G. von Rad, "The Origin of the Day of Yahweh," *JSS* 4 (1959), 97–108; A. J. Everson, "The Days of Yahweh," *JBL* 93 (1974), 329–337.
16. H. B. Huffmon, "The Covenant Lawsuit in the Prophets," *JBL* 78 (1959), 285–295.
17. Other occurrences of the "covenant lawsuit" in the prophets: Mic. 6:1–8; Jer. 2:4–13; Hos. 4:1–3.
18. R. J. Clifford, "The Use of HÔY in the Prophets," *CBQ* 28 (1966), 458–464; W. Janzen, *Mourning Cry and Woe Oracle* (*BZAW* 125; 1972); J. G. Williams, "The Alas-Oracles of the Eighth Century Prophets," *HUCA* 38 (1967), 75–91.
19. D. N. Freedman, "Divine Commitment and Human Obligation: The Covenant Theme," *Interpretation* 18 (1964), 419–431.
20. Clements, *Prophecy and Covenant*, p. 43, etc.
21. Raitt, *A Theology of Exile*, chap. 5.

22. E.g. S. Sandmel, *The Hebrew Scriptures: An Introduction to their Literature and Religious Ideas* (Knopf, 1963), p. 147.

23. A very helpful guide through the difficulties is provided by R. G. Bratcher, "A Study of Isaiah 7:14," *Bible Translator* (1958), pp. 97–126. Readers may be interested in comparing the homiletical treatments by Achtemeier, *The Old Testament and the Proclamation of the Gospel*, pp. 165–172, and McCurley, *Proclaiming the Promise*, pp. 108–118.

24. F. J. Helfmeyer, "'oth" (*TDOT* 1; Eerdmans, 1974, rev. ed. 1977), pp. 167–188.

25. See Bratcher, "A Study of Isaiah 7:14." For the view that Isaiah saw the Virgin Mary herself in a vision, see E. J. Young, "The Immanuel Prophecy of Isaiah 7:14–16," *Westminster Theological Journal* 15 (1952/53), 87–124.

26. K. Fullerton, "Immanuel," *AJSL* 34 (1917/18), 256–283; N. Gottwald, "Immanuel as the Prophet's Son," *VT* 8 (1958), 36–47.

27. The evidence is discussed by G. B. Gray, "The Virgin Birth in Relation to the Interpretation of Isaiah VII, 14," *The Expositor*, 8th Series, Vol. I (1911), 289–308.

Epilogue

1. It is interesting to note that in the series "Proclamation Commentaries: The Old Testament Witnesses for Preaching," R. E. Murphy, who writes on the Psalms (*The Psalms, Job*, Fortress, 1977), concludes with "The Contribution of the Psalms to Today's Prayer Style" (pp. 47–57). In a series designed to aid one to preach from the Old Testament, naturally he does not discourage preaching from the Psalter, but he has more to say about the Psalms and prayer than about the Psalms and preaching. This is not out of step with tradition, despite the many sermons which have been preached from the Psalter. Consider, for example, this passage from Calvin's introduction to his commentary on the Psalms: "The other parts of Scripture contain the commandments which God enjoined his servants to announce to us. But here the prophets themselves, seeing they are exhibited to us as speaking to God, and laying open all their inmost thoughts and affections, call, or rather draw, each of us to the examination of himself in particular, in order that none of the many infirmities to which we are subject, and of the many vices with which we abound, may remain concealed . . . In short, as calling upon God is one of the principal means of securing our safety, and as a better and more unerring rule for guiding us in this exercise cannot be found elsewhere than in The Psalms, it follows, that in proportion to the proficiency which a man shall have attained in understanding them, will be his knowledge of the most important part of celestial doctrine" (J. Calvin, *Commentary on the Psalms* (Eerdmans, 1949), Vol. I, p. xxxvii).

2. A similar judgment was made by C. Westermann, in his comments on the sermons in *Verküdigung des Kommenden: Predigten alttestamentlicher Texte* (Kaiser Verlag, 1978), p. 135, but he then goes on to do as I shall do, discuss those elements in the Psalter which do seem to be naturally and appropriately preachable.

3. Fuller discussions of these genres may be found in any of the modern introductions and commentaries. On the contemporary value of laments, see W. Brueggemann, "The Formfulness of Grief," *Interpretation* 31 (1977), 263–275.

4. One effort to show the theological importance of some of this material may be found in D. E. Gowan, *When Man Becomes God: Humanism and Hybris in the Old Testament* (*PTMS* 6: Pickwick, 1975).

Index of Biblical References

Old Testament

GENESIS

1–11	35, 41
1–3	5
2–3	156, 196
2:18, 22–24	93
6:9–9:17	41–47
9	88
9:8–17	135
12:1–3	48
12:4	48
12:10–20	3, 36, 48–53
14:1–17	36
15	88, 135
16:11	140
17	135
17:1, 7	48
21:1–20	40f.
24	36, 153
32:3–31	40
37–50	36, 63–64
38	153

EXODUS

4:24–26	16
13:17–14:31	26–34
13:18	26
15:1–18	30, 145
15:21	29
19	88
19:5, 8	135
21:1–23:19	89
21	92
21:20–21	91
22:16–17	92

22:21	91
22:26	128
23:6–8	128
23:9	91

LEVITICUS

17:10–14	95–99
19–26	89
19:14	94
19:18	83, 89, 94
25:39ff., 42	91–92
26	135
26:42	49

DEUTERONOMY

4:31	49
6:5	83, 88
6:21–23	28
12–26	89
15:12–15	92
18:22	77
22:28–29	92
23:7	90
24:7	128
26:5ff.	28
28	135
32	145

JOSHUA

2:18	4
3–4	28

JUDGES

3:15–29	153
4	153
5	145

9:7–21	103
13:3–5	140
14:12–18	103

RUTH

1–4	68–74, 153

1 SAMUEL

1:20	140
2	145

2 SAMUEL

7	17, 22, 135
9–20	15

1 KINGS

1–2	21
12:1–24	15
20:28	129, 140
22	129

2 KINGS

11	22–26
17:13	125

EZRA

3	21

NEHEMIAH

9	146

ESTHER

1–10	65–68, 153

JOB

1–42	112–115
1:1–2:13	112
11:1–20	104

28:1–27	112	30:5–6	105	46–51	147
42:7–17	112	30:15–31	103		
				EZEKIEL	
PSALMS		**ECCLESIASTES**		14:14–20	43
1	106–108, 146	2:14	112	20	28
4	146	3:1–9	115	25–32	147
8	146	4:5,6	112	33:10–20	128
11	146	5:1–7	104	36:26–27	136
16	146	5:18–20	115–118	36:27, 29	127
23	146	7:24	117		
27:1–6	146	9:1–12	115–118	**DANIEL**	
29	146			1–6	54–63
37	146	**SONG OF SONGS**		7–12	147, 151
37:25	105	1–8	v, 151	9	146
48	131				
49	111, 146	**ISAIAH**		**HOSEA**	
49:15	111	1:2–9	130–134	4:1–3	158
62	146	1:16–17	122		
73	111	5:1–7	103	**JOEL**	
73:23–24	111	5:8ff.	122	3	127
78:52f.	30	7:1–17	138–144		
89	135	13–23	147	**AMOS**	
103	146	14:4–21	122	2:6–16	128–130
105	28	29	131	3:3ff.	122
105:16–23	64	41:8	49	3:12	129
106:9–12	30	41:10	144	4:13	121
107	146	43:16f.	30	5:1	122f.
114	30	51:2	49	5:4–6, 14–15	129
131	146	51:9–10	30	5:8–9	121
135	146	54:9	43	5:11	123
136:13–15	30			5:15	123
		JEREMIAH		5:18–20	129
PROVERBS		2:4–13	158	9:5–6	121
1:20ff.	103	7	131	9:11–15	129
4:1–9	108–111	15:15–18	121		
6:20–7:5	104	17:14–18	121	**JONAH**	
8:1ff.	103	18:19ff.	122	1–4	54, 55, 74–78
8:22–36	105	23:9–40	77		
10:15	104	26	131	**MICAH**	
13:20	104	28	77	6:1–8	122, 158
14:20,21	104	29:15–23	77		
15:3–11	105	30–31	136f.	**HABAKKUK**	
16:4,9	111	31:31–34	134–138	2:4	111
16:8	104	33:14–26	135	3:17–19	111–112
27:14	101	35:18–19	123		
30:4, 15–16	103			**ZECHARIAH**	
				12–14	131

Apocrypha

1 ESDRAS		**ECCLESIASTICUS** (Sirac)		**1 MACCABEES**	
3–4	161	24	105	1	154
		24:23	112	2:53	63f.
WISDOM OF SOLOMON		49:15	64		
1:16–3:11	113			**2 MACCABEES**	
6–7	105			5–7	154
10:13f.	63f.				

New Testament

MATTHEW

1:1–17	147
1:18–25	141
1:23	139
2:15	31
5:17	82
5:18	80
5:21–47	82
12:1ff.	82
12:9ff.	82
12:39–40	75
12:41	75
24:37–39	43, 44, 46

MARK

2:23ff.	82
3:1ff.	82

LUKE

6:1ff.	82
6:6ff.	82
10:25-28	83
10:28	79
10:38–42	93
13:10ff.	82
13:14	83
14:1ff.	82
17:26–27	43

ACTS

2:25–31	158
2:30	146
7:9–16	64
7:36	31
8:32–35	158
13:16ff.	31
15:29	79

17:26–28	40

ROMANS

1:17	84
1:20f.	40
3:21f.	84
3:23, 24, 31	84
3:31	80
4	49, 88
6	84
7:6	79
7:7, 11	85
7:12	80, 85
7:24–8:1	85
8:2, 4	85
12:14–21	86
13:8–10	86
14:1–23	86
15:2	86
16:17–20	86

1 CORINTHIANS

1:24, 30	106
9:8ff.	79
10:1–13	31f.
11:3–16	93
13	71
13:7	56, 70
14:34–35	93

GALATIANS

2:19	79
3	49
3:28	92
5:2–12	79

EPHESIANS

1:3–14	50
2:11–19	19–20

3:28	93
5–6	85
5:21–33	93
6:2f.	79

PHILIPPIANS

4:4–9	118
4:11–13	109

COLOSSIANS

2:16	79
3	85

1 THESSALONIANS

5:14–18	85

HEBREWS

1	158
8:8–12	137
10:16–17	137
11:7	43
11:21f.	64
11:29	31
11:32–40	23, 24
13	85

1 PETER

2–3	85
3:20–21	43

2 PETER

2:4–9	43
2:5, 9	47

1 JOHN

3:11ff.	64
4:19	94

251
272

61716